Documentation, libraries and archives: studies and research   3

Titles in the series *Unesco manuals for libraries*:

Titles in this series:

Conservation and restoration of archive materials

by Yash Pal Kathpalia

Unesco Paris 1973

Published in 1973 by the United Nations
Educational, Scientific and Cultural Organization
7 Place de Fontenoy, 75700 Paris

Printed by Imprimeries Populaires de Genève

ISBN 92-3-101073-5

Preface

The historical material held in archives forms part of the cultural heritage of mankind, and the conservation of such holdings is of vital importance. In 1969, therefore, Unesco concluded a contract with the International Council on Archives for a manual on the conservation and restoration of archive materials. This manual, which accords particular attention to the specific problems encountered in regions with unfavourable climatic conditions, has been prepared by Yash Pal Kathpalia, M.Sc. (Chemist), Scientific Officer at the National Archives of India, New Delhi, and is based on his own research and experience.

The aim of the publication is to provide archivists and librarians responsible for manuscript collections with a survey of the methods, techniques and materials employed in the conservation and restoration of archive materials.

The author of the present document is responsible for the choice of facts presented and their interpretation; the opinions expressed are not necessarily those of Unesco or of the International Council on Archives.

Contents

List of illustrations

Foreword

The conservation of archive materials is a skilful art confined before the development of modern processes to a small number of institutions throughout the world, and utilizing methods dependent on the ingenuity and dexterity of the restorer. Although the intervention of science has led to a better understanding of the various causes and problems of deterioration and to the formulation of preventive measures, the use of orthodox methods and techniques has continued and is in all probability likely to continue; the processes used have withstood the test of time and proved their usefulness. They comply with the essential principles of repair, reversibility, for example, and may be easily adopted for preservation work in those developing countries which have opened or are in the process of opening their own archive centres and whose interest in the development of repair activities is hampered by lack of funds, facilities and trained personnel.

There is no short cut in this art and there is no school which exclusively provides training in the conservation and restoration of archive materials. The few institutions which do impart training confine their efforts to in-training for conditions and processes suitable to their own needs. Such institutions have mechanized their restoration units and are using modern preservation techniques.

In 1968, the Executive Secretary of the International Council on Archives (ICA), Mr Charles Kecskemeti, returning from the inauguration in Malaysia of the South-East Asian Regional Branch of ICA (SARBICA), paused in New Delhi to visit the National Archives. In his talks with me then, he suggested the need for a manual on the conservation and restoration of archive materials.

The present work is the outcome of those talks, and the product of the contract concluded between Unesco and ICA for its preparation, which was entrusted to the author.

I have attempted to include all the information available, together with details of the various processes and techniques employed and considered suitable for conservation and restoration work in various centres throughout the world. These processes vary from institution to institution and from country to country according to climatic conditions. Processes suitable for one are not necessarily suitable to others. More often than not, modifications have been necessary to suit the needs of individual institutions. Nevertheless, the principles remain unchanged. In writing this book I have drawn upon twenty years of professional experience both in India and in countries of Europe and America, and have described these processes which have proved their utility and suitability for conservation and restoration work.

Interest in archive preservation is world-wide. Most institutions are seeking aid from scientific institutions and organizations in the solution of their problems. Some are themselves engaged in preservation work and have set up their own laboratories. The tempo of work and the development of new procedures have been increasing and are certain to increase further in the coming years. New processes are already under investigation and a reappraisal of the entire problem of preservation on the basis of information provided by research is contemplated. Although one or two books on the subject have been published, most of the information concerning recent developments in archive conservation lies scattered in literature and journals which are not easily accessible and has not been published in a book form. Such information has also been collected as far as possible, and compiled in the present work for the benefit of the profession.

My thanks are due to Dr A. Wagner, Programme Specialist in the Division for the Development of Documentation, Libraries and Archives, Unesco, for his interest in this work, for the use of literature, and for photographs of the Kaschiermaschine; and to Mr Charles Kecskemeti, Executive Secretary of ICA, for help and encouragement, as well as photographs and literature. I am also grateful to Mr William K. Wilson, Chief, Paper Evaluation Section, United States National Bureau of Standards; to Mr George Daniel Martin Cunha, Conservator, Library of the Boston Athenaeum; to Mr R. D. Smith, Graduate Library School, University of Chicago and Barrow Research Laboratory, Richmond, Virginia, for providing the available literature, journals, books, various publications and information which have been of assistance to me in writing the present work.

My thanks are also due to Mr James L. Gear, Acting Director, Technical Services Division, United States National Archives; to Mr Pierre Durye, Secrétaire général des Archives Nationales, Paris; to the Bundesarchiv (Federal Republic of Germany); to Dr Guido Pampaloni and Dr Francesca Morandini of the Florence State Archives, for photographs used as illustrations in this book; and to my two colleagues in the National Archives, Mr R. Kishore for help and Mr P. L. Madan for drawings used in the book.

I shall be failing in my duty if I do not record my gratitude to the National Archives, New Delhi, the institution which initiated me into the profession. I am deeply indebted to Mr D. B. Wardle and Mr Y. Pérotin for scrutiny of the text and their valuable suggestions.

Finally, I crave the indulgence of the readers for the omissions which are inevitable in a work of this type.

Y. P. KATHPALIA

Introduction

The art of preservation is as old as human civilization itself. In a way it may be said to derive from the instinct of self-preservation common to all animate beings. Documents have existed in one form or another since man invented the art of writing, and it was natural for mankind to attempt to preserve them, in view of their value as testimony of a legal or some other kind. The methods adopted for the purpose have, however, differed from time to time, depending on the materials used in the creation of the documents.

With the progress of human efforts to translate thought into writing, the engraving of lengthy records on stone and metals gave way to writings on materials such as papyrus, bark, leather, parchment and palm leaf. These remained in use for a considerable time. Palm leaf in particular, despite the invention of paper and its universal use thereafter for the creation of records, was in use in the East as late as the nineteenth century. As we now know, all these materials, with the exception of stone and metals, are vulnerable: clay to worms; papyrus to insects and moisture; bark, wood and palm leaves to termites and other insects; and leather and linen to rot and insects. Learned people and scholars, alive to the importance of documents, developed ingenious methods of conserving them.

It has been reported that some three thousand years ago, papyrus scrolls were dried and unrolled after every rainy season, to determine whether the rain had washed off the ink writing. For protection against insects, humidity and dust, the Egyptians, Greeks and Romans stored their scrolls in cylindrical boxes of wood and ivory, while in India and elsewhere in the East fragile palm leaf manuscripts were protected first by fastening them between strips of wood or carved ivory and then by covering them with a cloth piece, called *bastas*. To maintain papyrus records in a good state of preservation, they were treated with cedar-wood oil, a preservative. Citrus leaves and citrus oil were also used for the same purpose. Shortly after the invention of paper, the Chinese began to treat it against insect attack with *huang-neih*, an extract from the seeds of the cork tree. This treatment was believed to preserve paper for several hundred years. Other materials used from time to time as insecticides included camphor, cloves and clove oil, oil of eucalyptus, musk, etc., but these provided little or no protection. Various authors of the ancient and classical periods have recommended the use of cedar oil, saffron and containers made of polished cypress wood to prevent insect damage to books. In fact, cedar oil was probably the first insect repellant ever used for the preservation of cultural property.

Certain aromatic flowers and leaves were inserted between the pages of books to protect them from insects. This practice was widespread and even now it is not entirely extinct despite the fact that its use is harmful. In some instances, the help of gods was sought. An invocation in an Arabic manuscript displayed in the museum of the Istituto di Patologia del Libro in Rome appeals for the protection of books and documents from moths. Special attention and importance were also accorded to the location of places where books and documents were stored. To ensure the best conservation of books, it was recommended that such places should as a rule face in an eastward direction.

Before the Middle Ages, preservation did not pose a major problem, largely because of the good quality of the materials used for the creation of documents and the limited number of the latter. Parchment and vellum, which had become common materials by that time, had greater durability. Initially, the skins were treated carefully with lime to protect them from deterioration. With the increase in demand, the processing period was shortened into days, and the quality declined. At the same time, old parchment manuscripts began to show signs of deterioration, presumably because of age, decay and other causes. In the Istituto di Patologia del Libro in Rome and elsewhere throughout Europe there are many early publications with relatively sound leather or vellum covers, but whose paper and parchment is affected by insects and mildew.

The problem of preserving records became acute with the invention of printing. In the early eighteenth century, increased demand for paper and a shortage of paper fibres to meet that demand led to changes for the worse in paper-making processes. It was then that the custodians of records became conscious of the need to take action to conserve and restore damaged and brittle documents.

Without referring to the very earliest stages, we may say that initially the restorer worked alone in his private and improvised workshop and discovered new methods which became jealously guarded secrets. The revival of faded writing on parchment in an infusion of certain flowers was one such discovery. The process was found to be effective and harmful neither to manuscripts nor to the restorer. Its secret, alas, died with the inventor. Some of the processes discovered were sound and are still in use. Examples include the covering of the documents with cloth to protect them from the action of light, their protection from insects through the use of such materials as clove oil, cedar oil and camphor, and the use of gelatine as size for preservation. The use of gelatine was later (1898) restricted, because 'it cost as much as the rest of the raw materials in the paper'. On the other hand, the use of hypochlorite as a bleaching agent, and of a great variety of materials and glues for reinforcement have resulted in damage. It is a well-known fact that some of the documents restored at that time have been completely ruined or lost, or damaged beyond repair. Such methods were largely based upon an imperfect understanding of the nature of the materials involved. It is only in the past hundred years or so that attempts have been made to understand why documents and the materials used in their repair behave in the way they do, and such investigations only gained momentum after the First World War.

An interesting report published in 1750 contains the following statement:

Really 100 years ago they made paper twice as good, as strong, as the paper they make now-a-days. Many scholars complain that in several places paper is not strong and white enough, but dirty and thin. . . . The main reason may be the great number of printing offices and the nearly unbelievable quantity of books which are printed every day, and for which the printers are not inclined to make great costs. And as the papermakers can hardly send enough paper to the printers, they become careless and covetous.

In 1829, Murray studied the problem and attributed the deterioration of paper to the harmful changes in papermaking practices, overbleaching and the use of raw materials of poor quality. To check acidity in paper, he recommended the use of syrup of violets, which as we now know contains anthocyanins and acts as a pH indicator changing from red to blue and vice versa at a pH of approximately 7.

In 1842, Faraday studied the deterioration of leather book bindings and stated:

Our loss in the destruction of books is very great . . . it is due to the gas as a whole, partly to the vapour that arises from the gas and partly it is due to the heat, to the state in which the air is kept in the room, the high temperature of the atmosphere conjointly with certain things which the leather dresser puts into the leather and the certain effects of the gas itself.

Current problems of preservation and restoration were reviewed by Leighton in 1858, with the conclusion that an improvement in the quality of paper was desirable.

It is clear that in the beginning advice was sought in isolated cases only, and that the investigation of the problems of conservation was of limited interest. Examples of the subjects that received attention include the study and prevention of damage caused by gas-lights, the treatment of infested materials, the reasons why paper was dirty and thin instead of strong and white, the effects of heat, and light, and the action of insects. These investigations later led to the systematic study of the conservation and restoration of record materials with the aim of preserving the cultural heritage for succeeding generations.

The first organized attempt was made by the Keeper of the Vatican Library, Cardinal Franz Ehrle, with an appeal at the International Conference of Libraries held in Saint Gall in 1898, for a reappraisal of existing restoration methods and for the aid of science. Cardinal Ehrle introduced the process of strengthening damaged manuscripts with a covering of transparent silk-gauze, and the use of new parchment and gelatine in the repair of parchment manuscripts. In England at about the same time, the Society of Encouragement of Arts, Manufacturers and Commerce received a report from the committee set up to examine the deterioration of paper. In 1900, the same society created a body to determine the cause of deterioration of leather bindings. Meanwhile, an archivists conference held in Dresden in 1899 and the International Congress of Libraries which met in Paris in 1900 considered the problems of conservation of written records. Between 1908 and 1911, the problem was also evoked in Germany, Italy and the United States of America.

The spread of awareness resulted, soon after the First World War, in important investigations by and co-operation between the various individuals and institutions concerned with the preservation of their holdings. Notable work was carried out in the United States of America, the United Kingdom, Italy, France, Russia, Sweden and Germany, and in India. A number of new processes and techniques for conservation and restoration were developed. Some of these, which are still in use, are discussed in the following chapters. The data collected during these early investigations forms the basis of our present knowledge which in its turn is being expanded with the aim of improving the art and techniques of conserving archive materials.

Among the problems investigated with a view to formulating counteractive measures were: atmospheric pollution and its effects on paper; the effect of acids and other impurities; the yellowing of paper; insect and fungus damage; the effects of climate, humidity, temperature, and other environmental conditions; and the effect of fumigants on paper. Investigations in the field of restoration concerned the development of generally applicable processes for the preservation of leather bindings of books and volumes; the fumigation of infested records; the reinforcement of brittle documents with cellulose acetate film and tissue paper applied under heat and pressure; the bleaching of spots on paper with Chloramine T, etc. The question of the permanence of paper was also examined and specifications for permanent paper and ink were elaborated. Equally important were the study of the artificial ageing of paper and the development of accelerated ageing tests. Physical tests for determining tensile strength, bursting strength and folding endurance, as well as the purity of cellulose or permanence of paper, and chemical tests involving cellulose content, copper number, etc. were devised and perfected as a means of evaluating the longevity and durability of paper.

It was only after the Second World War and the creation of bodies like the United Nations Educational, Scientific and Cultural Organization (Unesco), the International Council on Archives

(ICA) and the International Council of Museums (ICOM) that the problem was tackled at the international level. Most of the work, however, is still conducted by institutions such as the Barrow Research Laboratory, the National Bureau of Standards and the National Archives in the United States of America, the Public Record Office and the British Museum Research Laboratory in the United Kingdom, the Archives Nationales in France, the Archivschule in the Federal Republic of Germany, the Centro di Fotoriproduzione Legatoria e Restauro degli Archivi di Stato and the Istituto di Patologia del Libro in Italy and the National Archives in India, and by individuals devoted to the cause of conservation.

The stability of deacidified and laminated documents has been studied by Barrow, who has shown that the durability of sound, average quality paper is improved by the use of chemicals such as calcium and magnesium carbonate. Wilson and Forshee, of the United States National Bureau of Standards, have conducted a complete study of various laminating techniques which, in addition to assessing the efficacy of laminating processes, lays down specifications for an ideal cellulose acetate film for restoration purposes. Barrow, after prolonged research, has produced an alkaline paper, claimed to have a life expectancy of 300 years, for books and records, and has made a detailed laboratory study of the deterioration and durability of paper.

In England, Langwell has studied the problem of air pollution and its deteriorative effect on documents, suggesting a vapour phase deacidification process for counteracting acidity in paper and the Postslip Lamination Process for the restoration of documents. Further work on these problems is continuing.

In India, Kathpalia's investigation of restoration problems has led to the development of a solvent lamination process also known as the Indian Process of Lamination, adopted by a large number of institutions throughout the world. The silking process for the restoration of documents and the effect on the document and the reinforcing material of the paste used in the process has been studied by Kathpalia and Kishore, who recommend the use of an alkaline paste containing either lead carbonate or barium carbonate. The possibility has also been explored of using synthetic non-woven fibres such as terylene-tissue in place of tissue paper in the Solvent Lamination Process of reinforcement.

The problem of bleaching with chlorite has been studied by Gettenes and further investigated by Madame Flieder in France. The Istituto di Patologia del Libro in Rome has investigated the efficacy of Chloramine T, first recommended by Plenderleith in 1937 as an effective bleaching agent. Considerable progress has been made in the use of adhesives. New synthetic materials like soluble nylon and methyl cellulose, polyvinyl alcohol and polyvinyl acetate emulsions, and sodium salt of carboxymethyl cellulose (CMC) have been used for preservation work. In some cases, these synthetic materials have replaced the traditional pastes made from wheat starch or flour. Some of them, soluble nylon for example, are used as sizing agents.

Various scientific investigations of the causes of decay have shown that deterioration occurs mainly in one or more of the following physio-chemical situations:

1. Heat and exposure to light.
2. Moisture, which besides constituting a hydrolytic danger also favours biological attack and deterioration due to fungi, insects, etc.
3. Frequent and pronounced changes in temperature and humidity.
4. Acidic impurities, such as those present in the atmosphere of industrial areas, or in dust. Strong alkalis are also injurious and contribute to the deterioration of paper. Fungi, for example, grow very easily on alkaline paper.
5. Oxidizing agents.
6. Presence of heavy metals which, even in traces, catalyze oxidative degradation. Sulphuric acid is also formed from the sulphur dioxide present in the atmosphere.
7. Presence and use of acidic sizes, such as alum, rosin, etc.
8. Presence and use of acidic inks.
9. Use of fibres with low cellulose content and presence of non-cellulose materials of the lignin type, which are often acidic in nature or yield acidic derivatives upon decomposition. Such non-cellulosic materials are sensitive to deteriorative agents such as light.

Deterioration caused by the various agents enumerated above, i.e. light, moisture, heat, dust particles, insects and acids, differs from the deterioration associated with the normal ageing of paper. All papers, irrespective of the materials from which they are made, must deteriorate with age, even when storage conditions are ideal. Such deterioration can only be minimized or at best retarded. Deterioration due to all these causes can be counteracted by preventive measures and such measures constitute the conservation of documents.

Once the cause or causes of deterioration are established, it is possible to prevent, check and repair the damage. Much has already been done in this direction, and investigations are continuing. It now seems likely that, in contrast with the past, records can be kept properly and scientifically preserved. Institutions interested in the preservation of their holdings are taking encouraging steps to identify the causes of deterioration and the nature of damage to archive materials, seeking in the process the help of scientifically trained specialists. Indeed, some institutions, including the National Archives of the United States of America, the British Museum, the Archives Nationales, Paris, the National Archives of India, the Bundesarchiv (Federal Republic of Germany) and the Centro di Fotoriproduzione Legatoria e Restauro degli Archivi di Stato, Rome, realizing the gravity of the damage, have engaged scientific or technical staff for conservation purposes.

One of the methods generally employed for the identification of one cause of deterioration, namely acidity, involves the measurement of free acidity in paper by a pH meter. If a low pH is recorded, the deterioration of the document may be attributed to excessive acidity. A pH of 7 indicates a neutral state, less than 7 indicates acidity and over 7, alkalinity. The following shows the pH of papers stored in various archives in Europe from the fourteenth to the nineteenth century: 1346 (6.9), 1449 (7.2), 1515 (7.2), 1563 (5.9), 1661 (6.2), 1779 (6.7) and one from the nineteenth century (5.4). Some of the papers with a high pH value are still in good condition. The above figures also provide an indication of the characteristics of paper during different periods. From the eighteenth century onwards, when there was a great demand for paper for writing purposes, changes were made in methods of production, as a result of which the paper produced shows a decline in pH value.

Deterioration of this type, together with other indications, such as the extent of discolouration of the paper, insect damage, fungus growth, etc., yield a certain amount of information concerning the nature of the decay. The task, however, is not an easy one.

In many cases, despite the absence of such damage, the paper may be brittle. This is because one of the consequences of deterioration is a breakdown of the cellulose molecules on which the material strength of a paper largely depends. The length of the cellulose chains in the molecule may be determined chemically. The less the breakdown in the cellulose molecule, the less is the loss in the strength of the material.

To counteract the deteriorative action of acidity, remedial measures such as deacidification and resizing are applied. Such measures help to restore strength to the document paper and neutralize the free acidity. If there is no other damage to the document, no further action appears necessary, apart from storage in a suitable environment. Once, however, the paper has broken, or becomes fragile, restoration is the only solution. Here, laminating techniques involving the application of cellulose acetate film and tissue paper either under heat and pressure in a flat bed or a rotary type press, or through the action of a solvent, as in the Indian process, are used by most of the archive centres and institutions of the world in preference to the old methods of restoration, i.e. repair with silk (chiffon) or tissue paper by full pasting if the writing is only on one side. Another notable feature is the realization that proper storage conditions contribute to the longevity of archive materials.

As a result, new buildings which are insect-proof and air-conditioned and equipped with proper storage and shelving arrangements have been constructed, for example in Ghana, the United States of America, the United Kingdom and India, are in the process of construction or, as in the case of Florence, are being contemplated. Measures to minimize damage due to fire and acts of war are incorporated in the design of such structures.

Increased awareness in professional and administrative circles of the need to safeguard archive materials has led to an increased interest in preservation work. A number of problems are currently under investigation. It is hoped and believed that new methods which will be simple, cheap and more effective will be developed for the protection of archive documents and materials. The problem is not, however, as simple as it may appear to be. Every decayed document presents a different problem. A method that is effective in one case may not necessarily be effective in another. Even if a method is applied with confidence on the basis of tests devised as a result of modern knowledge, the behaviour over a long period under normal storage conditions of the materials involved cannot be foreseen, because the ingredients used in the manufacture of paper have varied from time to time and as a result of progress in manufacturing processes, and are as unpredictable in their behaviour as their composition.

The manner in which paper deteriorates is highly significant. The two characteristics involved are permanence and durability, the former being the capacity of paper to retain its original characteristics, i.e. its chemical stability, and the latter being a reflection of its capacity to resist the wear and tear of use, i.e. its physical stability.

The impermanence of archive material is related to the degradation of cellulose. As stated earlier, the mechanical strength of a paper depends in great measure on the length of the cellulose chains in the fibrous material used in its production, which may be determined chemically.

Certain materials have been found to protect or stabilize paper, and thus prevent degradation. The Egyptians used natron, a natural and impure form of sodium bicarbonate (baking soda), in mummification. It has been observed that certain mummy wrappings treated with this substance conserve an astonishingly fresh appearance. This condition of mummy wrappings some thousands of years old, constitutes important evidence of the stability of cellulose in the presence of moderately alkaline compounds such as sodium bicarbonate. Nevertheless, accelerated ageing tests have shown that this compound has a detrimental effect on paper, in contrast with its behaviour during natural ageing, as suggested by the mummy wrappings. This is an example of a material which performs well in normal ageing but not in accelerated ageing. Such situations call for knowledge of the materials involved, utmost care in judgement and the judicious use of the solutions, materials and techniques employed in conservation and restoration, together with the appraisal of test data so that errors may be avoided.

The task is therefore not only enormous but involves a knowledge of many different branches of science. As stated by Roger Ellis, those who undertake this work must be acquainted with the various methods of document repair and with the merits and demerits of each. They must study the ever-widening range of materials from which records are made or which may be used in their restoration and repair: paper and ink of every kind, carboard, parchment, vellum, leather, textiles, film, plastic, adhesives; and they should know all that is to be known concerning the behaviour of these materials, over long periods under varying conditions of storage or use. They must, therefore, be at least familiar with the basic principles of physics, chemistry, architecture and entomology. In other words, it has been realized that scientifically trained staff are an essential element of any archive institution, and that the trend is towards seeking expert advice and the help of scientists. The fruit of this policy is seen, as we have pointed out, in the tremendous amount that has been achieved since the Second World War, in both the conservation and restoration fields, by various institutions and individuals.

Systematic investigations have built up our store of modern knowledge concerning the constituent materials present in documents. On the basis of this knowledge, doubtful procedures and materials formerly used for conservation and restoration purposes have been eliminated, and replaced by standardized processes and materials. The need for storing documents in accordance with the best available criteria of conservation has been stressed, since no material can be preserved, even by best available procedures, if its conditions of storage are defective.

Interest has by no means declined. Research has increased during the last few years and is being carried out in many centres and laboratories throughout the world. Institutions contributing to the cause include the Barrow Research Laboratory, Richmond, Virginia, the National Bureau of Standards, Washington, D.C., the Institute of Paper Chemistry, Appleton, Wisconsin, the Graduate Library School, University of Chicago, Chicago, Illinois, and the Empire State Paper Research Institute, Syracuse, New York (United States of America); the British Museum Research Laboratory, London and Imperial College, London (United Kingdom); the Laboratoire de Cryptogamie, Musée National d'Histoire Naturelle, Paris and the Archives Nationales, Paris (France); the Biblioteca Nazionale Centrale, Florence, the Istituto di Patologia del Libro, Rome, and the International Council of Museums, Rome (Italy); the Timber Research Unit, Council for Scientific and Industrial Research, Pretoria (South Africa); the National Archives of India, New Delhi (India); the Council of Scientific and Industrial Research, Canberra (Australia); the Laboratory for the

Preservation and Restoration of Documents, Leningrad, and the Department of Book Hygiene and Restoration, Moscow (Union of Soviet Socialist Republics); the National Library, Sofia (Bulgaria); the Jewish National and University Library, Jerusalem (Israel); the National Archives, Petaling Jaya (Malaysia); the Archivschule, Marburg (Federal Republic of Germany); and a number of institutions in Poland, Romania and Yugoslavia.

Results of research are published in journals such as the *Journal of the Society of Archivists*, and *Archives—the Journal of the British Record Association* (United Kingdom); *The Archivist—Journal of the Society of American Archivists*, the *Library Quarterly*, Chicago, and the *Journal of the National Bureau of Standards* (United States of America); *Indian Archives*, New Delhi (India); the *Unesco Bulletin for Libraries*; *Archivum—Revue Internationale des Archives*, published by ICA, Paris.

Two new journals are devoted mainly to the preservation and restoration of records: *Restaurator*, Copenhagen (Denmark); and *Mitteilungen der Internationalen Arbeitsgemeinschaft der Archiv-, Bibliotheks- und Graphik-Restauratoren*, Freiburg im Breisgau (Federal Republic of Germany). Another journal, *Bulletin d'Information sur la Pathologie des Documents et leur Protection aux Archives de France*, was launched in 1961, but has given no sign of existence during recent years. Besides compiling information on preservation work being carried out in different localities, these journals help to stimulate interest in the preservation of written records as an element of the cultural heritage of the past, for generations of the future.

Among the subjects under investigation at the present time is the non-aqueous deacidification of documents. The Vapour Phase deacidification process and the Chicago Process which uses magnesium methoxide, are being scrutinized. Other notable activities concern the effect on paper of insecticides, cleaning methods and materials; the keeping quality of documents laminated with various plastic films by processes involving heat and pressure or the use of a cold solvent; the evaluation of traditional processes such as silking, tissuing, and backing with the use of one or more of the modern synthetic adhesives as a means of accelerating the restoration work; the strengthening of parchment; the comparison of gelatine and other sizing materials; the synthesis of new and effective fungicides and insecticides; the revival of faded writings; the microanalysis of ink with a view to determining its composition without damaging the document; the treatment of document paper with certain polymers to render it proof against fungus growth; the protection of cellulose from the deteriorative action of light through the use of metallic oxides; the restoration of coated papers; the permanency of microfilms and the prevention of rust formation and spotting on films.

There is a great need to evolve a restoration procedure which will strengthen brittle or damaged documents with the greatest possible degree of speed and safety. Such a procedure should at the same time be cheap and simple.

Much credit for development and research in the field of preservation should go to Unesco, which by sponsoring institutions for the study of the problems involved has made it possible for different countries to pool their knowledge and investigations in the quest for solutions.

Because of the great variety of the constituent materials of written documents and the large number of deteriorating agents, the problem of preserving documents is very complex. It is therefore essential to take action against such agents with a great deal of patience and care, and to use only materials whose suitability has been confirmed by long use and the test of time or which laboratory tests have shown to be effective and least harmful. The indiscriminate use of even those materials is likely to result in greater harm than good. In addition, the work of preservation should be entrusted to technically trained persons and not to those who are unfamiliar either with the material being used for preservation or with the constituent materials of the document itself. If, for example, the cleaning of documents is entrusted to inexperienced workers, the use of materials which are inferior or applied in inaccurate proportions may harm rather than help the documents. If deacidification is carried out incorrectly, through the use of a solution which is too concentrated or of low strength, or if the document is kept in contact with a solution for a longer time than required, the results are also likely to be harmful. Conservation and restoration work, if conducted in the wrong way, can lead to results contrary to that desired, namely preservation. If such disasters are to be avoided, it is advisable to entrust the work to qualified persons who have a technical and scientific background and who have received advanced professional training in the methods of conserving and restoring documents.

In the pages that follow, the various problems involved in the preservation of archive materials including microfilms, tapes and sound recordings have been described and discussed. The book has been planned as follows:

Chapter 1: Constituent Materials of Documents. In this chapter, the materials used in the creation of documents, such as papyrus, parchment, palm leaf, paper, ink, leather, textiles and synthetic materials are described. A short history of these materials is provided to enable the archivist, librarian and restorer to understand the nature of the deterioration to which documents are subjected and the effect of their constituent materials on their durability.

Chapter 2: Deterioration—Causes and Control. In this chapter the causes of deterioration in documents and the methods used to combat such deterioration are presented under three headings: (a) 'Biological Deterioration', i.e. the deterioration caused by micro-organisms, insects and rodents, and measures to counteract such deterioration; (b) 'Physical Deterioration', i.e. the deterioration caused by heat, light, moisture, etc., and measures to counteract or minimize the effect of such agents; (c) 'Chemical Deterioration', i.e. the deterioration caused by acids present in the paper, by ink, atmospheric pollution, etc., and measures to counteract their action.

Chapter 3: Principles of Repair. This chapter discusses the ways and means of undertaking repair, and the underlying reasons.

Chapter 4: Cleaning, Washing and Flattening. A relatively large number of documents require preliminary treatment if they are to be properly preserved. This chapter describes methods of cleaning, etc.

Chapter 5: Deacidification. Acidity is a major cause of deterioration in paper; its removal is a prerequisite of any type of restoration. Methods to combat the residual acidity present in the document are described in this chapter.

Chapter 6: Restoration. Over the years, a number of processes have been developed and used for strengthening brittle documents. Some of these processes are manual and the more recent ones are mechanical. This chapter describes each process and discusses its suitability and utility.

Chapter 7: Special Problems—I. Processes for the repair of maps and plans, documents damaged by water or fire, parchment and palm-leaf documents, and seals are described in this chapter, which also deals with the care of bindings.

Chapter 8: Special Problems—II. This chapter is devoted to the requirements for a small restoration unit, and to suitable materials for restoration and conservation purposes.

Chapter 9: Aids to Preservation. Proper storage, servicing and handling contribute to the keeping qualities of documents, and are thus dealt with in this chapter.

Chapter 10: Preservation of Microfilms and Sound Recordings. The technique of microfilming is now extensively used for reference purposes and for preserving brittle documents. Microfilms, like paper, themselves pose problems of preservation. The conservation of films and sound recordings, including magnetic tapes, are discussed in this chapter.

Each chapter has been illustrated where possible with diagrams or photographs. Six appendixes, giving technical details of materials and preparations, and a bibliography for further study are given at the end of the work.

1 Constituent materials of documents

From earliest times up to the present day, the substances used as vehicles for writing have been numerous. Whatever was convenient and available was used for the purpose—papyrus, cloth, wood, palm leaves, parchment, vellum and paper, until the latter replaced all the other materials.

Paper

The principal chemical constituent of paper is fabricated cellulose fibre which, unfortunately, does not exist in a pure state. Pure cellulose is permanent, but raw cellulose fibres contain fats, waxes, lignin and other impurities which, because they are harmful to paper and contribute to its deterioration, must be removed before a fibre of high quality is obtained.

The processes by which these substances are removed degrade the cellulose fibre. If they are not carried out properly, they weaken the fibre and break the cellulose into other substances, which, in turn, are harmful to the paper. The initial purity of the fibres used determines to a great extent the degree of permanence which may be expected of the paper produced. The physical strength of paper, i.e. its durability, is dependent upon the quality and length of individual fibres as well as on the bonding of the fibres.

The fact that books and documents more than five hundred years old, whose paper remains in good condition, are available in archives and libraries clearly shows that the paper made in the past was intended to last for centuries. Some of the papers are still as good as new. The efforts of archaeologists have unearthed a number of actual specimens or original papers dating back to A.D. 105, when paper was first invented in China.

The early paper-makers produced a lasting and durable paper. Although there is much evidence in literature to show that they gave considerable thought to the production of paper of high quality, a great deal of their knowledge was gained through trial and error.

As we now know, the early papers were produced by stamping or beating hemp, linen rags and ropes in mortars with water until a smooth paste of fibres was obtained. This paste was then diluted with water to a suitable consistency, mixed thoroughly and poured over a linen fabric stretched on a wooden frame mould. This mould was kept in constant vibration in all directions to ensure that the fibres were distributed uniformly. The greater part of the water filtered through, leaving a thin layer of wet and matted fibres on the fabric. This matted fibre sheet was dried in the sun, and then detached from the linen fabric base and cut to size and flattened. Later moulds were made of bamboo strips tied together with silk threads. Samples of paper so made are still in good condition; some of them are almost white, while others have discoloured with the passage of time.

This process of paper-making has not changed. The modern hand-made paper manufacturing technique employs a wooden mould with brass wires laid in parallel or woven across the frame. The newly formed sheet is stripped from the mould when slightly wet to economize on the number of moulds in use.

The paper formed in this way is sized with animal glue or starch to provide greater mechanical strength and the required surface characteristics. The size prevents the ink from feathering on the paper and acids in the bonding of the fibres.

Paper continued to be made from pure rags until the seventeenth century. No method was employed to bleach or camouflage discoloured rags as the supply of clean, new white rags or clippings from garment making was sufficient to meet the demand for writing and printing papers. This explains why so many of the records of that and earlier periods remain in an excellent state of preservation. Thereafter, the use of new and strong rags was confined to the best grades of writing and printing papers, while worn and discoloured rags were generally used for manufacturing inferior quality papers such as wrapping paper, cartridge paper, etc.

Towards the end of the seventeenth century, the demand for paper became great and soon the supply of new white rags was insufficient to meet requirements. As a result, rags of all kinds were treated in various ways to produce fairly white stuff for making paper, and the quality deteriorated. During the nineteenth century, even the linen wrappings of the ancient mummies of Egypt were removed and sold for this purpose. Many of these rags and wrappings were of low physical strength; quite a few contained almost every type of foreign matter, some of which was washed out during the paper-making processes. But even under modern methods of purification, old used rags do not make strong paper.

The use of low-grade rags for some of the papers made after 1700 accounts for their weakened condition today. The indiscriminate use of chlorine as a bleaching agent is one of the factors in the deterioration of the quality of paper. The blueing of paper made of yellowed and deteriorated rags is another; blueing gave the yellowed paper a relatively white appearance and made it possible to use low-grade rags for the production of writing and printing papers. The use of alum as a moderating agent resulted in paper which was acidic in nature.

MODERN PAPERS

Until 1861, almost all quality writing papers were made from rags, as the chemical processes required for converting wood and other materials like esparto and straw into a white and relatively pure cellulose fibre had not yet been developed commercially. In the raw state, wood, esparto, straw, etc., are impure forms of cellulose and require chemical treatment to liberate the fibre in the form most suitable for the production of good quality paper. Chemically produced fibres are fairly long, although much shorter than those of cotton and linen. According to studies made at the United States National Bureau of Standards, the sources of raw materials from which pulp is made are of secondary importance; the degree of purity and the subsequent treatment of the stock during the paper-making processes are of primary importance in the production of permanent papers.

Modern methods, except in the case of mechanical wood pulp (also known as groundwood pulp), involve the digestion of the raw material in large boilers under pressure, with the addition of calcium bisulphate in the sulphite process, caustic soda in the soda process and a complicated mixture of caustic alkalis, usually a mixture of caustic soda and sodium sulphide, in the sulphate process. These methods free the cellulose fibre from impurities and leach out or destroy lignin effectively, leaving the cellulose relatively free from attack. Very careful control of all the factors is required to produce a good yield of pulp and at the same time to remove all undesirable susbtances which, if permitted to remain, cause discolouration and premature deterioration of the paper. The process is usually completed by bleaching with chlorine. The resulting pulp is then thoroughly washed to remove the substances produced during the process.

Bleaching is an important operation from the point of view of permanence. If carried out too drastically, for example, the cellulose is degraded. Furthermore, if the substances produced by the bleaching agent on the impurities in the pulp are not removed, they hasten the deterioration of paper; the colour of the bleached pulp provides no indication of this possibility.

The fibrous material, i.e. the pulp so produced, is diluted with water and macerated in a beater to produce fibres of suitable paper-making quality. Variations in the duration of beating and the set of the beater knives and plates result in the production of entirely different papers from the same stock. During beating, the fibres are completely separated from each other, frayed, hydrated to a certain degree and cut to the right length. They are also provided with a surface corresponding to the grade of paper to be made. Modern beaters are generally constructed of iron and steel and may consequently add small quantities of iron to the paper pulp. This small amount of iron has some influence on the durability of paper (see Chapter 2).

The beating process is of great importance in paper-making. It determines the character of the final paper, and is therefore of significance to its durability, i.e. its strength. On the other hand, the operation of sizing carried out in the beater is probably the most important factor influencing permanence. Beating may be described as the process which determines the ultimate shape of fibres and consequently the properties of paper.

Sizing materials and others, such as loading materials, are then added to the pulp in the beater. Sizing consists of the addition of a diluted solution of rosin to the pulp and its precipitation on to the fibres by the further addition of alum. Sizing binds the fibre and prevents ink from spreading on the paper. It also contributes to the felting process during the formation of the sheet in the machine.

The alum-rosin combination increases the acidity of the mixture. If an excessive quantity of alum is used, the finished paper has undesirably high acidity and poor ageing qualities. The sizing process must therefore be carefully controlled in order to combine maximum strength in the paper with an acceptable level of acidity. Iron-free water and alum are used in paper manufacture to prevent discoloration during storage.

The pulp thus prepared in the beater is diluted to the consistency which suits the paper machine and which will result in the required thickness of the finished paper. It is then run into a long vibrating wire screen, which strains out the pulp and felts the fibres together. The paper is carried in a continuous sheet by the screen to the drier rollers, where it is pressed and dried.

High-grade record papers in finished form are frequently run through a bath of warm, diluted animal glue or starch to increase their strength and improve their surface and erasing qualities. Such surface sizing is relatively permanent and does not harm the paper.

Machine-made paper produced in this way is much smoother and more even than a hand-made sheet, and also has a more strongly pronounced grain.

Investigations have shown that bleaching with chlorine and other compounds and the use of alum in sizing are the principal sources of high acidity in modern paper. Papers made in the past contained alkaline compounds due to the use of (a) lye, made from wood ashes, for bleaching rags; (b) hard water, used in the paper-making process; and (c) chalk, used for whitening the pulp. W. J. Barrow has overcome this defect in modern papers, making paper from long, strong, well-furnished chemical wood fibres, sized with aquapel (non-acid) and loaded with calcium carbonate. This paper is alkaline and withstands the injuries caused by acid inks and atmospheric pollution.

In the selection of papers for permanent records, careful physical and chemical examinations are desirable as a means of determining their durability and permanence.

The durability of paper is determined mostly by physical tests. These tests simulate the stresses and strains of actual use of a book by bending the sheet of paper to and fro and subjecting it to the forces of pulling and tearing. The permanence of paper is related to its chemical properties, to the qualities of its fibres and to the process of manufacture. Chemical tests determine the acidity of paper, the purity of pulp and expected behaviour during ageing. The latter is determined through a combination of physical and chemical tests (see Appendix 1).

Tests such as those mentioned above have shown that the grades of paper which have the greatest permanence are those made from pulps with high cuprammonium viscosity, high alpha cellulose content, low copper number, low lignin content and low pentosan and gamma cellulose content. In other words, the factors which promote permanence in paper are: (a) purity of cellulose pulp; (b) high initial strength; (c) absence of loading; (d) minimum acidity—or better still, total absence of acidity; (e) minimum amount of residual chemicals; and (f) low rosin content.

To obtain a finished paper of the desired properties a number of variable have to be controlled and taken into account. These include the type of fibre used, the extent of cooking and bleaching and the degree of bonding between fibres, which determine to a large degree the physical properties of the paper. The amount of fibre treatment, formation on the wire, the amount of wet processing, methods of drying and the amount of calendering affect the degree of bonding.

Modern practices and manufacturing techniques have made it possible to obtain good quality paper from any fibre. In this connexion, standards for different grades of paper have been laid down in almost every country.

Palm leaves

Writing on palm leaves was practised until the nineteenth century or even later in some parts of India and Ceylon (now Sri Lanka).

There are two types of palm, the Talipat and the Palmyra. Leaves from each type were used extensively for writing purposes in southern India and to some extent in northern India and adjoining countries like Burma, Sri Lanka and Thailand. Numerous examples of records written on these leaves are to be found in private collections and institutions in Burma, Federal Republic of Germany, India, Japan, Nepal, Sri Lanka, Thailand and other countries.

PREPARATION OF THE LEAVES

Leaves from the palms are prepared for writing purposes in an ingenious manner. Strips 40–90 cm long and 4–7.5 cm wide are cut from the leaf, and boiled in water or milk. Any abnormal growth is then pared off with a knife. The strips are smoothed and their surface rubbed with gingili oil to adapt them for writing purposes. Desired lengths are then cut from the prepared strips, uniformity being rather a matter of length than of width. The leaves are thin and stiff but smooth, and some relatively flexible. Writing is accomplished by means of a stylus or metal pencil which cuts into the leaf. Some talipat leaves, however, are inscribed in carbonacious ink. In order to make the scratched writing visible, ink prepared by mixing oil with charcoal or a black pigment with water is rubbed over the surface of the leaf, thus rendering the letters discernible and distinct. Such writing cannot be effaced. Two holes are pierced on each strip and the leaves are then tied together with strings passed through the holes and attached between two wooden planks. They are finally wrapped in cloth which is usually red or yellow in colour.

The two varieties of palm leaves can be easily distinguished. Talipat leaves are thin and broad, and have clearly marked cross-veins in the form of rills. Their width varies from 4 to 8 cm and they taper gently from the centre towards the edges. Inscriptions are in carbonaceous ink. Palmyra leaves are thick and coarse, and have a pockmarked appearance. Their width varies from 3 to 5 cm. Their inscriptions are made by a stylus. Palmyra leaves came into use for writting at a much later date, in about A.D. 1675. They darken with age and the reproduction of older specimens presents very formidable problems.

Birch bark

A number of manuscripts on birch bark still exist in India and Nepal, and in certain institutions throughout the world. The earliest extant documents, believed to date from A.D. 450, are inscribed in Brahmi Script and were discovered in 1889 in eastern Turkistan.

Like the Talipat palm leaf, these birch bark manuscripts are oblong and have a string hole. They exist in two sizes, 28.5 by 6.5 cm, and 23 by 5 cm approximately. They are in typical Indian *Pothi* form, separate leaves being tied together in a bundle through the string holes in the sheets and attached between wooden boards.

Birch-bark manuscripts of the tenth and eleventh centuries are broader. They measure approximately 17.5 by 10 cm and have no string holes. Manuscripts of the later period have the form of modern books, i.e. they are folded in the middle to form a folio of two leaves or four pages.

The bark sheets consist of a number of thin layers and are prepared in various ways. As a general rule, pieces of bark measuring approximately 90 by 20 cm are cut from the tree, beaten to produce a hard surface and then smoothed for writing purposes by oiling and polishing. The bark is durable and immune from insect attack because of the presence of birch oil, a natural preservative chemical.

Papyrus

Papyrus was the chief writing material of the ancient Egyptians and is sculptured in roll forms on many of their temples. Papyrus documents dating back to antiquity, some in single sheets and many in roll forms, are still in existence.

The manufacture of this writing material, as practised in Egypt, has been described by Pliny. The technique is as follows:

Strips of stumps cut from the 'Cyprus papyrus' reed are laid side by side to the required width. Another layer of shorter strips is then laid over them at right angles. The two layers are then soaked in water (according to Pliny, Nile water was used in ancient Egypt), beaten to form a sheet and then dried in the sun. The two layers form a 'net' and impart a woven texture to the sheet. The upper layer is recto and the under layer verso.

The dried sheet is smoothed and polished with ivory, pumice-stone or a smooth shell. Several sheets are then joined together to form a roll. Writing on them is in ink probably made from a mixture of glue, lampblack and water.

The height of the roll has varied through the ages from 15 to 45 cm. The length has also varied, and rolls up to 30 m long, though rare, exist.

Papyrus was in use around the shores of the Mediterranean. During the Roman period it was universally employed for correspondence and legal documents. Its use for writing purposes diminished as parchment and vellum became available, and ended in the eighth and ninth centuries with the growing manufacture of paper. It may, however, have been manufactured in Egypt as late as A.D. 1050. Used for 4,000 years, papyrus could not survive a damp climate. The specimens which remain are kept in safe custody under lock and key, and more often than not facsimiles alone are found in libraries and other institutions.

Parchment and vellum

The use of skins became noticeable in about 200 B.C. More general use began in A.D. 1, but did not supersede the use of papyrus. The earliest extant examples date from A.D. 100. From the fourth century onwards the use of papyrus declined, and skins came into prominent usage as a medium of writing. Sheep, calf and goat skins were most commonly employed although other animals also lent their hides to culture. Over the centuries, the word 'parchment' came to signify the skin obtained from sheep and goats, while vellum referred to a fine quality of skin obtained from calf, kid or lamb, its quality depending on the youth of the animal. Vellum is the material used in the superb books of the middle ages.

Parchment is a very strong, paper-like material. Vellum on the other hand is finer, thinner, whiter and smoother than ordinary parchment. Both materials are strong and resistant to tearing, withstand considerable use without deterioration and are suitable vehicles for writing or printing. Parchment offers little or no resistance to the pen. It is almost white and can be written on both sides. The flesh side is somewhat darker, but retains ink better. Vellum is costly. Its hair side is slightly darker and yellow, while the flesh side tends to be nearer white. Before the widespread manufacture of paper, parchment and vellum were commonly used for books. Their use was later restricted to certain important documents.

The skin of such animals as sheep, lamb, goat or calf is cleaned of its hair and wool by washing and soaking in a lime pit, and then stretched on a frame and the remaining hair or flesh removed. It is then wetted, covered with powdered chalk and rubbed with pumice-stone. The treated skin is allowed to dry in the frame. All these operations are conducted with great care, to produce a skin of right structure capable of receiving writing on both sides.

Although parchment and vellum are stronger than paper, they are very sensitive to humidity. They are, in fact, more sensitive than paper to climatic variations. Most parchment documents are written with iron gall ink which has faded with time and acquired a brown hue.

The arrangement of the leaves of parchment and vellum books is essentially the same as that of the pages of modern books. In order to secure uniformity in tint, hair side is laid next to hair side and flesh side to flesh side in making up the quires for a volume. Hair side skins are sometimes most obvious in facsimile and at times give trouble in reproduction, the coarser structure obscuring fine pen strokes.

Leather

The skins of such animals as goats, sheep, cattle and lambs, etc., have been used for writing and binding purposes from the earliest times. Even in prehistoric times man knew how to utilize and preserve animal hides and skins. As we now know, these are preserved either by treatment with lime, described in the section on parchment and vellum, or by converting them into leather by chemical treatment and tanning. Another process for the preservation of skins involves treatment with alum; skins so treated being known as tawed skins.

There are two types of leather: vegetable tanned or mineral tanned. Vegetable tanned leather is made by treating skins with extracts from the bark of oak and hemlock trees. The tannins in the bark solution react with the proteins in the skin and convert it into leather. The actual process is, however, a complicated one, usually lasting months and involving washing the hides, loosening the air by lime treatment, scraping off the epidermis, soaking in bark solution and finally drying, finishing, polishing, graining, etc.

Vegetable tanned leather is water-resistant, flexible and permits artistic working. It also resists decay and the action of acids. The skin retains protective non-tans (water-soluble organic salts deposited in the leather during the tanning process) which prevent rotting by sulphuric dioxide. Some early tanned leathers have lasted very well.

To meet the increasing demand for leather in the nineteenth century, the tanning process was reduced from months to days, through the use of sulphuric and acetic acids. These acids dissolve the non-tans and leave harmful salts in the leather which cause rotting and decay of leather bindings, as revealed in many of the leather bindings of the nineteenth century standing on the shelves of archives and libraries throughout the world.

Mineral tanned leather, and especially leather tanned with chromium salts, is of good quality and durable. It is, however, stiff and thus unsuitable for binding purposes. Of the various types of leather used for binding, the best is vegetable tanned goat skin, commonly known as Morocco, Niger, Cape or Persian leather, and calf leather, although a number of other varieties, such as sheepskin, pigskin, cowhide, imitation goatskin, etc., have been used for this purpose. The latter, however, are not durable.

The most important factor in the preservation of leather is the tanning process. Untreated leather does not keep well, goes mouldy and is extremely sensitive to humidity. Tanning makes the leather pliable, resistant to decomposition or bacterial decay, especially when wet, and improves other properties, including its tensile strength. Nevertheless, like paper and palm leaf, leather is affected by extreme climatic conditions and polluted atmosphere.

Textiles

The textiles used for writing purposes are generally made from vegetable fibres such as cotton, flax and hemp. Silk and wool do not appear to have been used for archive documents. Textiles made from cellulose materials keep very well and resist normal deterioration. They are, however, easily damaged by insects and biological agents.

Inks

Ink is one of the most important components of records. In one form or another, it has been used for writing on paper, parchment, vellum, palm leaf and similar materials ever since man felt the need to record his progress, and is still indispensable for the creation of records and for activities connected with the day-to-day business of life.

Ink may well be defined as a liquid medium by means of which words or characters are recorded or drawn upon paper or similar material in more or less permanent form. Further, it is a liquid which is clear and not a suspension, is mobile but does not spread, has an intense colour which does not fade (essential for a good ink), is odourless and has little acidity.

CARBON INKS

Carbon ink was widely used for writing until the nineteenth century and is still preferred for fine work. Its use has been widespread all over the world, especially in the East.

Carbon ink, known as 'India ink', is made from lampblack or soot. The pigment is held in suspension in water by means of glue, gelatine or gum. Such ink is permanent and not at all harmful to the material written upon. Ink similar to 'India ink' but in a solid state is known as 'China ink'. These inks are carbon inks and black in colour.

IRON-GALL INK

Carbon inks, though permanent, can easily be washed off or removed with a wet cloth. To overcome this defect, iron-gall ink was developed for writing on parchment and vellum documents.

Iron gall ink is a combination of iron salts (green vitriol or copperas, i.e. ferrous sulphate) with the infusion of tannins obtained from nut galls. Freshly made, the ink has very little colour and cannot be used, but during storage gradual oxidation takes place and a blue-black colour is developed. The ink thus formed has a natural tendency to settle. The addition of substances like gum prevent this precipitation or sedimentation.

It has been observed that after writing on paper or parchment the oxidation of the ink continues. During this process, the ink fixes itself indelibly on these materials, the degree of indelibility depending on its tannin and iron contents. Such writing has remained legible for centuries, but has faded from black to brown, through the action of residual chemicals in the paper, and of light.

Oxidation of the ink leads to the formation of acid. This, together with the hydrochloric or sulphuric acid added to the ink to improve its flow, has an adverse effect on paper. The acid has burnt and in many cases perforated the paper. In some cases it has migrated to adjacent sheets and contamined them. Many examples of such damage exist in almost all archives. Vellum manuscripts, however, have not been adversely affected, presumably because of their alkaline nature.

The modern practice is to add a suitable dye, usually of blue colour, so that the ink writes blue, turning into blue-black as the writing oxidizes or matures. The added dye has little or no influence on the fastness of writing to washing, but gives an agreeably bold colour to the writing.

A variety of dyes have been used for this purpose. The first to be used was extract of logwood, which improves the colour of iron-gall inks and when heated with potassium chromate produces a satisfactory deep-blue solution. The greenish shade when writing changes to black on drying.

Next to be used was indigo, which increases the intensity of the ink. This was replaced by aniline dyes, which have become common constituents of iron-gall inks. Naphthalene Blue is one of the most common dyes used in the ink industry.

These inks are more or less permanent and contain iron in the form of ferrous sulphate. The proportion of ferrous sulphate varies with the type of ink required, such as permanent record ink, ordinary writing ink and fountain-pen inks. Formulae of the various inks are provided in Appendix 2.

A good ink should, as a general rule: (a) yield permanent writing which should become relatively black within a few days; (b) flow rapidly from the pen and penetrate the fibres of the paper without passing right through them; (c) neither gelatinize nor become mouldy in the ink pot; (d) have a minimum corrosive action upon steel pens; and (e) be neither sticky nor quick drying.

Modern inks

FOUNTAIN-PEN INK

Although extensively used for records where permanence is required, iron-gall inks cannot be used in good quality fountain pens as the acids which they contain destroy the nib. They have been almost entirely superseded by solutions of synthetic dyes which are free from acid and have the same tinctorial power as the modern iron-gall inks. Among the dyes used are Black Nigrosine, Fuschine, Brilliant-Orange R, Naphthal Yellow and Diamond Green. However, such inks have poor light fastness and hence are not permanent. They are soluble in water or other solvents, with the result that the writing spreads on becoming wet. These defects have been overcome by the use of certain substantive dyes which on drying adhere to the fibre. These inks are strongly alkaline with a pH of 12–13, and are fast to light.

BALL-POINT INKS

Ball-point pens do not function properly with iron-gall inks, mainly because of their acidity and muddiness. The inks used for such pens, whose formulae are secrets closely guarded by the manufacturers, are made from fast dyes (usually basic dyes), mixed with an oily solvent.

These inks are, however, not permanent. They are soluble in alcohol and other organic solvents and may be washed off without difficulty. They do not sink deeply into the paper and may thus be removed easily either by soaking in spirit or by an eraser.

Recently introduced inks are effective, and permanent in the sense that they cannot be removed with erasers without easily detectable damage to the surface of the paper.

PRINTING INKS

Printing inks are suspensions of pigments in various proportions in a varnish base. The proportion of the varnish oil varies from 70 to 78 per cent, while the proportion of pigment depends to a great extent on the character of printing required. Boiled linseed oil, a drying oil which solidifies as a result of oxidation on boiling, is commonly used as a varnish. The pigments commonly used are: (a) lampblack or amorphous carbon for black-coloured inks; (b) beryta white, zinc oxide, titanium oxide and antimony oxide for white inks; (c) chrome yellow and zinc chromate for yellow-coloured inks; (d) vermilion (Hgs), scarlet chrome and maddar (Alizarin) for red-coloured inks; and (e) ultramarine and Prussian blue for blue-coloured inks.

These inks are permanent and outlast the paper on which they are used.

TYPEWRITER INKS

Typewritten documents, especially copies, figure increasingly in archive collections and may eventually outnumber printed and written documents. Typewriter inks are fast to light, erasure and solvents. The ribbon of a typewriter is made from a thin, tough textile fabric impregnated with an oily base carrying oil-soluble dyes or insoluble pigments. The black pigment is usually some form of carbon and for this reason black ribbons can always be relied upon for permanence. The ink, because of the oily medium in which it is suspended, penetrates the paper slowly. After two days or so it becomes difficult to erase without damage to the paper.

The earliest inks used were strong solutions of aniline dyes in spirit or water. Glycerine was added in small quantities to prevent the ink from drying too rapidly. Modern typewriter inks are almost identical with printing inks, and insoluble pigments are used to a large extent.

INK FOR CARBON PAPERS

When only a few copies are required, tissue paper backed with specially prepared inks is commonly used. The ink consists of a wax base containing lampblack or wax soluble dyes, and is applied to thick, strong paper. The 'carbon' impresion left by the typewriter key on the paper can be erased easily with a pencil eraser. Being black, the writing is fast to light.

STENCIL DUPLICATING INKS

When more copies are required, the method of stencil duplication is employed. Inks for this purpose have special characteristics. They flow readily from the roller, do not clog the stencil sheet and dry readily on paper. The pigment does not separate from the medium either on the rollers or when spread on paper. These qualities are achieved by the use either of an essential oil or a vegetable oil or hydrocarbon of suitable viscosity.

Adhesives

It is important to use proper adhesives for the preservation of archives. The adhesives commonly used are flour or starch paste and glue. These have been used for binding records and, whenever necessary, for reinforcing brittle, broken or torn sheets. Every collection of records includes documents on which these adhesives have been used for repair and binding. Formulae of some of these adhesives are provided in Appendix 3.

More recently, a number of commercially available ready-made pastes have come into use. These pastes are for the most part of uncertain composition and documents treated with them have in some cases shown signs of decay. Carefully prepared preparations of polyvinyl alcohol are, however, reasonably safe and are used in many archive centres throughout the world.

Synthetic materials

Synthetic materials have been used recently with increasing frequency either in place of leather bindings, which are expensive, or for the protection of cloth bindings. The most commonly used are polyvinyl chloride, vinyl chloro-acetate and polyvinyl acetate. The former are unstable, become yellow with age and decompose to give chlorine or chlorides, which are harmful to archive materials. Vinyl acetates are relatively more stable and appear to keep well. Other synthetic materials which have been or are being used include cellulose acetate film for restoration purposes and carboxy methyl cellulose, soluble nylon and methyl cellulose for sizing and repair work.

2   Deterioration—causes and control

Depending upon natural and environmental conditions, paper is subject to attack from several sources. Heat, sunlight, moisture, dust and dirt are known to damage paper and cause deterioration in its properties. Similarly, acidic and other gases present in the atmosphere and harmful chemicals added during manufacture adversely affect the storage life of paper.

The agents which cause deterioration in paper may be broadly classified as: (a) biological agents; (b) physical agents; and (c) chemical agents. The degrading effect of these agents begins rather slowly and is likely to escape detection at an early stage unless constant vigilance is maintained.

Other causes of deterioration in archive materials include acts of God like flood and fire and acts of man like riots, deliberate destruction and mishandling. Another factor is improper conservation and restoration, due either to a lack of information or to the use of out-moded and outdated processes and materials.

Such deterioration can be counteracted by the use of modern scientific methods which already exist or are in the process of development as a result of research and investigation conducted by various institutions throughout the world.

Biological deterioration

Biological agents cause most damage in tropical countries. In countries like the United States of America and in cold climatic regions, the problem is less serious. This is not to say that it does

48

not exist in the libraries of archives of such countries, for most of the materials of which archives are composed are particularly susceptible to damage by biological agents. It is therefore desirable to be aware of infestation by certain biological agents like fungi, bacteria and insects, which have been observed to cause damage to archive materials.

FUNGI

Fungi are among the most important biological agents. Together with bacteria they are termed microbiological agents.

Fungi are actively responsible for the decomposition of cellulose; many are pigment forming and stain paper usually with yellow, brown and black spots, although some form colourless colonies and colouration of this type may also be due to other non-viable agents, such as iron and lignin. Most fungi destroy cellulose, stain block bindings and cause damage to glue, pastes, and other adhesives. Binding cords, leather, parchment, artificial leather and plastics are also affected.

The growth of fungi is influenced by such environmental factors as humidity, temperature, light and nutrients, the two most important of which are humidity and temperature.

Fungi spores, which are always present in the atmosphere, grow at temperatures near freezing as well as temperatures as high as 50–55° C. But a combination of high temperatures and moist conditions, such as exposure to steam for 15 seconds at 110° C, kill most fungi and fungal spores. They withstand prolonged periods of freezing or subfreezing temperatures, and grow and reproduce as soon as the temperature and other conditions favourable to their growth exist in the storage rooms. Below 70 per cent relative humidity (RH), however, the growth is nil. Higher RH produces variable rates of growth. At 80 to 90 per cent RH, for example, growth is considerable, and above 95 per cent RH it is abundant. It has been observed that the relationship between relative humidity and temperature is of importance and that optimum conditions vary. For example, the optimum temperature for growth of fungi at 95 per cent RH is 30° C, and at 100 per cent RH, 37.5° C. At 70 per cent RH the optimum temperature is considerably lower, i.e. 24–25° C.

Both light and darkness are conducive to the growth of fungi, so there is little to choose between the two conditions in the storage area. Although a certain amount of ultra-violet light is lethal to fungi, it also affects paper adversely.

Fungus growth may be affected by the presence of sizing or filling materials. Fungi have been observed to flourish on papers containing dextrine, starch and gelatine. Other nutrients which have an influence of growth of fungi are carbohydrates, the salts of metallic elements, amino acids, proteins and oxides of nitrogen.

Even the slightest trace of fungus or mould should be considered as a warning of infestation and an indication that temperature and humidity are above the limits of safety in the storage rooms. Generally, fungus or mould growth is abundant in damp places such as cellars and badly ventilated rooms. The presence of such growth may be easily recognized by the powdery mass formed on the surface of infested materials.

The action of fungi may be very slow, requiring from several months to two years before damage may be detected by normal means. The amount of growth may not be exactly determined from the intensity or extent of the area of discoloration, since some fungi grow with little colour production while others produce a great amount of colour with very limited growth. The acid produced by fungi also appears to influence the intensity of colour, the optimum pH being 4.8–5.6. The actual degree of destruction of cellulose in paper should, therefore, be determined by quantitative measurement of strength losses.

As a result of fungus growth, the cellulose fibres of paper become soft and weak, but may still be handled and folded without breaking; this fact helps to distinguish damage due to acid, where the paper becomes so brittle that it cracks on mere folding. Starch, glue, paste and adhesives are converted into other materials, and the paper becomes desized, soft and as absorbent as blotting paper. Ultimately it is reduced to pulp. Similarly, leather begins to rot, and the binding gives way. Fungi also affect inks, particularly iron-gall inks, which are susceptible and fade. In extreme cases the fading is complete and it becomes difficult to restore such writings.

Papers vary in their resistance to fungi. For example, machine-made papers are more prone to fungus attack than hand-made papers. This is probably due to the chemical treatment and other processes used during their manufacture. Generally papers with a pH of 5.5–6.0 are extremely resistant to mould. Certain less hygro-scopic papers, e.g. sized papers, specially rosin sized, and calendered papers, are resistant to fungi attack.

It has been observed that vegetable tanned leathers are more susceptible to attack by fungi and to mould growth than chrome tanned leathers. This is probably because of the chemicals used for tanning, for the collagen fibres in the leather are seldom affected.

Foxing

A common growth observed on old papers in muniment rooms is the brown spotting known as 'foxing'. These spots are independent of the mould growth and may occur even though the conditions which favour growth of fungi have been eliminated. Such stains are the result of chemical action between iron impurities in the paper and organic acids released by the fungi. The amount of moisture necessary for the spots to grow or appear is far less than that required to render mould growth visible. The extent of staining depends upon the impurities present in the paper. It has been observed that papers of the earlier period, i.e. the fourteenth century, which contain almost pure cellulose, are less foxed than papers of the eighteenth or nineteenth centuries, which are made from thin fibres and by machine.

Preventive measures

The elimination of mildew infection requires precautionary measures such as cleanliness in the restoration workshop and the maintenance of proper temperature and relative humidity.

Optimum conditions for checking the growth of fungus are a temperature of 20–24° C and relative humidity of 45–55. These may only be achieved by air-conditioning. If the control of temperature and relative humidity within these limits is not possible, efforts should be made to retard fungus growth by maintaining free circulation of air, which helps to prevent fluctuations in humidity and the consequent formation of pockets amenable to fungus growth. Assistance in the control of humidity is also provided by wooden furniture and curtains, which absorb moisture when relative humidity is high and exude moisture when it is low. An essential piece of equipment for the measurement of humidity is the hygrometer, with which every storage room in an archive institution should be provided. The hygrometer should be checked for accuracy at least once a month, with the aid of a psychrometer.

High humidity in a room may also be reduced through the use of machines such as dehumidifiers or by chemicals like silica gel, anhydrous calcium chloride and slaked lime. Dehumidifiers are effective when in round-the-clock operation with doors and windows closed. Doors should be opened as little as possible, and the air should be kept in constant circulation by means of exhaust fans. The dehumidifier has no effect on the temperature. Silica gel and anhydrous calcium chloride are also effective in a closed room. To dehumidify 25 m^3 of air space, approximately 3 kg of silica gel are required. As it absorbs moisture, the silica gel becomes pink and can be regenerated to its bluish colour by heating in an oven. Silica gel in bags of thin mesh cloth or packed in plastic net pockets should be distributed about the room. Anhydrous calcium chloride also absorbs moisture and is effective, but less easy to regenerate than silica gel. Another chemical which has been used is slaked lime in earthen pots. Once saturated, it cannot be used again.

Despite all these precautions, cases of mildew do occur in some parts of storage areas, even when air-conditioned. This is due to excessively tight stacking of volumes and books on shelves close to the floor, wall or ceiling. In air-conditioned areas, faulty ducts may be responsible. The remedy is to reshelve the volumes, circulate the air with fans to prevent the formation of pockets, clean the infested area and volumes, and redesign the ducts in the air-conditioned area.

Mildew on papers may be prevented by the use of preservatives or by treatment with fungicides. Experience and information available in the relevant literature show that untreated paper actively supports fungus growth and that once infested such paper cannot be reconditioned satisfactorily.

A wide variety of organic and inorganic compounds and chemicals have been recommended and are currently used for protection against microbiological attack. These include acetone, beta-naphthol, formaldehyde, para-nitrophenol, pentachlorophenol and its sodium salt, boric acid, salicylanilide, ontho-phenylphenol, 2-hydroxy-diphenyl amine, thymol, ethylene oxide, chloramine-T, etc.

The choice of a fungicide depends on such factors as toxicity to human beings, the nature of the paper, volatility, odour, reaction with other chemicals, cost and availability. For example, pentachlorophenol in 0.5 per cent concentration or more may prove dermatitic, but is harmless to man in 0.25 per cent concentration and is considered effective, and has been used for wrapping records with paper previously impregnated with 1 per cent solution of this chemical. Pentachlorophenol is, however, relatively volatile, and the treated paper has to be changed if the volume wrapped in it is used often. Low volatility is generally desirable.

Salicylanilide (trade name Shirlan) is non-volatile and long-lasting, and has proved useful as an inhibitor for brown stains and foxing, but is harmful to archive records, manuscripts, and books if not employed in correct concentration.

The use of boric acid or salicylic acid is restricted, as relatively large amounts are required for it to be effective.

Para-nitrophenol is effective, but leaves a light greenish tinge if used in higher concentrations.

Ortho-phenyl phenol is proving its worth as a fungicide and is used as a preservative in pastes employed for restoration work. It has low toxicity and is as wide-ranging as pentachlorophenol in its destruction of different types of fungus. It is stable and unlikely to break down or interact chemically with other substances. It is soluble in water and is alkaline; in 10 per cent aqueous solution it has a pH of 11. Tissue paper sheets impregnated with this solution may be used for interleaving documents or wrapping them, even in rooms which are subject to mould growth. They may be laid on shelves prior to arranging volumes and documents on them and also used for covering the tops of documents in such rooms. As its volatility is very low, impregnated tissue may be used for a period of from six to nine months without replacement. Recommended on the basis of tests by laboratories engaged in conservation work, it was utilized by the author in Florence in 1969, and a large number of documents damaged in the 1966 floods have been effectively protected by this compound against fungus growth. It is employed there in the form of a 0.5 per cent solution added to the paste used for restoration work.

Two most outstanding fungicides are sodium salt of pentachlorophenol (Santobrite) and sodium salt of ortho-phenyl phenol (Topane). Another variety, Preventol may also be used.

Ortho-phenyl phenol in 5 per cent solution has been used with successful results as a fungicide for leather.

Mould spores present in infested records are killed by exposure to thymol fumes. Thymol does not give permanent protection but is effective and easy to use, although caution should be exercised as it affects ink and attacks paint and varnish. It does not reduce mildew stains but inhibits mildew growth effectively. Virtually non-toxic and readily available, it may at times have a softening effect on parchment, vellum, size and glue, but the 'use of thymolized dusters can do little harm'.

Thymol fumigation

Infested documents or volumes are exposed to thymol vapours in a sealed chamber or a cabinet. A simple cabinet of size 150 cm length, 75 cm width and 135 cm height (approx. 5 ft by 2½ ft by 4½ ft) is made of wood, the interior of the cabinet being left unpainted and unvarnished. Soft rubber gaskets on the door render it air-tight. The cabinet is designed to accommodate loose papers, books, manuscripts, maps and prints. The material for fumigation is spread in an inverted 'V' on a removable framework of wire netting some 15 cm above the bottom of the cabinet. A 40-watt electric bulb is placed underneath a watch-glass containing thymol crystals. Heat from the lighted bulb vaporizes the thymol in the watch-glass. One hour of heating daily is sufficient to vaporize enough thymol to saturate the air inside the cabinet and fumigate or sterilize the documents and volumes which it contains. The recommended quantity of thymol is 120 grammes for every cubic metre of space. In recent experiments, the use of 20 grammes of thymol per cubic metre has proved effective.

Designs of three cabinets, two in use in the National Archives, New Delhi (Figs. 1 and 2), and the other (Fig. 3) at the Bibliothèque Nationale, Paris, are provided.

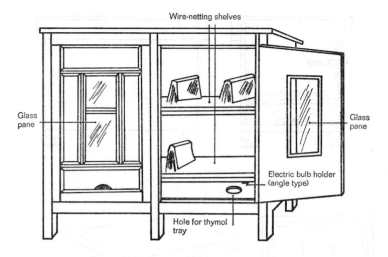

FIG. 1. Thymol fumigation chamber.

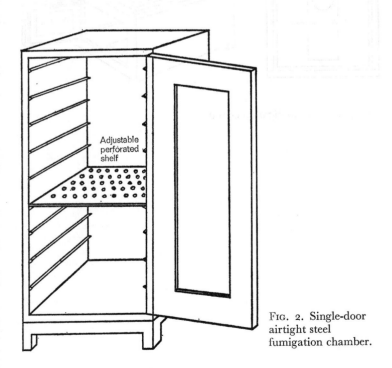

FIG. 2. Single-door airtight steel fumigation chamber.

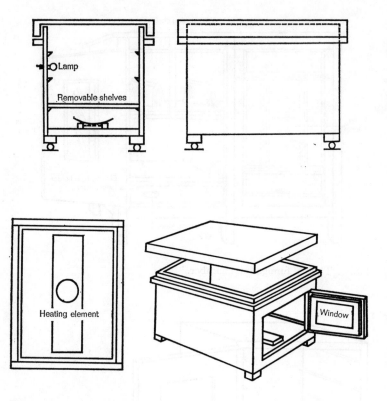

Fig. 3. Portable fumigation chamber.

Mallet fumigation chamber (Formaldehyde fumigation) [*Photo:* National Archives, Paris].

Vacuum fumigation chamber [*Photo:* Venice State Archives].

Thymol fumigation cabinet in use at the National Archives, New Delhi. [*Photo:* National Archives, New Delhi].

Damage by
cockroaches [*Photo:*
National Archives,
New Delhi].

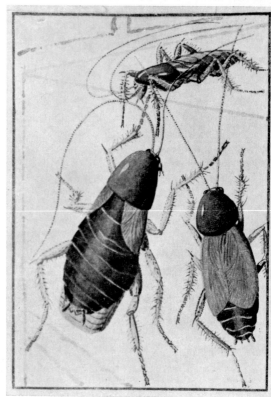

Cockroaches
[*Photo:* National
Archives, New Delhi].

White-ant worker
[*Photo:* National Archives, New Delhi].

White-ant damage
[*Photo:* National Archives, New Delhi].

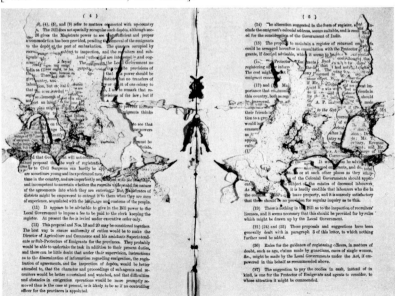

Book-worm damage [*Photo:* National Archives, New Delhi].

Water-stained and fungus-damaged document [*Photo:* National Archives, New Delhi].

The normal fumigation cycle is forty-eight hours for documents which have not been badly affected. In more severe cases, the cycle lasts from six to ten days depending upon the intensity of infestation. As mentioned earlier, thymol fumigation affects parchment and vellum. Damage to documents in these materials may be due to excessively long heating of the thymol crystals with subsequent crystallization on the document, or to placing the documents and volumes too close to the point of vaporization. It has been observed that parchment documents do not become soft or sticky as a result of this treatment if they are aired until free from the smell of thymol. If the fumigation has been properly conducted, the danger of mould redeveloping in the storage area is practically nil.

A fumigation chamber in the form of a room approximately 4.5 m long, 1.8 m wide and 2.4 m high has been designed at the Somerset Record Office, in the United Kingdom. The chamber has an extractor fan on a window on the outer wall to expel foul air, and an inlet vent in an inner wall to draw in fresh air. The fan's capacity is such that it can effect four air changes in an hour. Capable of functioning as an airing, drying and fumigation unit, the chamber may serve both as a fumigating unit and as an airing room in tropical countries where documents are easily attacked by mould.

If a cabinet or chamber is not available, mould growth may be checked by interleaving the sheets in books, volumes or even loose documents with tissue paper previously impregnated with 10 per cent thymol solution in alcohol. The treated tissue paper is inserted between every ten sheets or so and in a few weeks all mould growth is destroyed. This technique has also been sucessfully used to counteract mould growth on papyrus.

Even rooms infested with mould growth can be effectively sterilized by spraying a 10 per cent solution of thymol in alcohol with a 'swing fog' machine (a type of spray gun). This process is also used for checking mould growth on the infested material stored in the room. For the best results, all doors and windows of the room should be closed for at least twenty-four hours. If necessary, the room may be sprayed again after a week. Addition of Killopetra (three parts of ethylene dichloride to one part of carbon tetrachloride) to the spraying solution creates a 'smoke' which helps to make the spraying uniform. After treatment, the infested documents should be cleaned to remove all fluffy fungus growth.

Fumigation with ethylene oxide

In the early sixties attempts were made to devise an effective fumigation technique for use against fungi. It was observed that exposure of documents to 50 per cent mixture of ethylene oxide and air for twenty-four hours in a vacuum chamber 'had a definite destructive effect on fungi'. Documents treated by this procedure at the Archives Nationales, Paris, in 1960 have shown excellent results. Since ethylene oxide and air have a tendency to form an explosive mixture, the work should be carried out with care.

Disinfection of repositories

Before storing documents in the rooms of a repository subject to fungi, it is desirable to sterilize the affected rooms by spraying with a 5 per cent solution of lauryl-dimethyl-carboxy-methyl-ammonium bromide in methylated spirit. Its use in various archive repositories has been found to be effective. It is essential to wear a mask as the quaternary ammonium compound may cause irritation of the mucous membrane.

Another solution which has been used with success against fungus for sterilizing muniment rooms is an 80 per cent solution of triethylamine diborolactate decahydrate, dispersed in a vapour form at the rate of 5 cm per cubic metre of air. It is essential after treatment to check the documents for effectiveness.

Control of fungi by the use of ultra-violet light and gamma radiation has been attempted at the Lenin State Library in the U.S.S.R. Such treatment is, however, dangerous because of the harm caused by ultra-violet rays to organic materials such as cellulose, etc.

All these processes should be applied with caution and by technically trained persons. Any variation in the use of chemicals or techniques may aggravate rather than check deterioration.

Of the various processes described above, the use of the following is recommended on the basis of use and the experience of various workers in the profession: (a) thymol fumigation and vacuum fumigation with a mixture of ethylene oxide and air for fungus infested records and volumes; (b) Topane, a fungicide paste of sodium salt of O-phenyl phenol, for preventing fungus growth on repaired documents; (c) Topane-impregnated paper for wrapping records and for lining shelves; and (d) spraying with a 10 per cent solution of thymol in storage rooms infested with fungi.

INSECTS

Insects are dangerous to archive material and are a potential threat, particularly in tropical countries. In temperate regions, although the problem exists, it is not serious. Insects can be easily controlled by maintaining cleanliness and by periodic inspection of the storage areas, and by constant vigilance over new acquisition. Any area found to be infested with insects can be treated with insecticides and the affected documents fumigated.

Insects such as silverfish, cockroaches, termites, meal worms and the granary weevil are known to damage paper and other cellulose products. Those which occur widely and cause most damage and destruction to paper are the thysanurans (silverfish and firebrats), the various species of cockroach, the so-called bookworms and termites (white ants).

Thysanurans

These include various species, known as silverfish, fish moths, slikers or firebrats. They are nocturnal pests, cone-shaped, swift-running, and sombre coloured. They are found everywhere in buildings, but prefer dark corners. They are extremely prolific, dark spaces behind the books on shelves and in cabinets and drawers being favourite egg laying places.

These insects are fond of starch and glue, attacking stores of paper, bookbindings or letterings, rayon and similar materials. They remove glaze from paper and disfigure valuable etchings and prints by eating into the surface. They also damage photographs, labels, paper sizing, onionskin paper, cellophane and waxpaper.

Cockroaches

These are common household pests. They are brown or brownish, black or tan, shiny, flat-bodied and foul-smelling insects, which feed on many kinds of material and often eat the bindings or leaves of books and magazines and other paper products, parchment, leather and fabrics. They excrete a dark liquid which discolours any material over which they crawl, and deposit their eggs in filthy places where temperature and humidity are favourable. Several species of cockroaches are known.

59

Bookworms

Voracious eaters of nearly all kinds of materials, bookworms are particularly harmful to books, digesting cellulose and actually nourishing themselves with paper. They are difficult to combat. They deposit their eggs near the surface of book-bindings or on the edges of the leaves. Once hatched, the larvae eat their way to the interior of the book and return to the surface when prepared for the chrysalis stage. Finally the fully grown beetle emerges.

Psocids or booklice

Sometimes confused with the bookworm, these are pale, minute insects seldom found on books which are constantly in use and noticed only when they occur in large numbers. They feed on starch and glue in book bindings but because of their small size do little real harm.

Termites

Termites thrive in tropical and subtropical climates. Because of a superficial resemblance they are sometimes called 'white ants', although they are neither white nor ants. They are insidious pests and are fond of a diet of woody tissues. Invading dwellings, libraries, trestles, fence posts and storage areas, they attack any article of wooden origin or containing cellulose, such as stores of paper stock, carboard boxes, books, documents and blueprints. Since they avoid exposing themselves to air, they are seldom seen until great damage has been done. Many objects are attacked more or less incidentally and damaged or penetrated simply because they obstruct the passage to the food the termites wish to reach or stand in the way of emerging, winged adults.

Preventive measures

Sterilization

Prevention is the best cure for insect infestation. In the larger and better equipped archives, all new acquisitions together with any infested holdings are disinfected or fumigated in vacuum chambers.

Vacuum fumigation

A vacuum fumigation plant consists of a steel chamber of 10 m³ capacity and an accumulator, where a mixture of gas ethylene oxide and carbon dioxide used for sterilization is stored.

Books and documents to be sterilized are placed in the chamber in their containers either on trolleys or platforms. The steel door of the chamber is closed and the air inside expelled. Approximately 4.5 kg of ethoxide gas (a mixture of 10 per cent ethylene oxide and 90 per cent carbon dioxide by weight) are then introduced into the chamber. This mixture has been found to be effective against insects without causing harm to archive materials. The infested documents are maintained in this atmosphere for three hours, during which the gas is once circulated in the chamber by means of electric pumps. After three hours, all stages of insect life, i.e. eggs, larvae and adults have been destroyed. The gas is pumped out and the vacuum broken by admitting air into the chamber. The door is opened and the documents removed. Material so treated may be safely stored in the storage rooms without any fear of insect damage provided the area itself is free from insects. As stated earlier, the gas in the proportions used is absolutely safe, being neither inflammable nor harmful to man in the concentration used for sterilization.

Fumigation with formaldehyde

This method is used at the Bibliothèque Nationale, Paris, for the fumigation of books, documents and pastel drawings. Fumigation is carried out in a chamber of size approximately 1.20 m by 0.40 m by 1.10 m, which is large enough to admit a three-tier trolley. Documents are laid on the trolley while books are kept half-open with their pages spread to ensure that the vapours penetrate between the leaves. The chamber is hermetically sealed and formaldehyde at the rate of 250 grammes per cubic metre of space is sprayed inside together with a similar quantity of water to humidify the atmosphere to prevent cracking of leather or parchment. The temperature inside the chamber is maintained at 30° C. The documents are treated in this way for twenty-four to forty-eight hours according to the intensity of damage. After a few days they are checked to verify that the fumigation has been effective.

Fumigation and ethylene dichloride and carbon tetrachloride

Vacuum fumigation is an ideal method for disinfecting records from the points of view of speed, cost and thoroughness of the treatment, although fumigation may be carried out in airtight chambers if the bulk is small and vacuum fumigation facilities unavailable. The fumigant used is a mixture of three parts of ethylene dichloride and one part of carbon tetrachloride by volume. Half a litre of this mixture is sufficient for a chamber of 2 m³ capacity (1 m by 1 m by 2 m). The documents are exposed for a period of twenty-four hours, during which it is necessary to maintain a temperature of 23.85° C or above. If the temperature falls below 23.85° C, fumigation must be repeated. Fumigation is carried out by this process in a chamber called the 'Plymeth Fumigation Vault' at the Illinois State Archives Building, Springfield, Illinois.

Fumigation with para-dichlorobenzene

For small quantities of books, a simple method is fumigation with para-dichlorobenzene for at least a fortnight. Fumigation is carried out in an airtight steel almirah with perforated shelves. Books and documents are spread on the shelves and the fumigant is placed at the bottom on a watch-glass. For every cubic metre of air space 1 kg of para-dichlorobenzene is required.

Para-dichlorobenzene and Killopetra kill insects and their larvae, but not the eggs. It is therefore advisable to keep the treated books and documents under observation for at least a year, repeating the fumigation if insects reappear.

Other fumigants

Other fumigants available for use on archive materials include carbon tetrachloride, hydrocyanic acid gas, ethylene chloride and carbon dioxide, and methyl formate and carbon dioxide. These kill insects and larvae but not the eggs. As a general rule, therefore, treated materials are usually kept in isolation for three weeks. If the eggs hatch they are refumigated. These fumigants are 100 per cent effective in killing all storage insects within twenty-four hours without significant effect on the properties or stability of paper. Since they are poisonous, extreme care is necessary and they should be used under controlled conditions by specially trained staff. As a temporary expedient, or until fumigation is carried out, it is desirable to use petroleum base pyrethrum sprays or to spread sodium fluoride or a mixture of boric acid and starch, or to distribute naphthalene flakes tied in a mesh cloth at the back of shelves or cases to act as repellants.

As an alternative to fumigation, insecticides may be applied by brushing or by spraying as a fine mist.

If prompt action is taken insects may be eradicated from storage areas. They are vulnerable to one or more of the many powerful insecticides, such as dieldrin (20 per cent solution per gallon of water), oil solution of 5 per cent DDT, 2 per cent chlordane, 2 per cent malathion, 1 per cent lindane, or shirlan, a proprietary preparation containing salicylanilide. As far as possible, the use of oil sprays on records should be avoided, since their efficacity is offset by certain obvious disadvantages.

Shelves may be brushed or sprayed with insecticidal lacquers. Lacquers which have proved effective contain either dieldrin or chloro-naphthalene as their active principle. They should be thoroughly applied to the bookshelves, care being taken to cover all areas, including cracks, crevices and the underside of the shelves.

Termite control
To protect stored material against termites, the storage places should not be moist, warm nor unventilated. These conditions also lead to mould growth and to subsequent attack by insects. Termites infesting documents, books and other materials soon leave or die if they are placed outdoors during cold weather but away from direct sunlight. Fumigants, sprays, poisons and insecticides are of no permanent value in preventing termite damage to stored materials. The application of insecticides such as BHC (benzene hexachloride), DDT, chlordane, sodium arsenite, pentachlorophenol and copper naphthanate has, however, made it possible to protect such materials temporarily while they are removed from storage for use. These insecticides are applied near the termite tunnels, on top of their nests, or in cracks and crevices in floors and walls. The tendency of termites to lick each others' bodies and devour their own dead is utilized to effect their destruction by

placing a sufficient quantity of chemicals near their nests and tunnels. The use of white arsenic, DDT powder, 1 per cent solution of sodium arsenite in water, 5 per cent solution of DDT and also of dieldrex have proved satisfactory for this purpose.

When subterranean termites have gained access to storage areas, as a temporary measure the wooden shelves and almirahs are moved away from the walls and placed over plates or dishes of metal containing coal tar or creosote. All inlets such as joints, cracks or crevices in walls and floors should be immediately sealed with cement and concrete. Chemicals should be applied regularly twice a year, before and after the rainy season.

Wood-dwelling termites may be excluded by using the best materials treated against termite attack. Once termites gain access, however, only fumigation with hydrocyanic acid gas will rid the building of them. Expert handling is required, since some forty-eight hours are necessary for the fumigation treatment and a further forty-eight hours to air the entire building and eliminate the hydrocyanic acid gas before it is re-opened. For temporary relief, fumigation with methyl bromide for twenty-four hours may be carried out.

Excellent control of drywood termites in infested timber may be obtained by brushing or spraying the wood with BHC, DDT or chlorodane dissolved in mineral spirits. Such treatments not only eliminate the infestation but also prevent subsequent attack for a long period. When the infestation is deep-seated, only fumigation with methyl bromide or hydrocyanic acid gas as described above will kill the termite colony.

Rodents

Rodent attack on paper and paper goods poses one of the most difficult problems of protection in the entire field of preservation. Damage to stored materials, where such infestation occurs, may amount to as much as 20 per cent of the total holdings.

Fungi and bacteria derive their food from the cellulose constituents, adhesives as other organic compounds of the paper, while insects, during the process of eating and burrowing through paper, come in contact with or ingest toxic or repellant materials incorporated in the paper. Rats and other rodents, on the other hand, attack paper mechanically without ingesting any appreciable amount and even without allowing the particles to come into contact with their digestive systems. The use of any toxic material in the paper is, therefore, ineffective against them.

The most effective way of combating such pests is to eliminate them through campaigns or to adopt rodent-proof constructions and use materials repellant to rodents.

A satisfactory rodenticide or rodent repellant must be non-toxic to the personnel handling it; it must not contaminate or cause skin irritation under conditions of use. It should have no adverse effects on the properties of paper, such as strength, durability, resiliency or its bacteriostatic or fungistatic characteristics. It must be free from objectionable odour and taste, capable of application under the usual manufacturing conditions and effective under normal handling and storage conditions.

To this end, several thousand chemicals have been listed, but to date no satisfactory compound has been discovered, possibly as a result of the very rigid requirements. It is noteworthy that the most effective compounds are those which contain nitrogen and sulphur and that a correlation appears to exist between rodent repellency and fungistatic activity.

Mouse repellants include flake naphthalene, which may be scattered around stored articles, powdered sulphur and lime, tung oil, coal tar, creosote, pine tar, copper oleate, kerosene and oils of citronella, cedarwood, wintergreen and peppermint. Materials such as sodium silicate, plastics such as polymethyl methacrylate resins, drying oils such as ground tung oil and some synthetic resins, when incorporated in paper, impart physical resistance to rodent attack.

One rodenticide which has found wide application is 3-alpha acetonylbenzyl-4-hydroxy coumain, marketed under various trade names such as Warfarin. This is very effective and the concentration of 0.025 per cent recommended in baits for rat and mouse control is so low that there appears to be little or no danger to other animals in its use. However, it is toxic and would kill any warm-blooded animal if consumed in sufficient quantity. It is, therefore, recommended that baits of Warfarin be set only in rodent-infested places which larger animals cannot enter.

Other chemicals for general use are red squill, alpha-naphthyl thio-urea, zinc phosphide, arsenic oxide, strychnine alkaloid and calcium cyanide dust, which is also used as a fumigant rodenticide. These, together with thallium sulphide and sodium fluoroacetate

(Compound 1080), are very poisonous and extreme care is necessary in their use. They must, in fact, be used only by specially trained persons under carefully controlled conditions.

Physical deterioration

Agents which cause physical deterioration are light, heat and moisture, which bring about photochemical, hydrolytic, or oxidative changes in paper. This deterioration differs from the damage caused by insects, moulds or use, and its outward signs are yellowing and progressive embrittlement which eventually prevents ordinary handling. Such deterioration is caused by subtle chemical changes which affect not only the chemical properties of the material but also the rate and course of subsequent ageing processes.

The extent of deterioration may be detected and determined by measuring the amount of alpha-cellulose, the copper number, the viscosity in cuprammonium solution, and the folding, bursting, and tensile strengths, etc., of paper (see Appendix 1).

Low viscosity and high copper number indicate deterioration, and the folding endurance test gives the best measure of the physical effect of ageing on paper. Methods of performing these tests are detailed in the TAPPI and ASTM standards for paper and paper products (see Appendix 1).

LIGHT

All natural, animal and vegetable fibres gradually lose their strength on exposure to sunlight, the rate of deterioration varying with the intensity of the light, the temperature, and the humidity of the atmosphere. A major cause of such deterioration and weakening of fibres is the ultra-violet element of sunlight, although deterioration of cellulose and other materials in documents, textiles and paintings is also caused by radiant energy.

The change occurs whether the light is natural or artificial, but due to the relatively low intensity of artificial light sources the rate of change of colour may be so reduced that it may only be assessed after a prolonged period of time. Long-term exposure to artificial light may cause as much fading as exposure to sunlight over shorter periods.

The yellowing and eventual embrittlement of newsprint or similar paper is a familiar phenomenon. It has long been assumed that yellowing occurs whenever paper is exposed to radiant energy over a sustained period. Work conducted at the United States National Bureau of Standards indicates that some types of paper bleach when irradiated in air if the temperature is not allowed to rise much higher than 30° C during the process, otherwise they yellow. In other words, discolouration of paper is a combined effect of light and heat. The two processes, bleaching and yellowing, occur simultaneously. Whether the change is provoked by radiant energy or by temperature rise is indicated by the net observable effect. Thus, if a white paper turns yellow when irradiated, photochemical reactions have probably not played the dominant role, and reactions other than photochemical have been involved, although paper containing lignin yellows in air or oxygen even in the absence of heat but bleaches in an oxygen-free nitrogen atmosphere. Papers scorched brown at very high temperatures or yellowed at 100° C to a state resembling that of paper 250 years old have been bleached by light.

High-grade papers, for example, bleach instead of yellowing and also become brittle, while groundwood paper such as newsprint, containing a minimum amount of iron, insufficiently purified cellulose, or considerable rosin sizing, is more adversely affected by exposure than high-grade papers.

Studies on the deterioration of irradiated cellulose products show that the greatest damage is caused by ultra-violet energy of wavelengths shorter than 360 millimicrons and that damage is appreciable up to 500 millimicrons.

Sunlight and artificial sources rich in ultra-violet rays are particularly destructive. Light and near ultra-violet radiation cause loss of strength and oxidation of cellulose. The rate of deterioration is relatively rapid. As a result of radiation, oxidized cellulose becomes susceptible to damage by reagents which otherwise have no effect on unoxidized cellulose. Oxidized cellulose also discolours more rapidly in darkness.

In the presence of free resin and sulphuric acid, the effect of light on cotton, rag and purified wood-pulp paper is much greater than on inferior paper. The deacidification of document paper is, therefore, essential.

Although resistance to the influence of sunlight depends on the type of paper and the cellulose material present, all papers are prone to damage from this source. According to Launer and Wilson, the photochemical stability of papers is related to the nature and origins of the materials used in their manufacture and declines in the following order: new rag, refined sulphite, old rag, soda sulphite and newsprint. The accidental or deliberate presence of resin, glue, alum, iron, lignin or other substances has a strong bearing on degradation by light. Materials subject to deterioration by light include binding materials, cord, thread cloth and parchment, various types of plastics, rubbers, adhesives and inks, as well as a considerable number of dyes. Deterioration due to sunlight is reflected in loss rather of folding endurance than of tearing and tensile strengths.

Ideal protection of paper against sunlight is provided by storage places without windows and lighted when necessary with low-wattage lamps. In windowed rooms, the windows should be provided with opaque shades or heavy curtains, or the paper should be kept in closed containers. The permanent exhibition of valuable paper documents is inadvisable and unless special precautions are taken to reduce to the greatest possible extent the period of exposure to light, temporary exhibits are to be preferred. Sunlight should be prevented from falling directly upon paper either in store or on display by the use of opaque blinds and curtains. The intensity of the lighting, whether natural or artificial, should not be excessive, for while there is little to choose between tungsten and fluorescent lighting from the point of view of fading effect, the intensity of the light source is an important factor. For the internal lighting of showcases, however, fluorescent tubes are preferable to tungsten lighting as they are cooler in operation. It is essential that auxiliary equipment such as chokes, etc., be mounted outside the case where they are also readily accessible for servicing. The intensity of roof lighting should be controlled. Light through vertical windows may be diffused by blinds of the Venetian type. In certain cases, windows may be fitted with special protective glass which excludes the most harmful rays. Such glass cuts out a portion of the spectrum and thus restricts the over-all lighting to a certain extent. Special glasses reduce the tendency to fading, but it should be added that no glass is available which will entirely prevent the fading of dyestuffs. While glass containing cerium and cobalt oxides affords the best protection to written paper against ultra-violet discolouration, glasses which are red, green, lemon-yellow, dark-brown, yellow or light brown in colour provide some protection against sunlight for double-sized rag paper, resin sized 50 per cent rag, 50 per cent sulphite paper and free sulphite paper. Of these, brown-yellow glass possesses the best shielding ability.

Certain special optical filters on the market are claimed to eliminate harmful rays. These filters are colourless and therefore do not interfere with the viewing of documents. They are obtainable in form of plastic sheets—usually perspex—in which a special chemical has been incorporated so that there is a sharp cut-off in the transmission curve in the region of 400 millimicrons. One of the most effective of these is known as Oroglas 11 UF. An American firm has produced a solution which may be either brushed or sprayed on glass to achieve the same purpose.

The enclosure of objects in an inert atmosphere has also been used successfully to protect them from light damage (NBS Circular no. 595, 181, Preservation of the Declaration of Independence and the Constitution of the United States). This method should be used with caution. Certain substances, such as Prussian Blue, fade by reduction in an inert atmosphere.

HEAT AND MOISTURE

Paper in storage deteriorates with time, however perfect the conditions. This change, which takes the form of yellowing and subsequent embrittlement is known as 'natural' ageing. Deterioration increases with an increase in temperature, and even exposure for short periods to high temperatures causes paper to become yellow and brittle. Low temperatures, however, retard the process of ageing.

The changes in paper exposed to high temperatures, for example at 100° C for seventy-two hours, may be determined by the so-called accelerated ageing test, which is widely used for measuring the stability of paper. Baking at 100° C for seventy-two hours has been found to be equivalent to twenty-five years of storing under normal storage conditions.

Comparison of the data obtained from samples after four and eight years of normal ageing and from samples subjected to accelerated ageing has shown that stability is related to chemical purity, retention of fold endurance revealing that the papers retained the same relative order of stability. In other words, the same types of chemical change occur during eight years of natural ageing as under accelerated ageing. From the presence of high alpha cellulose content, low copper number and moderate acidity in the samples so compared, Scribner concluded that the cellulose of the stable papers remains in good condition.

Heat tests on papers made from rags and possessing the characteristics of good book paper led to no appreciable change, thus indicating that such papers are quite stable, while the same tests on papers produced from a mixture of sulphite pulp and soda pulp showed that they are less stable than those made from pure fibres. These tests also revealed a close relationship between the cellulose purity of the fibres and the stability of unsized papers made from them. Paper strength decreases with increasing filler content, which itself depends on the amount rather than the type of filler. Non-alkaline fillers, if used in right proportions, have no harmful influence on stability, while calcium carbonate fillers have a protective or inhibiting effect on ageing. Acidity is an important factor, the attack on cellulose increasing with increased acidity in papers.

While a combination of heat and low humidity causes paper to dry out and become brittle, damp heat makes the paper soggy and encourages the growth of moulds. In order to preserve paper in good condition for a long time, it is essential to maintain both a moderate temperature and moderate humidity. Constantly maintained temperatures of 20–24° C and relative humidity of 55 per cent have been found to assist in the preservation of paper records. Even a poor-quality paper, which under normal conditions would have relatively poor chances of surviving deterioration, may be kept for a considerable time under these controlled conditions.

It is not easy to maintain satisfactory atmospheric conditions day after day in a private house or in a safe or storage room. Fortunately, the presence in the house of hygroscopic materials like carpets, curtains, cotton wool and other textiles helps to control excessive humidity and tends to stabilize the atmospheric conditions. For minimizing the effect of changes in humidity, documents should be wrapped in paper, or preferably in textiles—cotton and linen materials being the safest.

Excessive humidity weakens the tissue and promotes the growth of micro-organisms which feed upon size, cellulose, paste and leather, etc. If this trouble is checked at once by drying the affected papers, little harm is done, but if the process is allowed to continue, the paper becomes yellow and stained with coloured spots, i.e. mildew sets in. Since the real source of the trouble is damp and stagnant air, appropriate action should be taken as described above in the section dealing with biological deterioration.

Chemical deterioration

Cellulose is attacked slowly by acid even under the most favourable conditions of storage and becomes discoloured, fragile and brittle. If, however, the paper is stored under conditions of excessive heat and moisture or exposed to light, for example in the tropics, these changes are accelerated considerably. The distinction between deterioration of paper due to chemical agents, i.e. acidic gases, etc., and deterioration due to physical agents, i.e. heat, light, use, etc., is a distinction between classes of reagents rather than between types of reaction occurring in the paper. Such deterioration differs from the impairment caused by biological agents.

Degradation of paper by chemical agents may be caused by acidic gases or smokes in the atmosphere, dust, inks, etc., or by the adverse action of chemicals used in the manufacture of the paper itself.

ATMOSPHERIC CONTAMINATION

Atmospheric contamination is a major cause of chemical degradation in paper. The contaminants involved are the oxides of carbon and nitrogen and, more particularly, of sulphur, which require moisture and free-air circulation to be active as deteriorating agents. Most of the damage caused to paper is due to the oxides of sulphur present in the atmosphere mainly as a result of the combustion of coal and oil, particularly in industrial areas. Sulphur dioxide gas is itself quite harmless to paper and bookbinding materials, including leather, and it has been demonstrated that properly packaged materials of proper moisture content are not affected, even in heavily contaminated environments. But the traces of iron and copper present in paper or leather are capable of catalyzing sulphur dioxide gas into sulphuric acid. Reaction between this gas and the oxygen and water vapours present in the atmosphere also forms sulphuric acid, which is extremely harmful to paper, acting as a catalyst, removing the water molecule from within the cellulose molecule or causing mild oxidation which results in the cleavage or degradation of the molecule.

Considerable attention has been paid to the effect of sulphur dioxide on paper and to its removal from the air of storage areas or muniment rooms.

The first systematic study was made in 1898, when the Committee of the Royal Society of Arts on the Deterioration of Paper reported that illuminating gas causes deterioration in all grades of paper. In the present century, work on the same lines has confirmed that acidic gases in the atmosphere contribute substantially to the deterioration of record papers and that embrittlement may be attributed to action of traces of sulphur dioxide in the atmosphere on traces of metallic impurities in the paper. It has been observed that the paper of books stored in urban areas is more acidic than that of books kept in rural locations. This is attributed to the fact that the atmosphere of the latter locations is less contaminated.

To determine the effect upon paper of sulphur dioxide in the low concentrations commonly found in large cities, a series of commercial papers of different fibre composition was exposed to an atmosphere containing from 2 to 9 p.p.m. of sulphur dioxide at 30° C and 65 per cent RH for 240 hours. Marked deterioration and an abnormally high acidity in the papers were observed in every case.

In another series of tests it was noticed that certain high-grade, high alpha-cellulose content papers deteriorated to a greater extent than lower-grade paper, which clearly shows that a high-grade paper gives no sure guarantee of resistance to sulphur dioxide. Furthermore, paper exposed to concentrations of sulphur dioxide in an urban atmosphere showed marked deterioration in as little as ten days. It was observed that temperature and humidity play an important part in the deteriorative action of sulphur dioxide, susceptibility to sulphur dioxide being considerably greater at higher temperatures and higher humidities.

In yet another series of tests, samples of paper were exposed to sulphur dioxide fumes. It was observed that different portions of the same paper exhibited different physical conditions and chemical compositions after exposure. Areas near the edges, i.e. those most exposed to the fumes, were most seriously affected, and were found to have the lowest pH values, the highest titrable acidity, the highest content of water-soluble sulphate, the highest copper number and the lowest alpha-cellulose content. These tests showed that when alpha-cellulose content, pH value and folding endurance decreased, the copper number increased. Increased acidity caused a decrease in the folding endurance which appears to be the most conclusive index of deterioration. This finding has been confirmed by other studies.

One exposure test showed that rag ledger paper and highly purified wood-fibre bond paper were least affected, while chemical-wood book paper, an English rag paper sized with glue and rosin, a sized and supercalendered chemical wood book paper, a 75 per cent rag-laid antique book paper, a 100 per cent rag machine-finished book paper and a white sulphite writing paper showed marked deterioration.

In a handbook containing at least three kinds of paper and exposed to the atmosphere of London on an open shelf from 1919 to about 1939 and in a storage vault for the next seventeen years, one section was observed to be only moderately damaged while the other two showed quite serious embrittlement. This indicates that quite similar papers may differ greatly in their susceptibility to atmospheric damage, that high quality in papers is no guarantee that they will absorb less acid than those of poor quality and that storage in a closed vault is very effective in preventing atmospheric damage.

Another study indicates that the greatest absorption of acid occurs in the outer edges of leaves.

The above observations clearly explain why book edges deteriorate rapidly whereas the centre of book pages usually remain for a long time intact.

EFFECT OF DUST

The harmful action of sulphur compounds is aggravated by dust and dirt, which are sources of both physical and chemical degradation. Dust is not an inert material, and provides acid radicals as well as metallic ions which may sometimes provoke degradation. Dust films attract moisture which is essential for the chemical action of gaseous atmospheric contaminants. Since most dust and lints are hygroscopic, they tend to maintain a higher moisture level on a surface than would exist if they were absent. It is therefore essential that records be kept clean.

It should, however, be stressed that the removal of such harmful agents from the atmosphere results in only a token reduction of the total deterioration of paper. It has been observed that different books stored under identical conditions show different degrees of deterioration. For example, the leaves of volumes which are only from thirty to fifty years old are cracking while those of seventeenth-century and even earlier volumes remain flexible and strong. It is therefore clear that the storage conditions alone cannot be responsible for the marked deterioration of the comparatively newer volumes. Despite this fact, far too little attention has been paid to the identification or removal of the other probable causes of deterioration, for example agents introduced into the paper during manufacture and the use of inks, etc.

HARMFUL CHEMICALS

Among the factors affecting paper at the time of manufacture and responsible for its subsequent deterioration are imperfect methods of digestion, excessive use of alum, rosin sizing and residual chlorides from the bleaching process. The oxidizable carbohydrates found in chemical wood fibres also contribute to the chemical degradation of paper. A small amount of degradation could be due to the deterioration of cellulose, but failure to wash the chlorides from the fibres and the use of alum in sizing probably account for most of the acid present.

Most early materials have shown amazing stability under storage conditions in which modern papers would last only a few decades. Manuscripts on palm leaves, birch bark, papyrus, parchment, vellum, and even on hand-made papers manufactured more than four centuries ago are still available in our libraries and archives. Linen rags were the principal source of cellulose fibre in the manufacture of the earliest papers, and many of these have lasted well. Several investigators have found that the strongest early papers are either only very slightly acidic (pH 6 and above) or mildly alkaline and attribute these conditions to the presence of mainly calcium and magnesium compounds, which may have been introduced during the bleaching of rags with extracts of wood ashes, when the rags were washed with water containing bicarbonates of these elements or when lime was used in the preparation of pulp. Regardless of the source of these compounds, it has been found that their presence in paper is associated with preservation; such papers are still in existence while more acidic papers of the same period are today either quite brittle or have altogether disappeared.

The use of potassium aluminium sulphate (alum) in sizing before the end of the seventeeth century was only the first of a number of additions which threatened to shorten the life of the paper. Alum is a relatively acidic substance, and the quantity employed should not therefore greatly exceed that which is necessary to precipitate the resin fully. In actual practice, however, this is by no means the case. It has been observed that it is easier to overdose with alum than to underdose, for alum is regarded as a cure for many paper-making troubles, such as froth; a certain excess of alum is also essential if the best results are to be obtained with certain colours.

Traces of chlorides left as a result of insufficient washing or after the bleaching process help to intensify the deteriorative effect of excessive alum in paper. This is probably due to the reaction between the aluminium sulphate and the chlorides, and the formation of aluminium chloride which in the presence of moisture and heat produces hydrochloric acid, one of the most potent of all acids in its attack on cellulose.

Under pressure of a rising demand for paper, paper-makers found that they could utilize weakened rag if its yellow tint could be corrected by blueing or if they could bleach other discoloured and often weak materials with chlorine. Such sources of cellulose could not satisfy the spiralling demand. From 1860 onwards, other sources of cellulose like grass, wood, etc., were tapped, and the substances steadily established themselves as raw materials. The chemical treatment which they required issued new threats to the permanence of paper either by leaving undesirable constituents of the raw materials themselves or by leaving unwanted residues or effects when reagents such as chlorine, sodium hydroxide, sodium sulphate, calcium bisulphite, etc., were used to remove those constituents. As a result, paper in books from twenty-five to fifty years old has deteriorated and become useless although kept under the same storage conditions as the thousands of books printed or written four or more centuries ago which are available in our libraries and records rooms and whose paper is still white, strong and flexible.

ACTION OF INKS

The history of inks also provides a clue to the acidity due to harmful chemicals used in the production of paper or documents.

During the middle ages, carbon inks were gradually supplanted by iron-gall inks. Because of the interaction of ferrous sulphate with tannins, sulphuric acid was formed in these inks in varying degrees of concentration depending upon the concentration of the chemicals. Documents, damaged by highly acidic inks are commonly found in libraries and archives, and the damage is invariably extensive. It has been observed that inks of high acid content often eat holes into paper, while low acid inks cause little or no damage. This could be due to the fact that the alkalinity of the paper in some cases counteracts and neutralizes the acid, which would also explain why the damage caused by these inks to documents on vellum and parchment, which have high lime content, is small.

PRINTING AS A CAUSE OF DEGRADATION

Printing may be said to have ushered in the modern age of paper by stimulating the need for and use of paper and advancing the technology by which those needs are met. On the other hand, printing has resulted in the progressive loss of permanence in paper which it might have appeared to ensure, mainly because of the use of materials such as straw, esparto grass, wood pulp, bamboo, flax, rayon, cotton linters and alphapulps, or a mixture of these, instead of rag for the production of papers of inferior quality which have deteriorated.

PREVENTIVE MEASURES

Such inferior papers, eaten away and weakened by acid due to atmospheric gases or the chemicals used in their manufacture or introduced by inks, etc., require care and attention. Air-conditioning of storage areas and libraries, and neutralization of excess acid are among the suggested remedies. The intake of air in storage areas, libraries and archives should be washed in an alkaline solution during its passage through the air-conditioning units. For the removal of harmful sulphur compounds it is recommended that the wash water be kept at pH 8.5–9.

NEUTRALIZATION

From the above it would be logical to expect the stability of paper to be improved through the use of agents capable of effectively neutralizing its excess acidity. Pioneer work in this direction has been done by William J. Barrow, who has suggested a method subsequently accepted even by the supporters of orthodox methods for the restoration of documents, like Roger Ellis, who states: 'It may be said here in passing, but with emphasis, that Mr. Barrow's technique of deacidification seems a wholly admirable development.' Since then much work has been done on similar lines, as will be shown in Chapter 5.

3   Principles of repair

Documents which come to restoration centres for repairs have deteriorated through the action of biological, physical or chemical agents or their combined effect or have been damaged by floods or fire. More often than not, these documents are the only surviving copies and they are thus of great value to scholars and administrators alike. For this fact alone, notwithstanding their other qualities, documents have been and must continue to be preserved.

The repair of documents does not mean merely strengthening them by applying paper and paste. The work requires a thorough knowledge of the nature of the documents and of the various processes of repair to which they have been subjected in the past and which they are about to undergo. The slightest error in undertaking the work without first understanding the nature of the problem may result in irreparable damage to the document or even total loss. Documents which have been damaged beyond repair, by the adoption of wrong techniques, by hasty work, by the use of materials of unknown composition and doubtful durability are not uncommon.

The document restorer must therefore be acquainted with the various methods of document repair and their respective merits and defects. He must have knowledge of the materials used for creating records and of the materials which have been or may be used to conserve and restore them. He must, for example, know the composition of various kinds of papers and inks—the two materials which have consistently been used for creating records since the invention of paper, and of other materials such as parchment, vellum, leather, textiles, palm leaves, bark paper, boards, films, plastics and adhesives which have been used in the past or which are still in use. In addition, he should have some notion of their keeping qualities and durability under varying conditions of storage and use.

Before any attempt is made to undertake repairs, the documents should be thoroughly examined to ascertain the extent of damage or degradation, after which a decision may be taken concerning the nature of the treatment necessary for increasing their longevity or strengthening them.

The principles of repair are universal, regardless of climatic conditions. Once these are grasped, and with a reasonable amount of experimentation, it is not difficult to find solutions to meet local needs. The difficulties encountered often differ in degree rather than in kind. However, for such work experince and knowledge of the right type is necessary.

Examination

NATURE OF THE MATERIAL

The restorer should ascertain whether the document is on paper and, if this is the case, obtain an approximate idea of the type. He should proceed in the same way in the case of parchment, palm leaf, bark paper or other materials. If the document is bound, note should be taken of the colour and type of the binding, the manner of stitching, the number of gathers, etc.

EXTENT OF DAMAGE

Examination of the document will reveal whether the document is yellowed, soiled, damaged by insects, fungi or water or by a combination of these; whether it has become soggy or the sizing material has given way; whether it is broken in pieces or breaks when touched; whether parts are missing; whether it is folded and does not open flat without breaking at the folds, etc. Complete notes should be kept of all these observations. If the document is bound, a note should be made of whether the stitches have given way, or the back has caved in, or the covers have become detached. If the document contains charts, maps or seals, the conditions of these should be noted. In the case of seals, for example, it should be carefully noted whether the seal is broken, dry or cracked, or whether any writing on it is smudged. Further record should be made of the colour of the seal, and of its method of attachment, even if the seal itself is missing. In the case of maps or charts, attention should be directed to their condition, noting whether they have been superficially damaged; whether the ink and colour have flaked off or are in the process of doing so, and whether they may be folded without injury to themselves or to other documents in the collection.

TYPE OF INK

The next step is to note whether the ink is soluble in water. This may be done by placing a drop of water on the writing, allowing it to soak in and finally drying the treated portion with a blotter. If the ink is water-soluble it will leave a mark on the blotter. Great care must be taken with coloured documents as any spreading of the colours might mar their appearance. Note should also be taken of whether the ink has faded or has flaked off, or has burnt the paper where the lines are heavy on the document, and whether it has sunk deep into the fibres and affected the other side. The latter phenomenon is a clear indication of the acidic nature of the ink employed.

ACIDITY

Acidity in paper may be determined by measuring the pH of an aqueous extract of a portion of the document. A pH of 6.2 or lower is a sure indication of the acidic nature of the document, which should be deacidified before restoration (see Chapter 5).

NUMBERING

Numbering of the documents, whether in loose form or bound in a volume, should be checked. If any discrepancy is observed, the documents may be renumbered in the centre or in the right-hand corner of the bottom of each sheet. A distinctive mark of the repair centre should be inserted at the beginning and at the end of the renumbering. This generally takes the form of a line below the first number or a circle or some other shape around the initial and final words. Numbering may be facilitated by reference to catchwords. Care should be taken to ensure that the pieces of broken sheets are properly marked as sub-numbers of the relevant page, e.g. 346a, 346b, 346c, etc., so that they are not misplaced. At the end of a series or volume the number on the final page should always be underlined and the word 'End' written beneath or after it, i.e.:

$$\frac{346}{\text{End}} \text{ or } 346/\text{End.}$$

If the papers include outsized sheets or maps or charts which cannot safely be kept with the remainder, they should be set aside, blank sheets being inserted in their place and indicating where removed sheets have been stored. If the number of such sheets is small and where it is possible to fold them, care should be taken to ensure that the fold lies across a blank area free of writing. The sheet should be folded from the other margin or from the foot. Double folds should be avoided, as the meeting of two folds weakens the document.

Rules for repair

After the examination described above, the process of restoration which will strenghten the document and ensure its durability during storage and handling should be selected. Before beginning the work, however, the rules set out below should be recalled.

The originality of the document should not be disturbed in any way and the repair must be neat and tidy. The restorer should preserve as far as possible the original condition and appearance of the document, repairing it only when it becomes necessary to prevent the paper and other document materials from decaying or tearing further. In the case of seals which are badly cracked or of which portions are missing, restoration may be undertaken. But no attempt should be made at reconstruction, which would destroy their validity. Documents should not be trimmed to remove decayed edges, as such trimming impairs their originality. For the same reason, patches should not be pasted merely to strengthen one portion of a document or with the aim of flattening out a crease. Such work, besides looking ugly, harms the document.

It is therefore essential that documents in good shape and condition should not be repaired merely for the sake of repair. Once their strength is impaired, however, extensive restoration becomes necessary. In such cases, the strength of the reinforcing materials becomes the strength of the document itself, in other words, the keeping qualities of restored documents depend upon the quality of the materials used for their restoration.

In the case of a volume, the sequence of the sheets should not be disturbed unless this becomes necessary for the protection of the document itself and for its proper storage. Heavy volumes are not easy to handle and have a tendency to break, which may result in damage to the document. Such volumes, for proper preservation, safe handling and storage, may be broken into convenient parts and then bound. For this purpose each sheet, whether repaired or unrepaired, should be guarded, in order to ensure uniform size and facilitate its flat opening.

The nature and extent of the repair should be evident. If a portion of a document is missing or if the document has large holes, the restorer should first replace the missing portion or fill the holes with new material of the same kind. Documents on paper, for example, should be repaired with paper, and documents on parchment with parchment. Care should be taken to ensure that the grain of the paper or parchment used for the purpose lies in the same direction as that of the document itself. This ensures that the amount and direction of swelling on wetting and shrinking on drying will be identical in the document and in the reinforcing material.

Paper or parchment used for filling lacunae should never be tinted in order to harmonize with the document under treatment. Such tinting amounts to faking and disturbing the originality of the document, and is contrary to the basic principle of repair of archive materials. The nature and extent of repair should, therefore, clearly remain evident.

Documents written on one side only may be backed with the same type of material as that used for the documents themselves. Documents written on both sides should be repaired with tissue paper or chiffon (silk gauze) using an adhesive, or with a combination of cellulose acetate film and either tissue paper or chiffon applied under heat and pressure or with the use of a solvent such as acetone. This procedure ensures a homogeneous document with the same properties as the original and responding uniformly to variations in temperature and humidity and the effect of time and handling. Such repairs should be made evident by leaving a 2 mm margin round the document.

The writing should not be marred or impaired in any way. No attempt should be made to replace vanished writing. If the writing has faded, it should not be brightened by overwriting or through treatment by any of the chemical methods suggested for its revival. With the passage of time such chemicals weaken the paper and often result in complete loss. Faded writings, if they contain iron, may be easily deciphered and photographed, if necessary, with the use of ultra-violet or infra-red rays.

Writing which has become loose through decay of the prepared surface on which it is inscribed, should be fixed by the use of materials and adhesives whose constituents are known and which will not harm the paper or other document material in any way.

Any acidity present in the document paper or ink should be neutralized by use of methods described in Chapter 5. Great care should be taken with inks or colours soluble in water. These should first be protected by painting with a 5 per cent solution of cellulose acetate in equal volumes of acetone and amylacetate, with a 5 per cent solution of methamethylcrylate in acetone or benzene or with a 5 per cent solution of soluble nylon. All this work should be carried out with care and by trained technicians under supervision.

The process applied should be reversible. All repairs should be carried out with processes which not only impart strength to the document but which may also be reversed by the restorer if the original is required later for some reason. A number of processes which have withstood the test of time and have been used with considerable success in the past are available for this purpose. Being slow and time-consuming, however, they have not been applied to the vast amount of records which call for the attention of the restorer. To speed up repair work, newer techniques have been developed which, unless they are properly studied or investigated and applied with care, cause more damage to the document instead of strengthening it. The merits and demerits of these processes are described in Chapter 6.

A document is unique, and the restorer should select a process which is certain to cause little harm or one which is reversible. The process selected should in no way diminish the document's utility by obscuring the writing or smudging the ink or by damaging or weakening the document material. An ill-conceived method of repair is likely to harm rather than strengthen the document in the long run. It is therefore essential to use a process of proven suitability which may be easily reversed later or during restoration itself.

The process adopted should provide maximum reinforcement at minimum cost. Archives all over the world are faced with the problem of finding money for conservation work. This is because conservation requires the use of the best materials, which are costly, and because the quantity of documents requiring repair is vast. It is therefore essential to use processes which provide maximum strength, i.e. both durability and permanence, and which at the same time are economical. One such process is Solvent Lamination, which requires no expensive equipment, is easy to apply and employs the cheapest tested materials which have proved to provide maximum protection. It does not, however, accelerate restoration work to the extent required for dealing with the amount of documents in need of reinforcement. On the other hand, it permits the individual treatment of documents which is so important for permanency. The cost of restoring a document of foolscap size amounts to less than 10 cents a sheet. Other equally effective processes are discussed in Chapter 6.

Materials used for repair should be durable and permanent. A well-repaired document or volume is a product of sound materials and good craftsmanship. It can remain durable only when all the materials used are mutually compatible and equally durable. For example, the use of water-repellent materials on water-absorbent paper, leather, etc., causes mechanical instability which does the document greater harm than good. Adhesives, threads or other materials, if they are not of best quality, have a similar effect. The compatibility of materials is therefore an important factor in durability.

Unfortunately, traditional materials are now less-widely used because of their high cost, and modern machine-made substitutes are not as durable as those made by hand before the age of mechanization. Furthermore, the tremendous advance in modern technology has led to the production of many synthetic fibres and materials claimed to be effective and without any harmful effect on paper. The indiscriminate use of such materials may, however, have effects contrary to those desired. The only sure procedure is to use materials which have been tested and found useful after thorough scientific examination. For this reason, it is essential that an archive institution should either possess or be in contact with a laboratory to test the materials, to which problems may be referred and from which advice may be sought. The restorer, will, therefore, use only those materials whose behaviour has been tested over a long period of time, relying on processes which are traditional, in the sense that they have been tested and found safe and are of proven utility, rather than untried processes whose chief characteristic is sophistication.

4   Cleaning, washing and flattening

A document which has accumulated a lot of dust, has pencil marks or is otherwise soiled, spotted or stained, and is folded, requires cleaning, washing and flattening.

Techniques for the purpose require a good knowledge of the constituent materials of the document, together with common sense. Before applying them, the restorer should have a clear idea of the document's capacity to withstand such treatment.

Cleaning

BRUSHES AND COMPRESSED AIR

The basic method of cleaning paper is by gentle dusting with brushes which though time-consuming is effective and does not harm the document in any way. The process may be accelerated by the use of an ordinary household vacuum cleaner with brush attachment which is effective in removing dust from documents record volumes.

If, however, the number of documents in need of cleaning is large, the use of compressed air rapidly gives good results. The air is supplied by a compressor of 300–350 litres capacity in which the air is maintained at a pressure of 3–4 kg per sq cm. A blow gun fitted with a pressure control directs a blast of air along the sides and edges of the volumes or bundles of documents in such a way that all free dust is blown off without damaging them. The full pressure of the air is never directed straight at the documents themselves. With controlled blast, even brittle documents may be effectively cleaned. This process is conducted in a specially designed air-cleaning unit connected to a suction fan by ducts. Dust blown off by the blast of air is drawn away from the worker by means of the suction fan and carried to a chamber fitted with renewable cellulose filters which trap the dust particles, and the dust-free air is returned to the room. The filters themselves are cleaned by vibration; the dust settles at the bottom of the chamber and may be collected for analysis of the solid contaminants which it contains.

This air-cleaning equipment is costly and mainly used in institutions which have large holdings of archive documents and whose acquisitions are frequent and numerous. Satisfactory equipment for smaller holdings consists of an air-cleaning unit comprising a compressor, a tube fitted with a suitable nozzle and valve to control the blast of air and a fume hood fitted with an exhaust fan. Dust-laden air is sucked in by the exhaust fan and expelled outside the building. This removes the need to employ dust-trapping filters.

ERASERS

Surface dirt and superficial soiling, pencil and finger marks may be easily removed by soft rubbers or other non-abrasive erasers, such as sponge rubber, art gum, soap, kneaded erasers and synthetic erasers of materials such as vinyl. Kneaded erasers are perhaps the most gentle in their action, removing dust and pencil marks as easily as a blotter soaks in ink. Vinyl eraser is also very easy to work with, although it has a tendency to pick up its own crumbs; like all plastic materials it should be used with care, as it has the ability to affect other resins that may be present on the paper of the document. It may, however, be safely used on printed documents.

A material often used and recommended is bread crumbs. This material does clean the paper, but if the crumbs themselves are not thoroughly removed after treatment they cause spotting on the paper. The author believes, therefore, that it is safer and more desirable to use only those methods which have withstood the test of time and have proved their usefulness.

In addition to the erasers mentioned above, a number of materials used in the dry-cleaning industry have been recommended, for example 'Opaline' dry-cleaning bags and soaps. The Opaline dry-cleaning bag is a mesh bag containing either rubber or a dust eraser soap. Heavy films of loose dust may be removed simply by rubbing the bag gently over the surface to be cleaned. Its action is, however, no stronger than that of erasers and it is useful rather for removing loose dust rather than fine particles embedded on the surface of the document. When the surface of the bag becomes dirty through use, it is twisted and shaken. The dust particles fall away, leaving a clear surface for re-use. Among other new materials mention may be made of a wall-paper cleaner available in cans from paint and hardware stores. Of the several varieties on the market, 'Absorene' has proved suitable for very large and dusty surfaces. It is similar in its use and effect to the kneaded eraser.

All these erasing-type devices have been found to have no ill effect on paper when carefully used and removed from the surface of the document. The results of experiments by the American Library Association, involving microscopic examination and accelerated ageing tests on paper cleaned with them, indicate that the common erasers, Opaline bags and Absorene wall-paper cleaners may be safely used on paper.

Technique

For cleaning with any of the erasers described above, the paper, which must be neither weak nor brittle, is held firmly. The eraser is then applied at the centre, and moved lightly in one direction from the centre of the sheet to the edge, to prevent the wrinkling and tearing which any other motion may provoke. After cleaning, all traces of crumbs are carefully removed from the paper. Otherwise, they result in further damage to the paper.

This process is useful in removing surface dirt, pencil marks and soil stains. More persistent spots or stains may be removed by washing or solvent treatment. Before subjecting the document to such treatment, however, it is necessary to remove all pins, clips and rubber bands. These should in fact be removed even if the document requires no treatment, otherwise they will leave their own stains on the paper. The deterioration of rubber bands leaves brown stains and corroded clips and pins are difficult to remove

Washing on floating platforms in thermostatiscally heated wash basins [*Photo:* National Library, Florence].

Washing in a tray containing water. Sheets interleaved with wet-strength resin-sized paper [*Photo:* National Library, Florence].

Spot bleaching with hypochlorite
[*Photo:* National Library, Florence].

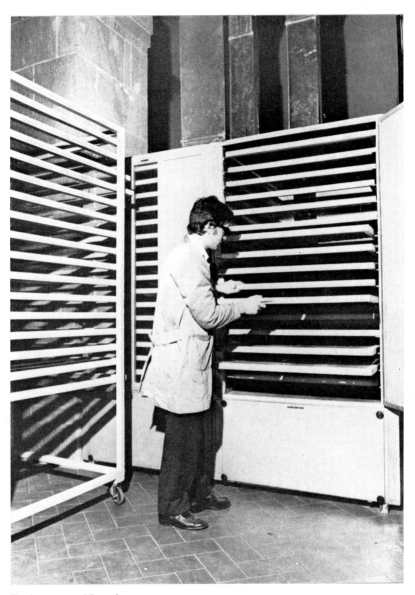

Drying oven with racks.
Also, a view of trolley where drying racks can be placed after taking them out of the drying oven.
[*Photo:* Florence State Archives].

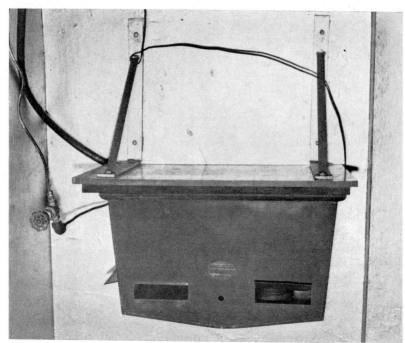

Pettifoger for humidification of folded papers.
[*Photo:* United States National Archives, Washington].

Air cleaning units for cleaning documents with compressed air.
[*Photo:* United States National Archives, Washington].

from paper and leave rust stains. Such stains are difficult to remove and often result in further damage to the document.

Washing

Washing is good for old paper, and has been observed to increase the mechanical strength of dry and brittle paper by re-establishing some of the broken hydrogen bonds in the cellulose molecule. Simple washing in clean, preferably distilled water helps to remove dark, soluble matter and some free acid from the paper. It also reduces water stains and permits the removal of wrinkles and other distortions. However, water has a tendency to 'set' surface dirt, which should be erased or removed by any of the techniques described above, before washing.

Some inks are adversely affected by water and these also require pretreatment. The first step, therefore, should be to test the effect of water on the writing of the document. For this purpose, a little water is applied to the writing in a corner of the document and allowed to soak in. A blotter is applied firmly to the writing. If it becomes stained, it is clear that the ink is soluble in water. Such writing should be bathed with a protective solution of cellulose acetate in acetone and allowed to dry before the sheet is immersed in water. Printing inks and iron-gall inks are not affected by water and may be washed without any danger of running or smudging. Other inks, however, have a tendency to smudge and wash off and should be protected in the manner described above or with a 5 per cent solution of soluble nylon.

Technique

For washing with water, an enamelled tray, similar to those used in photographic work and large enough to accommodate the sheet, is very suitable. The tray is filled to about half its capacity with distilled water. Prior to immersion in the water, each sheet is supported on plastic netting or if this is not available, on a waxed paper sheet. Brittle or broken sheets are supported on both sides to prevent damage or the loss of broken pieces. The sheets must be handled with great care. Thus supported, they are immersed by sliding them edgewise in water until they become uniformly wet. Ten sheets may be immersed together in this manner. They are then shaken gently several times and allowed to soak for a further 30–60 minutes. At the end of this period, the tray is gently rocked for a moment, and the soaked sheets are removed one by one by means of the supports and placed in an empty tray to drain off the excess water. They are then rinsed in clean water and dried carefully between clean sheets of blotter on a glass plate, pressure being exerted to remove the remaining water. The blotters are changed when necessary. The sheets are allowed to dry slowly in a gentle draught of air, and are finally allowed to dry completely under slight pressure between fresh blotters. Care should be taken not to apply excessive pressure as this imparts unequal characteristics to the sheet on drying. The drying process is completed by passing each sheet through a heated mangle or ironing by hand, the heat being applied to the document through the blotter and not directly. Finally, any protective coating applied to the writing is removed by sponging with cotton dipped in acetone. The process may be continuous if after each set of sheets has been removed from the washing-tray, another set is immediately immersed. The water in the tray should preferably be changed after each washing. Alternatively, washing may be done in running water. For removal of paste and glue, the water should be luke-warm, and deacidification (see Chapter 5) is advisable for removal of acidity in papers with a low pH.

Washing in this manner renders the sheets relatively free from paste, glue and other water-soluble substances which either mar their appearance or cause their premature deterioration.

Generally speaking, hard-sized smooth papers are easier to wash as they retain a certain amount of strength when wet and it is easy to remove dirt and mud from their surface; soft, heavy papers, on the other hand, are difficult to wash as they become weak and fragile on wetting and retain stains tenaciously. With a little care, however, the work can be done properly.

FLOOD-DAMAGED DOCUMENTS

Documents damaged in floods and with deposits of mud are washed in thermostatically controlled stainless-steel sinks containing a mixture of water and 0.05 per cent Preventol,[1] as a fungicide. The solution is kept at approximately 40° C. The sheets are washed on floating wooden boards held still by stainless-steel angle irons, which are also used to hold the sheets in alignment under water during washing.

The sheets are interleaved with a wet-strength paper. Resin sized, this paper has the property of retaining most of its dry strength when wet, and acts as a support to the sheets. Each sheet is washed separately, very soft brushes being used to remove dirt, mud, etc., sticking to the paper. The brushing is in an outwards direction in order to avoid tearing or scuffing the paper. All pressure should be avoided, and any traces of mud remaining after the initial brushing are removed by gentle brushing over and over again until they disappear. This process is repeated with the other sheets.

After washing, the sheets are placed in a solution of Preventol bath (0.5 per cent) as a fungicide for about thirty minutes and then pressured to remove excess water.

One material often recommended for washing and removing mud and grime from paper is soap solution. Being a chemical compound, its action is specific. For this reason, washing with soap of unknown composition and chemical action should not be attempted. On the other hand, detergents such as Lissapol N, etc., have no harmful effects on paper and may be used safely. Documents so treated should be thoroughly washed in running water to remove any traces of the compound, which might later cause degradation of cellulose. In Florence, flood-damaged records have been successfully washed with Lissapol N (5 per cent).

Washing is carried out in a tepid solution (30° C) of Lissapol N (5 per cent) in specially prepared wash basins which are electrically heated and thermostatically controlled. The sheets are interleaved with water-resistant, resin-sized 'overlay paper', and placed in the bath for about thirty minutes. During the washing process the sheets are cleaned gently with a soft brush to remove loosened mud, after which they are washed for a further thirty minutes in running water. The washed sheets are then spread on drying racks of plastic

1. Preventol is the trade name of Ortho phenyl phenol manufactured by Byers. Sodium salt of Ortho phenyl phenol is manufactured by Imperial Chemical Industries (ICI) under the name of Topane.

wire netting fixed in wooden frames which are specially designed to fit into drying trolleys. These trolleys are introduced into the drying ovens where hot (approximately 38° C), filtered air is blown through perforated tubes over the sections. The hot moist air is allowed to escape from the top of the ovens. When dry, the sheets are removed and assembled, interleaved with waxed-paper and placed under pressure.

PRECAUTIONS

If proper care is not taken during washing, more harm may be done than good. A number of precautions are therefore essential: (a) the ink on the document should be protected if it is soluble in water—coloured inks and drawings should always be protected; (b) all documents which require washing should be supported while wet to prevent tearing of the sheet and to permit safe handling; (c) drying and pressing should be done with care. Uneven drying of the paper causes a good deal of distortion, as does uneven or excessive pressing. If a wet document is pressed too hard, all natural distortion is removed, leaving it with the flat appearance of a poor facsimile. Excessive pressure also leads to dimensional distortion, particularly in case of etchings, engraving and seals. Drying with blotters, with the application of just enough pressure to ensure flatness and uniform drying, is the best method. Replacement of blotters, with a consequent periodic release of pressure on the sheet allows it to contract more or less naturally as it dries; (d) finally, washing should never be carried out piecemeal, as this results in staining, uneven wrinkling and curling of the paper. The entire sheet should be washed. Coated and glazed papers should never be washed with water as this dissolves the surface and ruins the paper beyond repair.

More recently, the use of enzymes for washing paper has been advocated. Enzymes are complex organic substances which break materials such as glue and starch and other adhesives into products soluble in water. Enzymes are, however, effective only under controlled conditions of temperature, water purity and pH, and their utility is therefore limited. Moreover, little is known of their effect on paper itself. Until more data is available it would be wise not to use them for washing and removing stains on paper.

REMOVAL OF STAINS WITH ORGANIC SOLVENTS

Washing followed by sizing often suffices to remove stains and impart body to an otherwise brittle paper. Organic solvents, which are perfectly safe, must frequently be used to remove more tenacious stains. With these solvents, it is not necessary to treat the entire document, as their application, unlike that of water, does not result in appreciable expansion of the paper. It is safe to treat only those parts which require cleaning with a non-linting cotton swab dipped in the selected solvent.

The different solvents used for removing stains do, however, affect printing and coloured inks, causing them to run and leave new and unexpected stains on paper. It is therefore advisable to test the fastness of the ink to the solvent chosen. The process is similar to that used for testing the fastness of ink to washing, with the difference that a specimen of the writing, instead of being tested with a drop of water, is rubbed gently with a cotton swab dipped in the solvent and then pressed with blotting paper. If the blotter is stained, the ink is soluble in the solvent. Black typewriter inks and carbon copies run or smudge in such solvents, and should be protected before the document is cleaned. One protective treatment is starch sizing, but the cleaning of such documents should always be approached with caution.

The selection of a suitable solvent for the removal of stains is essential to successful cleaning. Stains of oil, paint and adhesive tapes are safely removed in benzene or carbon tetrachloride, or in a mixture of these solvents. Lacquer stains may be removed by treatment with acetone, while those of Sellotape and wax are removed by treatment with a mixture of benzene and toluene, and stains caused by shellac and mildew respond to treatment with alcohol. Each of these solvents has individual characteristics which indicate its use for specific purposes.

The utility and suitability of solvents for the removal of different stains and the traces left by adhesives used for reinforcing documents, are set out in Table 1 which may be used as a guide for the selection of the most appropriate solvent.

The solvents which have been found most useful are hexane, toluene, acetone and pyridine. Hexane and toluene are effective for removing stains caused by grease, oil and wax. A mixture of these two solvents is also effective in removing deteriorated pressure

TABLE I

Stain	Solvent
1. Paint	Mixture of alcohol and benzene, or pyridine followed by thorough washing with water, or turpentine
2. Lacquer and varnish	Acetone, or methylated spirit, or pryidine, or dilute ammonia water for old spirit varnish
3. Shellac	Hexane, or toluene, or mixture of benzene and toluene
4. Oil	Hexane, or toluene, or carbon-tetrachloride or benzene
5. Fats	Alcohol, or petroleum ether, or pyridine
6. Wax	Petrol, or hexane, or toluene
7. Grease	Hexane, or toluene, or petrol (white), or naphtha, or hexane
8. Resins	Alcohol, or pyridine
9. Adhesive tape	Carbon-tetrachloride, or benzene
10. Pressure-sensive tapes (Sellotape)	Mixture of hexane and toluene, or mixture of benzene and toluene
11. Duco cement	Acetone
12. Rubber cement	Mixture of benzene and toluene
13. Glue	Warm water
14. Paste	Water
15. Tar	Benzene, petrol, pyridine, carbon-tetra-chloride
16. Mildew (mild stains)	Ethyl alcohol, or benzene
17. Tea or coffee	Potassium perborate
18. Rust	5 per cent oxalic acid (not recommended for weak papers)
19. Mud	Water or ammonia

sensitive tapes. Acetone is effective in removing many types of lacquers, plastics and spirit varnishes while pyridine has been found to be effective for fats, oils and resin stains, but is drastic in its action and should be used with caution.

The use of solvents or their mixtures requires a certain amount of experience, practice and discretion, together with knowledge of the solvents themselves. Care should always be taken to avoid any damage and rough treatment to the document.

Technique

The paper is laid with the stained side down on a white blotter. The portion to be treated is cleaned with cotton dipped in the selected solvent and then sponged from the back. The stain is softened by the action of the solvent and transferred to the blotting paper. The paper is then placed on a new blotting paper and sponged again, the process being repeated till sponging leaves no significant residue on the blotter. The paper is then turned over and treated in the same way. This procedure helps to prevent the stain from spreading and leaving a new stain on the document which would thus require recleaning. The treated document is then allowed to dry. It requires no ironing or flattening.

A somewhat different technique must be employed for removing old sealing wax. The paper is first moistened with water by pressing between wet blotters. The wax is carefully scrapped off with a sharp knife and final traces are removed by pressing the paper between white and clean blotters with a heated iron.

The misinformed use of pressure-sensitive tapes (also known as Sellotape) for mending torn documents is by no means uncommon. Such tapes are difficult to remove without damage to the document. However, the following treatment is suggested.

Provided that its ink is not soluble, the document should first be soaked in water. If the tape curls and wrinkles, it may be peeled off by means of a pair of tweezers, and any adhesive residue removed by sponging with either benzene or trichlorethylene. If, however, it is not possible to soak the document in water, or if the treatment is not effective, the edges of the tape and underside of the paper should be treated with either benzene or trichlorethylene. After thorough soaking, the tape may be removed, but not its stain. The intensity of the stain may in some cases be reduced by final sponging of the residual adhesives by either of the solvents mentioned above; failing this, little more may be done to remove the stain completely.

Other stains resist removal even after the most careful treatment with the best possible solvents. Such stains, if they are on documents of foolscap size, may be removed by subjecting them to solvent treatment in a soxhlet apparatus. In the soxhlet, the paper is washed repeatedly with newly distilled hot solvent, which removes even the residues of stains. This process is non-mechanical and the treatment, which is entirely chemical should be carried out in a properly ventilated room.

All organic solvents (see Table 1) used for stain removal are inflammable and to a certain extent poisonous. They should be handled with care and cleaning operations should be carried out away from any naked flame and in a well-ventilated room or under fume hoods fitted with exhaust fans.

OTHER STAINS

The stains encountered on old documents are often due to 'foxing' or to ink. Foxing is caused by mildew, and takes the form of a spotty brown discolouration observed on documents and prints which have been stored in damp rooms for a considerable time. The 'foxed' area is more acidic than the unfoxed or clear part. Difficult to remove by solvent treatment, it may be effectively removed, like ink and other stains, by bleaching.

Bleaching

Bleaching is somewhat drastic. It tends to weaken the paper and fade the writing on the document, although carbonaceous inks are not affected. It is therefore desirable to examine the effect of the bleaching agent on a few sheets of similar nature but of no value before subjecting the affected document to this treatment. Archive documents may be treated by bleaching if their paper is in good condition and if the stain is highly objectionable. Otherwise, the stain should be left untreated.

A number of bleaching processes which do remove stains unfortunately weaken the paper. These processes are therefore not recommended for archive documents on brittle, thin or otherwise weak paper or on a paper of poor quality, and should be used only in those cases where they will do more good than harm.

Hydrogen peroxide
In suspension in ether, this is a mild bleaching agent and should be tested on the stain before any other. The suspension is prepared by mixing equal quantities of ether and hydrogen peroxide (20 vol.) in a glass-stoppered bottle. When the bottle is shaken a certain

amount of hydrogen peroxide, which is otherwise immiscible with ether, mingles with the latter. When the liquid is allowed to stand, it separates into two layers, with an ethereal layer at the top and the hydrogen peroxide at the bottom. This ethereal solution contains enough hydrogen peroxide for bleaching purposes, and may be applied on the stain by means of a cotton swab.

Chloramine-T

This is a white powder which disintegrates on contact with air. It is generally used in the form of a 2 per cent solution prepared by dissolving 113.5 grammes of powder in 5.6 litres of water. The solution is painted on the surface to be bleached with a fine flat brush. The treated sheet is placed between blotters, covered with boards and pressed. After about an hour the sheet is removed, and if by that time the stain has not been bleached, the process is repeated until a satisfactory appearance is achieved.

Chloramine-T is effective in removing 'foxing' stains, and was first suggested for this purpose by Dr H. J. Plenderleith. It is very mild in its action and leaves no destructive residues on paper. Nevertheless, the treated sheet should be rinsed in running water for at least fifteen minutes, as it has been observed that the dried residues of the bleach remain active and may bleach adjacent sheets of paper. Coloured documents are particularly vulnerable to damage if the bleach residues are allowed to remain on the paper.

A chemical similar to chloramine-T is halazone, which is available in tablet form. A solution of five tablets in 100 cm^3 of water is as effective as chloramine-T.

Hypochlorites

Hypochlorites were already used for bleaching in the nineteenth century. The common bleach used at that time was bleaching powder, i.e. calcium hypochlorite. This has now been replaced by sodium hypochlorite, also known as chlorinated soda or *eau de Javel*, which is more convenient.

Bleaching with sodium hypochlorite is conducted in three stages. The first bath consists of a mixture of 5 per cent sodium hypochlorite solution and concentrated hydrochloric acid, in proportions of 5.5 per cent to 0.5 per cent. The second bath consists of 0.5 ml of concentrated hydrochloric acid in 2,700 ml of water and the third bath of 2 ml of concentrated ammonia in 9 l of water. The sheet of paper to be bleached is placed successively in the three solutions, the time spent in each bath depending on the extent and nature of the stain. In a typical operation it is placed in the first bath for five minutes, then transferred to the second bath and allowed to remain there for a further five minutes. Finally, the paper is transferred to the third bath, where it is allowed to remain for some ten minutes. The treated sheet is thoroughly rinsed in running water for another twenty minutes.

Another technique involves the use of a stronger bleach. A 10 per cent solution of sodium hypochlorite is prepared. Only 5 per cent of this solution is put in a bath and the document to be treated is immersed in it. If the paper of the document becomes soft through the action of this solution, it is transferred to a bath containing a solution of 5 ml of concentrated hydrochloric acid in 1,150 ml of water. The treated document is finally placed in a bath containing 2 per cent solution of sodium thiosulphate, which acts as an anti-chlor and counters the residual chlorine, before being washed in running water to remove all traces of residual chemicals.

Sodium chlorite and chlorine dioxide

Bleaching with sodium chlorite and chlorine dioxide is less simple than bleaching with chloramine-T. This process, developed by Gettens, is based on the bleaching action of chlorine dioxide gas, which is generated from sodium chlorite. The three methods of treatment are described below.

In the first method, a 2 per cent solution of sodium chlorite is prepared by dissolving 113 grammes in 5,600 ml of water. This solution is then mixed with 140 ml of 40 per cent formaldehyde. The sheet to be bleached is immersed in this mixture for between fifteen minutes and an hour, depending on the intensity of the stain. It is then removed with the aid of its support and washed in running water for at least fifteen minutes to remove any traces of the bleaching chemicals. Sheets treated in this way do not acquire the brilliant white colour caused by other bleaches. After treatment, they are dried between blotters under slight pressure, the blotters being changed when necessary.

During the bleaching process, chlorine dioxide is released as a result of the interaction of sodium chlorite and formaldehyde. Because of the pungent smell of this gas, it is advisable to conduct the bleaching in a fume cupboard fitted with an observation window and an exhaust fan to expel the gas. This process is useful in bleaching strong papers.

The second method involves bleaching with an aqueous solution of chlorine dioxide. The gas is prepared by the interaction of sodium chlorite and sulphuric acid in a gas generator or is purchased in a cylinder form, and bubbled through water, where it goes into solution. The material to be treated is supported by glass or plastic netting and immersed in the solution for some fifteen minutes, after which it is removed and washed thoroughly in running water.

This method is of advantage in bleaching operations, such as those involving prints and drawings, where only a minimum amount of immersion is desirable. Like the first one, it should be carried out in a fume cupboard.

For prints which cannot be immersed at all, and for use only when neither the first nor second methods are applicable, a third method has been developed. Here, chlorine gas is generated as described earlier, but instead of passing through water, is allowed to come into direct contact with the surface of the document in a sealed chamber. The document to be bleached is dampened with a sponge and placed in the chamber which, like the fume cupboard, is fitted with glass to permit supervision of the bleaching process. During the bleaching, products of the interaction of the gas with the stain are deposited on the surface of the document, and should be sponged off. If this is not done, the stain reverts to its original colour.

Potassium permanganate
This process involves the use of two baths, one of potassium permanganate to oxidize the stain and the other to reduce the oxidized product to colourless or soluble substances, which are then washed out with water.

The operation is a simple one. The sheet to be bleached is immersed for about five minutes in an aqueous solution of potassium permanganate. The strength of solution depends upon the intensity of the stain to be bleached and varies from 0.5 to 5 per cent. The addition of a small amount of orthophosphoric acid to the solution increases the action of the permanganate. It has been observed that phosphoric acid in a small concentration is not harmful to paper.

After about five minutes, the sheet is removed from the permanganate bath and placed in a second bath to reduce the resultant brown stain. A number of solutions for the second bath have been recommended and used, including sulphuric acid, potassium bisulphite, oxalic acid, sodium sulphite, sodium hydrosulphite and citric acid, all of which have been found to reduce the physical strength of paper. Oxalic acid is the most potent in this respect, and should under no circumstances be used with documents on paper.

For the second bath, the solution which has been found to cause least harm to paper and to be effective in reducing the brown stain from the first bath is a 5 per cent solution of sodium hydrosulphite in water. After reduction, which takes some five minutes, the treated sheet is washed in running water for five minutes and then immersed in a dilute solution of ammonia in water before being finally rinsed in running water for fifteen minutes. This process has proved to be quite safe for bleaching works of art and documents on paper.

A variation of bleaching with potassium permanganate has been described by Minogue. In this process, a solution of potassium permanganate (one part to sixteen parts of water) is prepared. The paper to be bleached is first immersed in a bath of water and then in the potassium permanganate bath for about thirty seconds. It is then removed and washed in running water for some ten minutes. Under the influence of the permanganate the paper acquires a uniform brown colour. Placed in sodium metabisulphite solution (one part to sixteen parts of water), the paper turns white. If the stain persists, the process is repeated. The bleached paper is finally washed in running water for at least fifteen minutes, dried and then toned to the required creamish colour by dusting with a finely divided mixture of yellow ochre and precipitated calcium carbonate.

As a result of bleaching, paper is considerably weakened and should be restored by any of the processes described in Chapter 6 to prevent its subsequent disintegration.

INK STAINS

Paper disfigured by ink stains must be considered separately because any treatment which removes the ink stain not only weakens the paper but also affects the writing. Iron-gall ink stains are bleached with a 3 per cent solution of oxalic acid, while water-soluble ink stains are bleached with sodium hypochlorite. The treated sheets should be thoroughly washed to remove all residual chemicals, which otherwise affect the paper adversely. Carbon and India inks are not affected at all by bleaching.

The various processes described above may be attempted in the following order for bleaching stains:

1. Chloramine-T is the least drastic of the bleaching agents and is convenient to work with.
2. If chloramine-T does not prove effective, one of the methods involving sodium-chlorite and chlorine dioxide should be used. A fume cupboard is essential to safeguard the persons carrying out the operation.
3. If a fume cupboard is not available, the potassium permanganate-sodium hydrosulphite process should be employed.
4. The use of hydrochlorites should be avoided whenever possible, as they degrade the cellulose, although they give good results on strong paper and when employed by experts.

Notwithstanding the objections that hydrochlorites degrade cellulose, prints treated in this way so far have shown no actual damage. Hypochlorites have been extensively used and with great success on papers damaged in the Florence floods in 1966. Solutions as strong as 10 per cent or even stronger have been used on paper and prints without any noticeable damage, although it should be noted that most of the books and documents treated are on good, strong paper. The process adopted is as follows.

The sheets are interleaved with wet-strength paper of the type used during washing. After immersion in a bath of tepid water to relax the paper fibres, they are placed sheet by sheet in the bleaching bath and kept there for a period ranging from thirty seconds to five minutes until the stains disappear.

The solution strength varies from 3 to 10 per cent concentration of sodium hypochlorite according to the intensity of the stain.

After bleaching, the sheets are immersed in an anti-chlor solution (sodium thiosulphate) for some thirty minutes. They are then placed in rinsing sinks, where they stay for at least four hours under cold running water.

Care should be taken during the process of bleaching, and the following precautions observed:

The treated material should be washed thoroughly in running water to remove the end-products of bleaching and the residual chemicals.

The document must be supported either with a glass plate or plastic netting before immersion in the bleaching solution or during washing. Wet-strength papers may be used in place of supports.

Bleaching should be conducted in a well-ventilated room fitted with exhaust fans. Work with pungent gases like chlorine should be carried out in fume cupboards.

Portions of the document other than those which are to be bleached should be painted with a solution of cellulose acetate in acetone or covered with a sheet of cellulose acetate film moistened with acetone; these may be removed without difficulty after the bleaching process has been completed.

In the case of colour prints, whose treatment differs from that of black and white prints, a knowledge of ink and colour is desirable.

Finally, and in view of the undisputed importance of archive documents and the nature of the treatment, the work should be carried out only by or under the supervision of scientifically trained persons.

Flattening

Flattening comprises the removal of folds, wrinkles and curls and is carried out prior to the actual restoration of documents. Folded documents have a tendency to break at the folds if they are handled extensively without prior flattening. Every time a folded document is opened and refolded, the fold is weakened until it eventually breaks. Once this has happened the only remedy is restoration, a costly process.

Most folded documents, if properly flattened, do not require extensive repairs, but may be docketed, used and kept safely for years to come. The process of flattening is a simple one. The paper is opened carefully and spread as smoothly as possible on plastic netting fitted in wooden frames. Some fifteen to twenty such frames may be loaded on a trolley, each frame being capable of taking four foolscap size sheets. The trolley is then placed in a humidification room measuring 2.4 m by 3 m and equipped with 'Pettifogers' —a device which injects steam into the room—or with any other mechanical humidifier. Relative humidity of 90 to 95 per cent is maintained in the room. The spread sheets absorb moisture uniformly from the moisture-laden air. When they have become thoroughly damp, the sheets are removed. Each is then placed between blotters and ironed until all folds, creases and wrinkles are removed. Care should be taken to ensure that the sheet is protected from direct contact with the iron, which may be of the ordinary household electrical type. Damping only at the folds should be strictly avoided as the water on drying will leave stains on the document. The entire document sheet should be wetted uniformly.

If a humidifying machine is not available, each sheet should be supported on a plastic wire net and dipped in a bath containing water, as in the washing process, and then flattened. This, of course, is a time-consuming process.

Most documents which have been washed or bleached or flattened, do not require any further treatment except resizing, which imparts the strength necessary for safe handling. Resizing is the last step in the restoration process and is carried out in cases where the document requires no further treatment for handling or after the document has been repaired and strengthened by the manual process of repair using paste. The technique of resizing is discussed under 'Restoration' in Chapter 6.

5 Deacidification

A major cause of deterioration in paper is acidity, caused both by the materials used in its production and by atmospheric contamination. This deterioration occurs as a result of hydrolytic action on cellulose, the main ingredient of paper, and is measured in terms of the hydrogen-ion concentration in the water extract of a sample of the affected paper. The lower the pH, the greater is the deterioration in paper. This is also reflected in decreased strength, which may be measured by the tear-resistance test, and loss of flexibility, measured by the folding endurance test. Deacidification of such papers is known to reduce the rate of deterioration.

In the early forties Barrow recognized that the built-in acidity of paper had a greater effect on its deterioration than atmospheric contamination and advocated the deacidification of documents. In 1969 the problem was reviewed and examined by Smith. In addition, a number of workers throughout the world have contributed much to our present knowledge of deterioration due to acidity and deacidification processes.

It has been observed by Smith that the pH value required for stable permanent paper has altered with the passage of time. In the early twentieth century, permanent book papers required a pH of 4 (hot water extract). In 1928 this figure was set at 4.7 or preferably higher. By 1935, it was realized that low pH was a cause of early deterioration in paper and the figure was raised to a minimum pH of 5 for good quality book paper. In 1937 the figure was raised by Grant to pH 6. He observed that for permanent paper the value of the hot water extract should not be less than pH 6. Lewis, in 1959, stated on the basis of tests that papers in good condition had a pH of 6.3 and 6.5. Barrow later also stated that the most stable papers show a pH of about 7 (cold extraction) while the least stable show a pH of 5, and that a pH of about 7 is desirable for maximum conservation. Smith suggests that the most desirable pH value is 7, i.e. neutral. An evaluation by Kathpalia of papers dating from the fourteenth to nineteenth centuries (see Introduction, page 15) has shown that papers with pH above 6.7 are in excellent condition while those with pH ranging from 6.2 to 6.7 are in good condition, and that all these papers are free from fungus stains.

It is now well known that a pH of 4 is far too acidic for papers which, under this condition, rapidly become brittle. It is also known that if paper is to resist fungus growth, it should be slightly acidic. In 1959, Barrow developed a grade of paper from chemical wood, which has a pH of 9 and which on the basis of tests may be expected to last for approximately 300 years. It would thus appear that a pH value of about 7 is most suitable for permanent papers and should be incorporated into standards for such papers.

As a result of the studies referred to above, a number of processes have been developed which effectively neutralize the deteriorative action of free acidity in paper. The various processes developed may be classified either under wet or dry methods.

Wet methods

These methods are based on an invention by Otto Schierholtz at the Ontario Research Foundation in Toronto and patented as early as 1936. The technique consisted of immersing paper in or spraying it with an aqueous solution of barium, calcium or strontium bicarbonates or hydroxides. The immersion time varied from five seconds to about two minutes. The wetted paper was then dried. As a result, carbonates of these metals were deposited on the treated paper.

To increase the neutralizing potential of these compounds, Schierholtz recommended carbon-dioxide treatment to convert hydroxides to carbonates and that the suspension of carbonates be allowed to settle on the treated sheets. He reported that a more concentrated bicarbonate solution could be prepared by using carbon dioxide gas under pressure and advised that the pH of a water extract from paper treated by this process should exceed a value of 6.5 and that a deposit of up to 2 per cent by weight might be required for stabilizing groundwood papers like newsprint. He claimed that treatment in accordance with his discovery would make alum-rosin sized papers more durable with age.

Some of the early methods developed since then and widely used utilize Schierholtz's invention. Those which proved useful and are worthy of mention are given below.

THE USE OF TWO SOLUTIONS

Calcium hydroxide and calcium bicarbonate

This process involves treatment of a document for twenty minutes each in two solutions. The first solution, which consists of 0.15 per cent calcium hydroxide, neutralizes the acid present in the paper, while the second solution, of 0.15 per cent calcium bicarbonate, converts the excess calcium hydroxide to calcium carbonate, which is deposited on the paper under treatment as a fine precipitate. This precipitated calcium carbonate acts as a buffer against acid attack and protects the document against further deteriorative action.

Calcium hydroxide
For this solution, 454 grammes of high-grade calcium oxide are placed in an enamelled container or glass bottle and 2,280 ml of water are added. The water reacts with the calcium oxide and during the reaction considerable heat is released. After about ten minutes the solution is stirred and poured into a bottle of 23 l capacity. The bottle is then filled with water, stirred with a wooden or glass rod, and set aside to allow the particles to settle. When the solution becomes clear, it is strained off and discarded. The bottle is refilled with water, stirred and set aside again until the particles have settled. This liquid solution contains approximately 0.15 per cent calcium hydroxide. It is decanted and used for deacidification purposes. The bottle may be refilled three times, the contents stirred and the resultant clear solution used for deacidification without affecting the efficacy of the process in any way.

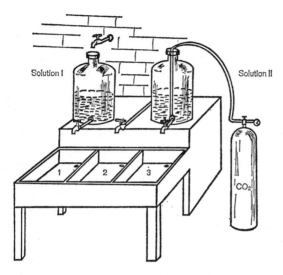

Fig. 4. Deacidification with Barrow's process.

Calcium bicarbonate

For this solution, 454 grammes of calcium carbonate are mixed with water in a 23 l bottle. The bottle is then filled and carbon dioxide gas is bubbled through the solution for from fifteen to twenty minutes. The resultant calcium bicarbonate solution is milky, and of approximately 0.15 per cent strength. Unlike the first solution, it must be prepared afresh each time the bottle is emptied.

Technique

Three enamelled trays or sinks are arranged as shown in Figure 4. Sink 1 is almost half filled with the first (calcium hydroxide) solution. Sink 3 is similarly filled with the second (calcium bicarbonate) solution, while Sink 2 is left empty. Documents in batches of ten or so are supported or interleaved with either bronze wire mesh or plastic wire netting and then placed one at a time in Sink 1, where they remain immersed for twenty minutes. They are then removed with the aid of their supports and placed in Sink 2 for about two minutes to drain off the excess calcium hydroxide. They are then placed in Sink 3 and allowed to remain there for the next twenty minutes. As a result of interaction between the two solutions, calcium bicarbonate is deposited on the surface of the documents. After twenty minutes the batch of documents is taken out of Sink 3 and placed in Sink 2 to drain off the excess calcium bicarbonate solution. Meanwhile a fresh batch of documents is placed in Sink 1 and the process is repeated (see Figure 4).

The treated documents are spread with their supports on drying racks, as in Figure 5. When dry, they are placed between blotters and pressed. Badly damaged or broken sheets are transferred very carefully to the blotters and given only a slight nip.

Investigations on the basis of artificial ageing tests have shown that hydroxide and bicarbonate of calcium are effective in counteracting acidity in paper and also in stabilizing it. The small amount of calcium carbonate precipitated as a result of soaking in these solutions appears to have no harmful effect on the paper.

Two objections have, however, been raised against this procedure. First, damaged documents which are falling to pieces offer poor resistance to soaking, and second there is no guarantee that the chemical processes will proceed as planned.

Werner, who examined these matters in detail, concluded that even badly damaged documents may be treated with these solutions with the help of the bronze wire mesh and that no further damage occurs. He maintains that there is no uncontrolled deacidification and that the pH of the documents treated in this manner is about 7.3. On the other hand, Langwell has stated that the process is uncertain. In his view, there is no proof that the pH value never exceeds 8 or that the possibility of alkaline damage may be excluded. A study by Kathpalia shows that this process cannot be used for all types of documents and that the pH value rises as high as 9.2 in deacidified papers. Barrow has claimed, however, that the high alkalinity indicated by pH 9.2 has no deteriorative effect on paper. In later works, he has lowered this figure, stating that 'the deacidified sheet generally has a pH 8.5 or slightly above'. It is clear that a detailed study of the mechanism of the reaction is required.

Nevertheless, the utility of the process has been proved. It has now been in use for over twenty-five years and no adverse reaction has been noticed or reported, so that it may be said to have withstood the test of time. But soaking papers in two solutions is a lengthy and costly operation, and new deacidification processes have been developed.

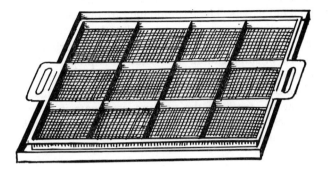

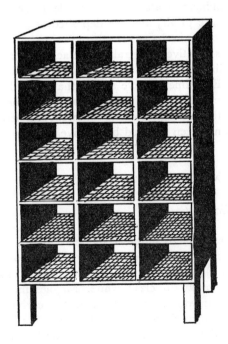

FIG. 5. Tray for deacidification and drying racks.

Calcium and magnesium carbonates

Calcium and magnesium compounds, probably in the original form of carbonates and phosphates, are found together in well-preserved old papers. These compounds are obviously not harmful to cellulose. Experiments have shown that the treatment of papers with a solution of calcium and magnesium bicarbonates offers possibilities of stabilization. The solution is prepared by passing carbon dioxide for two hours through a mixture of 1.5–2 grammes of calcium carbonate and 15–20 grammes of magnesium carbonate and about one-tenth of the calcium carbonate is converted to bicarbonates. When the undissolved particles have settled, the clear solution is decanted for use.

Technique

The papers to be treated are soaked in this solution for about twenty hours, preferably overnight, after which they are air-dried. The mixture of bicarbonates, being unstable, reverts to carbonates through exposure to air, and are deposited as a fine precipitate over the surface of the paper.

This process effectively neutralizes the acid in the paper, which becomes alkaline and retains this alkalinity even after accelerated ageing tests. Experiments have shown that treated papers show ten times more stability than untreated samples. The drawback of the process is the overnight soaking required, and perhaps because of this it has not been adopted by archive institutions.

THE USE OF A SINGLE SOLUTION

Magnesium bicarbonate

Forty grammes of magnesium carbonate are placed in a 23 l glass container which is then filled with water. Carbon dioxide gas under pressure (Fig. 6) is bubbled through the solution until its colour changes from milky to clear white. Magnesium carbonate is slightly soluble in water. Under the action of carbon dioxide it is converted into magnesium bicarbonate, which is soluble in water. The clear solution of magnesium bicarbonate thus prepared may be used immediately.

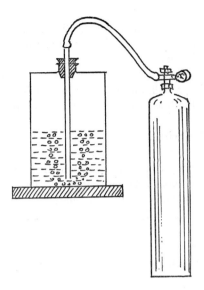

Fig. 6. Preparation of magnesium bicarbonate solution.

Technique

The solution is poured into a tray or sink. Documents supported on plastic wire mesh are placed in the solution one by one, the plastic wire mesh acting as an interleaf, and are immersed for some twenty to thirty minutes. They are then removed and dried in air. The unstable magnesium bicarbonate reverts to magnesium carbonate and carbon dioxide gas released.

As a result of its neutralizing action on the acid in the paper, the alkaline solution of magnesium bicarbonate changes colour from clear white to light yellow and finally amber. As soon as the solution changes to amber, it should be discarded and fresh solution used for the next batch of papers. One or more sheets may be deacidified at a time depending on the depth and amount of solution in the tray or sink, but the sheets should not be packed tightly, and enough space must be left to allow the solution to circulate freely around each sheet. This process effectively neutralizes the acidity in paper.

The use of magnesium carbonate for deacidification was first tested in 1957 by Gear at the United States National Archives. At about the same time, while working on the problem of stabilization of modern book papers, Barrow tested the mixture of calcium and magnesium bicarbonates described above under deacidification processes involving use of two solutions. Barrow later adopted the process of deacidification with only one solution—magnesium bicarbonate—using a technique similar to Gear's and involving the immersion of individual sheets in a saturated solution of magnesium bicarbonate.

Deacidification with a single solution is an effective method of stabilizing paper. According to Barrow, 'the nature of the process limits its application to relatively strong sheets such as are found generally in new books'. Three years later, he expressed the opinion that 'only leaves or sheets in relatively good condition are suitable for deacidification by this process'. As yet, no adverse effects resulting from the use of this process have been reported.

Deacidification by spraying with a solution of magnesium bicarbonate

Barrow has experimented with a deacidification process involving the spraying of brittle papers, maps and bound books with a concentrated solution of magnesium bicarbonate prepared by dissolving 25 grammes of magnesium carbonate in 1 l of water and passing carbon dioxide gas through this solution for two hours or slightly longer.

Technique
The solution of magnesium bicarbonate is applied evenly on both sides of the document by means of an electric sprayer of the type used by painters. During the process a white mist is produced which floats in the surrounding air and gradually settles on near-by surfaces. The spraying should therefore be carried out in a fume cupboard or a laboratory-type hood. The treated document is covered with aluminium foil to prevent evaporation and left overnight to allow the sprayed solution to soak in. Tests on treated samples reveal satisfactory deacidification.

Spraying with magnesium bicarbonate is less effective than soaking because the latter procedure permits the chemical to penetrate the innermost cellulose fibres. Moreover, spraying causes cockling in document paper which becomes more pronounced as more solution is applied. The addition of 10–25 per cent ethyl alcohol slightly reduces this cockling on drying. According to

Barrow, spraying does not impart as high a degree of stability as soaking, but is far more rapid and therefore more economical. It is useful for maps and written documents or prints which feather. But spraying only the un-inked side and allowing the magnesium bicarbonate solution to migrate raises the question of complete deacidification throughout the sheet. Spraying poses the same problem as soaking and is not suitable for general application. Indeed, the Barrow Research Laboratory is the only institution to have adopted this process.

Lime water

This process involves immersion in a saturated solution of calcium hydroxide, which is prepared from lime (calcium oxide) as described above under deacidification with two solutions. With the passage of time, the calcium hydroxide is converted by the action of air into calcium carbonate. This process is suitable only as first-aid treatment for papers which are slightly acidic, and as such has been used at the Public Record Office, London.

Inhibitors

The use of inhibitors for deacidification has been advocated by Langwell. The treatment involves immersion in an aqueous solution prepared by dissolving a mixture of disodium pyrophosphate (42 grammes), potassium ferrocyanide (5 grammes) and washing soda (14 grammes) in 4.5 l of water. The potassium ferrocyanide crystals dissolve with some difficulty, and are finely powdered beforehand. The inclusion of washing soda in the mixture prevents the solution from imparting a greenish colour to the paper when iron is present, and a pinkish colour in the presence of copper.

Technique
The solution is poured into a sink or tray. Papers for deacidification are immersed one at a time in the solution, care being taken to ensure that each is submerged before the next is added, until there is barely enough liquid to cover the last sheet. The wet pile is lifted and placed on a glass sheet, and excess solution is expelled with the aid of a roller. The sheets are then removed one by one and dried.

The rate of soaking may be accelerated by the use of a warm solution or by adding a few drops of a good quality nonionic spreading agent.

The acidity of the solution is measured with the help of neutral litmus paper. In the freshly prepared bath, the colour of the litmus paper is purple; when the solution becomes acidic, the colour changes to red. At this stage, it is desirable to discard the liquid and use a fresh solution.

This process is not suitable for papers which are brittle, in pieces or too weak to handle in the wet state. It is also unsuitable for documents written in water-soluble inks. It is therefore advisable to test the inks for solubility before immersing the documents. On the basis of available information, it appears that no institution is using this process, which is perhaps, therefore, of purely academic interest.

Other processes mentioned in the relevant literature include the use, by Russian workers, of pH buffered solutions of borates and phosphates.

APPRAISAL

The wet methods described above make it possible to stabilize paper by (a) neutralizing free acidity and (b) depositing salts which subsequently act as buffers against readicidification. These processes also help to dissolve many of the harmful products of deterioration and possibly improve fibre-to-fibre bonding as a result of the initial wetting and subsequent drying under pressure.

On the other hand, these processes have a number of obvious drawbacks. Wet, weak paper is easily damaged by handling. Such treatment therefore requires a high degree of skill.

Not all documents may be deacidified by wetting. For example, the ink may feather or be washed out, and broken pieces may be lost. In some cases, wetting leads to slight discolouration. Distortion also occurs in some cases, as papers on wetting absorbs almost twice its weight in water and consequently expands, while on drying it cockles; a slight increase in thickness usually occurs as a result of the relaxation of the fibres while wet. Finally, these processes are costly and time-consuming, as each sheet has to be treated individually.

These objections are, however, more than compensated by the proven effectiveness of these processes, the two most commonly used being deacidification with (i) calcium hydroxide and calcium bicarbonate solution and (ii) magnesium bicarbonate solution.

Non-aqueous deacidification

Considerable research is being devoted to improving the existing techniques, to accelerating the process of deacidification and rendering it applicable for the treatment of bound volumes and to reducing the cost of operations. In this connexion, a number of investigators have voiced the theory that a deacidification solution containing organic solvents might provide a remedy for difficulties caused by the use of water. Similar hopes were expressed by the International Institute for Conservation of Historic and Artistic Works in 1968, when its Committee for Paper Problems reported that 'a non-aqueous means of deacidification that would not be harmful to paper, pigments and the various media must be developed'. A number of non-aqueous deacidification processes have been mentioned in literature, but their use has usually been confined to small-scale deacidification operations in the laboratory, mostly for experimental purposes, and none of them has yet been adopted for general use, in contrast with aqueous deacidification processes. A brief résumé of the situation is provided below.

Non-aqueous deacidification treatments involve the use of a non-aqueous solution containing a deacidification agent and an organic solvent. The advantage of using organic solvents is that they are available as liquids over a wide range of temperature and may be blended to obtain the desired working requirements and properties. These solvents also evaporate quickly even at room temperature, so that the problem of drying and cockling do not arise.

On the other hand, all these organic solvents are either inflammable, toxic or more or less expensive. Some are poisonous or hazardous to health and others dissolve or cause feathering in dyes and inks used on paper. Substances such as magnesium acetate, barium hydroxide, cyclohexylamine and its carbonate and acetate and magnesium methoxide have been tested in this connexion.

MAGNESIUM ACETATE

Magnesium acetate has been found to deacidify paper and improve the permanence of paper. Wilson and Forshee in 1959 recommended its use as an acid inhibitor in cellulose laminating films. Magnesium acetate is soluble in methyl and ethyl alcohol, and a 2 per cent solution in 95 per cent methylated spirit has been shown to effect satisfactory deacidification. Documents for treatment may either be soaked in the solution or brushed or sprayed with it. Spraying can be carried out with reasonable safety on bound volumes. Barrow, however, during his tests on spray deacidification processes, and presumably on the basis of erratic results, eliminated magnesium acetate as lacking in effectiveness.

BARIUM HYDROXIDE

Baynes-Cope of the British Museum Laboratory has developed the use of barium hydroxide in methyl alcohol for the deacidification of documents written in water-soluble inks or which have become fragile and cannot be treated by aqueous processes without fear of damage. A 1 per cent solution of barium hydroxide is formed by dissolving 1.86 grammes of barium hydroxide octahydrate in 100 ml of methyl alcohol and applied to the document either by brushing or spraying if the paper is fragile or by immersion. The treated document is hung for air drying. The barium hydroxide is subsequently converted to barium carbonate through the action of carbon dioxide in the atmosphere.

A number of precautions should, however, be taken in applying this process as (a) barium and most of its compounds are toxic, although in the concentrations employed the toxicity problem is not likely to arise; (b) methyl alcohol fumes are both explosive and toxic; and (c) many coloured inks, including ball-point pen inks, are soluble in methyl alcohol.

The use of this process, as correctly pointed out by Baynes-Cope, is limited to the deacidification of single documents which cannot be subjected to aqueous deacidification, i.e. to documents written in water-soluble inks and to vellum. In India, the National Museum has experimented with the process, reporting sucessful results with a 0.5 per cent solution rather than the 1 per cent solution recommended by Baynes-Cope, although no test data have been published by the museum.

MAGNESIUM METHOXIDE

Magnesium methoxide is commercially available as a 5 per cent by weight solution in methyl alcohol and can be produced in the laboratory. Solutions of magnesium methoxide in methanol are stable up to concentrations of 8 per cent by weight and metastable from 8 to 11 per cent. Sheets requiring deacidification are dipped into the solution, agitated for a few seconds until wetted, and then removed and hung up to dry. The pH shifts to 10. On drying the paper cockles, but to a less extent than drying treatment by aqueous processes. Magnesium methoxide reacts immediately with the moisture present in the air to form magnesium hydroxide, which acts as a stabilizer.

The process has certain disadvantages, which are being eliminated. According to Smith, the instantaneous reaction of magnesium methoxide with the moisture absorbed by the paper produces a thick magnesium gel which hinders uniform treatment. The paper swells and cockles on drying. Inks, dyestuffs and other coloured materials are dissolved or adversely affected. These problems, can, however, be resolved by controlling the duration and conditions of treatment. Magnesium methoxide and its reaction products are not detrimental to paper permanence.

The deacidification of books has also been attempted by the use of magnesium methoxide at low temperature in autoclaves.

Dry methods

Gaseous or vapour media have been used for the deacidification of documents, as they present certain obvious advantages. For example, wetting of the document is not necessary and penetration by the gases or vapours is complete and uniform.

AMMONIA

The first gas to be used was ammonia, which is cheap, safe and easy to use. It is suitable for deacidifying records written in water-soluble inks and also those containing dyes and colours.

Documents and books requiring deacidification are exposed to dilute ammonia (1 : 10) in a sealed chamber. It has been observed that the ammonia vapours counteract the acidity in the papers after a period of exposure varying from twenty-four to thirty-six hours. This treatment does not affect either the durability of the paper or the water-soluble inks. The pH value is raised to between 6.8 and 7.2. No deposit of any reaction compound is left on the surface of the paper.

This process is used in the National Museum, Delhi, and also in the U.S.S.R. However, Barrow has reported that the paper reverts to acidic conditions within twenty four hours and that after fifty-four days the pH of the treated paper reverts to that which it possessed when the treatment was begun. Kathpalia, on the other hand, has found that papers deacidified by this process as early as 1957 in the laboratory have not been adversely affected, and that the pH has declined from 7.1 to 6.5 over a period of thirteen years. The difference between these findings is due to the fact that in the process adopted by Barrow the samples were treated only for eighteen hours, in contrast with the twenty-four to thirty-six hours suggested by Kathpalia. It has also been observed that the treated papers do not discolour in any way. It is reasonable to assume that documents treated in this manner will keep well if stored in a non-contamined atmosphere.

VAPOUR PHASE DEACIDIFICATION

In this process, cyclohexylamine carbonate is used for deacidification. Cyclonexylamine carbonate is a dry white powder, acidic rather than alkaline, and soluble in water and in organic solvents such as methyl alcohol. Excluded by its acidity as the deacidifying agent, on vapourizing it probably reverts to the alkaline chemical cyclohexylamine, which would therefore appear to be responsible for the deacidification.

Sheets of paper impregnated with cyclohexylamine carbonate are inserted at twenty-five page intervals for books printed on heavily sized or coated paper and at fifty-page intervals for books printed on porous paper. The impregnated sheets can also be used with manuscripts placed in containers. In each case, the sheets should be slightly larger than the materials to be treated.

The documents so treated are then placed in an air-tight chamber or container or in a tightly closed plastic bag. The deacidification process normally takes two weeks, after which the impregnated paper should be removed and the pH measured.

Langwell recommends 10 grammes of cyclohexylamine carbonate for deacidifying 2 pounds of loose papers contained in a box. This means that in a large archive collection with very many documents requiring deacidification, a huge amount of the chemical would be required. Russian workers have found that the maximum concentration of the chemical should not exceed 0.001 grammes per cubic metre (i.e. one part per million in contrast with the one part per thousand suggested by Langwell) if the safety of those working with it is to be protected. Cyclohexylamine carbonate, like cyclohexylamine, has dangerous properties and is dangerous to health in high concentrations, as it releases strong alkali, which may cause irritation to the respiratory system as well as skin irritations. Prolonged breathing of the vapours should be avoided and the hands protected by rubber gloves. The process should be used with care and should not be used where documents are stored in air-conditioned rooms.

Work conducted at the Barrow Research Laboratory indicates that treatment with cyclohexylamine carbonate provides adequate deacidification and prolongs the retention of acceptable physical properties of acidic and non-acidic paper. The treatment, however, results in the destruction of rosin sizing, decreased brightness and yellowing of acidic paper. The laboratory draws attention to the disagreeable odour of cyclohexylamine carbonate and to the precautions which must be taken to avoid hazardous effects to which those who handle cyclohexylamine carbonate or books and papers treated with it may be exposed.

Archive materials are unique and require not only specialized but also individual treatment. Only these processes which have proved useful and which have caused no harm may be considered to be effective. For deacidification purposes, the only processes adopted and confirmed by use in various archives are (a) deacidification with the use of two aqueous solutions, calcium hydroxide and calcium bicarbonate; (b) deacidification with the use of a single aqueous solution, magnesium bicarbonate; and (c) gaseous deacidification with ammonia which, although called in question presumably as a result of improper tests, has also proved useful and harmless.

The other deacidification processes are of academic interest and still in the development stage. Of these the most promising appears to be that which involves the use of magnesium methoxide in a non-aqueous solvent.

One final process, not yet mentioned, which marks an interesting and promising development worthy of further study, combines both deacidification and strengthening in a single operation. This process was developed in 1965 at the Washington State University College of Engineering. Paper to be deacidified is impregnated with a solution of sodium salt of carboxy methyl cellulose (CMC), which has been observed not only to neutralize the acid but also to increase the folding strength. While the neutralization effect remains, even after heat-ageing, the treated paper becomes stiff, although it has been further observed that the addition to the CMC solution of a non-volatile plasticizer (for example, a small quantity of wet strength resin) helps to maintain its flexibility.

6   Restoration

Most documents which have been cleaned, washed or deacidified and flattened, require either resizing, or minor repairs followed by resizing, to restore their mechanical strength. Documents which have yellowed or become brittle and are in an advanced state of deterioration require more extensive repairs. A number of processes are employed for reinforcing such documents, namely: (a) tissue repair; (b) chiffon repair (or silking); (c) mounting; (d) inlaying; (e) machine lamination; and (f) solvent lamination. All these processes have certain disadvantages and limitations. Their use, therefore, depends on the nature of the document, its constituent materials and the extent of damage. The work of reinforcement requires considerable skill, and its quality and effectiveness will depend on the knowledge and experience of the restorer.

With the development of the modern techniques of machine and solvent lamination, the use of more traditional processes such as tissue or chiffon repair (silking), mounting and inlaying has more or less declined, although these processes are still used in many archive centres, both in the East and the West and continue to prove their worth. They are also employed in cases where lamination is impossible or undesirable.

Minor repairs

Minor repairs are effected on documents which are only slightly damaged or torn. An adhesive, which may take the form of a synthetic (polyvinyl acetate) paste, a solution of cellulose acetate film in acetone, or flour paste is applied to the torn portion and tissue paper is laid over the tear and pressed down. The process is repeated on the other side of the document. When the paste dries, the excess tissue paper is scraped off. This technique strengthens the torn portion or fills gaps in the sheet. Alternatively, strips of tissue paper impregnated with polyvinyl acetate may be employed. These are prepared as follows:

A dilute solution of an internally plasticized polyvinyl acetate emulsion, such as Tixicote VJC 555, is prepared by rapidly mixing one part each of the emulsion, water and ethyl or methylated alcohol. A sheet of tissue paper is laid on a glass plate, and the solution applied either by spraying or with a brush. The tissue is then allowed to dry. When dry, glass plate and treated tissue paper are immersed in water. After a few minutes, the impregnated tissue paper may be peeled off and hung up to dry again. When required for a repairing operation, the tissue paper is cut to size, leaving a serrated edge. The paper is then applied to the torn portion of the document, covered with a silicone paper and pressed with a warm iron. The adhesive with which it is impregnated is softened, and attaches the tissue paper firmly to the document.

The author had an occasion to work with impregnated tissue paper at Florence, where the technique of preparation differs slightly from that described above. The emulsion is applied evenly to the glass plate, and the tissue paper sheet is then placed gently over it. Any air bubbles appearing are gently dabbed with a cotton wool pad to place the tissue in close contact with the emulsion, and excess emulsion outside the tissue-covered portion is removed with a moist pad of cotton wool or a fine sponge.

When the tissue paper has dried, its surface is rubbed with a hard paraffin wax block and then lightly dusted with calcium carbonate. The tissue is removed by lifting one corner with the help of a spatula and peeled away from the glass. The adhesive-coated side of the tissue has a fine glaze and can thus be applied without difficulty. Sheets prepared in this way are interleaved with silicone paper or waxed paper for storage.

The repair of torn papers or papers with missing portions is carried out in a manner similar to that described above, heat being applied by means of a flat soldering iron kept at approximately 90° C.

Minor repairs are suitable for strengthening one portion or mending a single tear in a document. But such repairs in a number of places in the same document amount to patching, which adversely affects the life of the paper and at the same time imparts an ugly look to the repaired sheet. Moreover, in the case of old documents, the paper is strengthened wherever minor repairs have been carried out, while the rest of the paper remains weak. This often leads to tearing or breaking at the points where the weak and strengthened portions meet. Furthermore, it takes longer to patch a sheet in a number of places than to reinforce it completely. Therefore, minor repairs should be limited to a minimum.

Sizing

Most documents which have received preliminary treatment such as cleaning, washing, deacidification, etc., require no further treatment apart from sizing, which imparts the necessary strength for safe handling. Sizing is the final step in the process of restoration and is carried out on documents which require strengthening but not restoration, as well as on documents repaired by traditional processes.

Before sizing, tests must be made to ensure that the ink of the document does not run. Writing which is soluble in water should be protected by the application of either polyvinyl alcohol emulsion or a solution of cellulose acetate film in acetone. Such documents, as well as other documents with coloured writings, should be sized separately.

SIZING PROCESSES

A 2.5 per cent solution of glue and water is prepared. The solution is heated to 43–45° C, and sheets for treatment are supported on plastic wire-net screens, passed through the hot size and then removed and placed in a tray to drain off excess size, before being hung up to dry.

Another sizing solution is made from gelatine. Dissolve 30 grammes of best-quality gelatine in 1 l of water. The solution is heated gently to prevent burning of the gelatine and consequent browning of the solution, which should be clear. The solution is strained through cloth and used hot, at a temperature between 43° and 45° C.

In this process a number of sheets are placed in the bath at the same time, removed and pressed between boards to drain off excess size, and then separated one by one and spread to dry or hung up to dry on a line. Care should be taken to ensure that the sheets do not stick together. After drying they are either run through a mangle or ironed.

Size prepared from fragments of parchment in the same way as the gelatine size and applied by brushing over the document is used by the Public Record Office, London, on sheets repaired by traditional processes.

Resizing by the above processes hardens the paper and tends to reduce water staining. If the leaves have surface grime, pencil marks, etc., they must be cleaned (Chapter 4) before sizing, otherwise these marks are fixed indelibly.

Mildewed papers may also be sized. They should, however, be first treated with thymol in order to kill the mildew (Chapter 2). Before immersion in the sizing bath they are placed for treatment in a 1.5 per cent solution of thymol in alcohol. The temperature of the sizing bath should be kept below 43° C, to prevent the vaporization of thymol deposited on the sheets during the preliminary treatment.

SYNTHETIC SIZES

A number of synthetic compounds are used as sizes. These include the following:

Methyl cellulose (trade name Glutofix). A solution of this compound is applied by means of a brush on repaired, and unrepaired but washed and deacidified sheets alike.

Another material which has proved useful for sizing, as well as repair work, is soluble nylon (trade name Calaton). Fifteen grammes of soluble nylon powder are dissolved in 1 l of alcohol by heating on a water bath at 40° C. The documents to be sized are dipped in this solution. In the course of this operation, alcohol vapours are given off, so that it is necessary to carry out the work in a fume cupboard, or in a well-ventilated room fitted with exhaust fans. No naked flame should be allowed in the vicinity during the operation.

Repair processes[1]

TISSUE REPAIR

The document to be repaired is first laid on a glass-topped table or an alkathene sheet, or on a perspex sheet using terylene (polyester) cloth as a support, and is uniformly wetted by means of a sponge dipped in water. Tissue paper slightly larger than the sheet is then applied to the document with a thin paste (Appendix 3). The paste may be applied to the document and the tissue paper laid over it gently to avoid any creases or air bubbles. Alternatively, the tissue paper itself may be first coated with paste. In each case the result is the same. The document is then turned over with the help of another alkathene sheet or terylene cloth and the other side is treated in the same way. It is then lifted and spread on a plastic net frame for drying. If terylene cloth has been used then the sheet is lifted together with the support and set aside to dry. Finally it is trimmed, leaving a slight margin of tissue paper on all sides, and pressed.

CHIFFON REPAIR (OR SILKING)

The process of repair with chiffon (silk gauze) is similar to tissue repair except that the chiffon is cut slightly smaller than the document and the paste applied from the top after it has been laid over the document. The reverse side of the document is treated in the same way. Chiffon has a tendency to fray at the edges. The repaired sheet is, therefore, framed all round with hand-made paper.

Chiffon must never be stretched over large holes in a document as it may fray and tear. In such cases the holes are first filled or

---

1. Details of equipment, etc., will be found in Chapter 8.

covered with tissue paper or hand-made paper patches slightly larger than the hole. Considerable skill is required to effect a repair of high quality.

MOUNTING

Documents written on one side are strengthened by mounting them on hand-made paper using thick flour paste (Appendix 3). Plans and other outsized papers, which are likely to suffer if kept folded, are cut into suitable sections which are then mounted on linen or paper, provision being made for a narrow margin between the sections. This margin makes it possible to fold the repaired sheet to the desired size.

INLAYING

Sheets which are weak and relatively small in size are inlaid, i.e. framed in new sheets of special hand-made paper. This method is generally used for the pages of books and occasionally to separate documents of uneven size whose sheets have decayed and become too brittle to handle with safety.

A hand-made paper sheet is cut to be required size. The outline of the document is traced on the paper, and the portion inside the outline, leaving a margin of 3 mm all round, is cut out. The document is then laid in place, i.e. framed by applying paste to the edges, smoothed and placed between waxed or silicone paper under pressure. Very brittle documents may be repaired with chiffon or tissue paper before inlaying.

Documents repaired by the above process are pressed before they completely dry. For this purpose they are placed between two sheets of waxed or silicone paper and placed in a press, where they are maintained under gentle but not excessive pressure until they are dry. It is essential that the repaired documents are dried under pressure. Documents containing seals should never be placed in the press, and should be pressed gently by some other means. The pressed documents are then trimmed to size, leaving a margin of 2 mm all round. Care must be taken to ensure that no part of an original document is cut or trimmed.

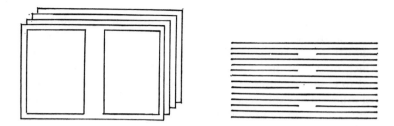

FIG. 7. Lamination: arrangement of sheets

LAMINATION

This process involves hot-sealing a deacidified document with cellulose acetate film of 23 microns (0.00088 inch) thickness and tissue paper in either a steam-heated flat-bed hydraulic press or an electrically heated roller press.

A 'sandwich' or 'envelope' is prepared by assembling the materials in the following order: tissue paper; cellulose acetate film; document; cellulose acetate film; and tissue paper.

The deacidified documents of the volume are placed in such a way that there is a gap of 5 cm in between the sheets 1 and 8, 2 and 7, 3 and 6, and 4 and 5 respectively of a section. The arrangement of the sheets is in step formation in the manner shown in Figure 7.

Thus from eight loose sheets, four pairs of sheets are obtained. These when placed one inside the other and on folding in the centre give what is known as a section or signature. This is repeated with the next group of eight sheets and so on till all the sheets of the volume have been enveloped. On lamination, this gap portion (laminated tissue) becomes strong enough to serve the purpose of 'guard' for stitching the documents into file covers. For the purpose of binding into a volume, the laminated guard can be strengthened by putting in a slip of either bond paper or muslin cloth.

During the preparation of a sandwich or envelope of paired documents, as described above, all loose fragments and the edges of the documents should be carefully fastened to the acetate film in their proper places with a cotton swab or an artist's brush dipped in acetone. Each sandwich or envelope is then placed between two sheets of 'Taflon' (tetrafluorethylene, a synthetic resin-coated glass fabric) before feeding it into the press.

In the case of hydraulic (flat-bed) lamination, the sandwich is covered with stainless-steel plates and a double thickness of blotters before being placed on the platen. This is to absorb any inequalities which may exist on the surface of the platen or in the sandwich and to ensure uniform pressure on the material to be laminated, regardless of any differences in thickness at the edges of the document. One or more sandwiches may be placed on one platen. In the latter case, the order of the various material on each platen is: stainless-steel plate; blotters; Taflon; sandwich or envelope; Taflon; blotters; Taflon; sandwich or envelope; Taflon; blotters; stainless-steel plate.

For satisfactory and uniform lamination no more than two sandwiches or envelopes should be placed on each platen. On the basis of research carried out in 1954–57, the United States National Bureau of Standards has in fact recommended that two sandwiches or envelopes be placed on one platen. Depending upon the size of the sheets or platen, four to eight sheets can be arranged in one envelope.

The temperature required for laminating paper documents varies from 140–150° C, and the pressure from 22–36 kg/cm^2 depending on the condition and type of paper. Between two-and-a-half and three minutes are usually required for lamination, and the entire process, i.e. of heating and cooling, takes from seven to ten minutes. The cellulose acetate, because of the high pressure, penetrates the pores of the document paper as well as the tissue paper.

Steam at a pressure of 5.5 kg/cm^2 (8 lb/in^2) is passed into the platens. As a result, the temperature rises to the required 150° C within two minutes. Simultaneously, pressure is applied to the platens. After three minutes, the escape valve is opened and the platens are cooled by passing water through them. The required pressure is maintained throughout this operation. When the platens have cooled, the pressure is released and the laminated documents are removed.

In the case of rotary lamination by the Barrow or Arbee processes, a sandwich or an envelope containing the document is placed between dry blotters and heated for 30–45 seconds at 180–190° C in the flat-bed platen. The heated sandwich is then passed between two rollers under pressure ranging from 25 to 40 kg/cm^2. The passage of the documents through the heated rollers takes

Pasting guard strip at the fold.
[*Photo:* National Library, Florence].

Document after repair with solvent lamination.
[*Photo:* Florence Archives].

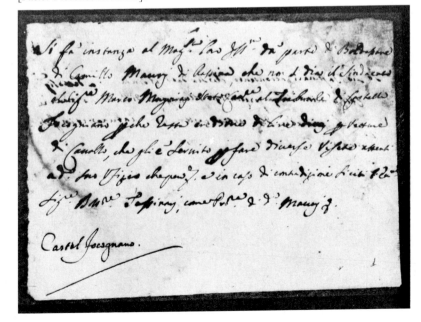

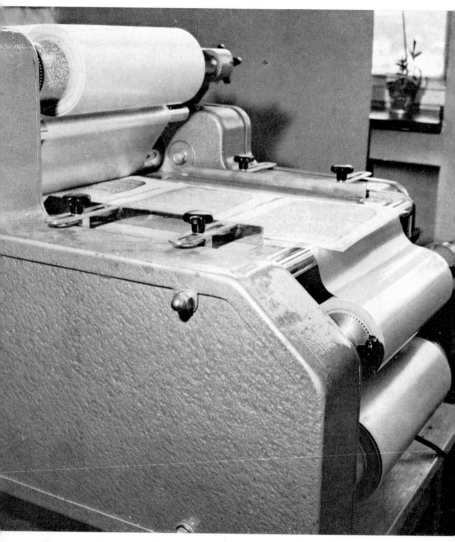

Hennecke Process. Machine K42 for lamination.
[*Photo:* A. Wagner].

Flat-bed hydraulic laminator.
[*Photo:* United States National Archives, Washington.]

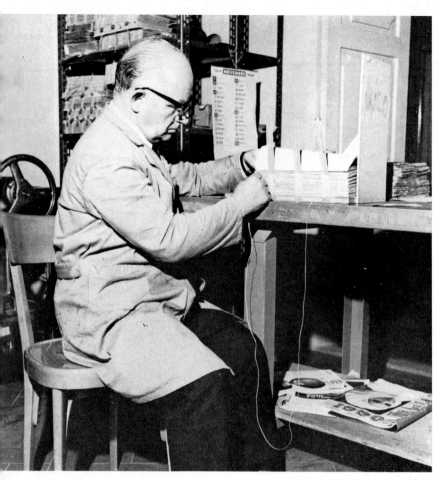

Stitching on tapes or leather strips.
[*Photo:* Florence State Archives].

Gold tooling of bound volumes.
[*Photo:* National Archives, Paris].

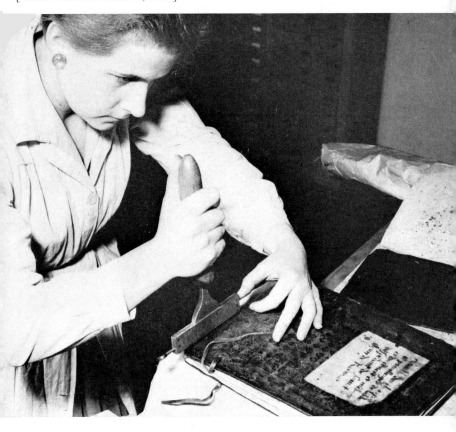

Binding unit [*Photo:* National Archives, Paris].

Author imparting training in solvent lamination process.
[*Photo:* Florence State Archives].

Mašino-Impex laminator (Florence).
[*Photo :* Florence State Archives].

Arbee laminator.
[*Photo:* United States National Archives,
Washington].

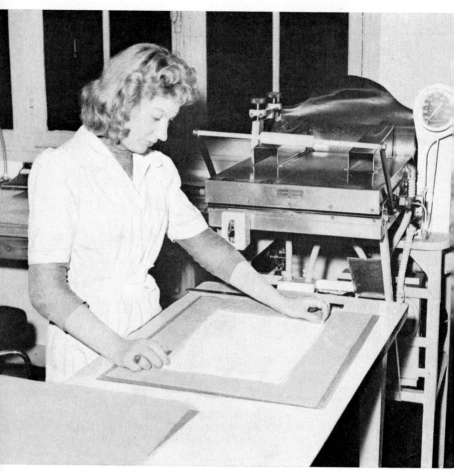

Preparing sandwich of a document prior to lamination. Barrow laminator.
[*Photo:* National Archives, Paris].

another thirty seconds. The resultant laminate is similar to that obtained from the hydraulic flat-bed press, but with the very important difference that here the cellulose acetate more or less acts as an adhesive and there is very little penetration inside the document paper itself.

The repaired documents are then placed between sheets of waxed or silicone paper and kept under pressure overnight. After this, they are trimmed as in the case of repairs with tissue paper.

The lamination of plans and charts is similar to that of other documents. These are, however, backed with cloth, and cellulose acetate film alone, instead of cellulose acetate and tissue paper, is applied to the face. The sandwich or envelope in such cases is composed as follows: cellulose acetate film (two sheets); plan or chart; cellulose acetate film (two sheets); cloth. The temperature and pressure applied are slightly higher, i.e. 150–$155°$ C and 25–40 kg/cm^2.

As already mentioned, one difference between the two methods of lamination is in the performance of the cellulose acetate with regard to the document paper. The differences between the techniques themselves may be summarized as follows:

The cost of both types of equipment is relatively high, and they

Rotary lamination	Hydraulic (flat-bed) lamination
The press comprises a heating oven and cylindrical pressure rollers. Heat is applied to the document sandwich or envelope as it lies flat in the oven, and pressure is applied to it as it passes between the rollers. The repaired document is then cooled by exposure to air.	The press consists of steam-heated and water-cooled platens, brought together by hydraulic pressure. The sandwich or envelope of documents is placed between the platens, and heat and pressure are applied simultaneously. The repaired documents are then cooled under pressure by circulating cold water through the platens.
More heat is applied in the roller press than in the flat-bed press, but for a shorter time.	Temperature and pressure controls are more accurate in the flat-bed press than in the roller press.
Only one sandwich or envelope of documents can be processed at one time.	Two sandwiches or envelopes of documents can be processed in each operation of the press.

are thus beyond the reach of smaller institutions. The National Archives of the United States of America and the National Archives of India have installed flat-bed hydraulic laminators, while rotary laminators are in use in a number of archive centres in the United States, Puerto Rico, France, Belgium, Poland, Italy, and in the British Museum, London, etc. A new type of rotary laminator, specially made by Arbee Co., N.J., and somewhat cheaper than the other two, has been installed at the United States National Archives and in other centres in the United States. Another machine is the Mašino-Impex Laminator manufactured at Zagreb, Yugoslavia, which uses (a) 'Moviphan' and (b) polymethacrylate, film instead of cellulose acetate. At Zagreb, documents treated with polyethylene film have been found to give a better laminate, while experiments have shown that the delamination of such documents in decalyne or benzene is possible without any risk.

Apart from the high cost of these laminators, the great heat required (approximately 150° C) is considered a disadvantage. Nor do these machines accelerate the process of restoration to any great extent, for apart from the application of heat and pressure in the press, all the stages in the process, i.e. the preparation of the materials for feeding into the press, the removal of the reinforced laminate, the pressing of the repaired sheets and finally trimming, involve manual operations.

OTHER LAMINATING TECHNIQUES

Many other hot sealing processes may be adopted for archive use. These were developed as alternatives to the processes involving the use of expensive machinery and undesirably high temperatures for lamination. All use coated plastic films. Those which deserve mention are the Morane, Mipofolic, Genotherm, Hennecke, Postlip Duplex and Dispro processes.

Morane process

This process was developed by the Morane Plastic Co. Ltd, Ashford, Middlesex (England). Here, the document is laminated either with a cellulose diacetate for a glossy finish or with a cellulose triacetate film for a matt finish.

The process of lamination is carried out by placing the document between two sheets of the plastic film selected according to the finish required under slight pressure at a temperature of 80° C. Pressure may be applied either by a photographic dry-mounting press or by an ordinary household electric iron heated to the required temperature.

The chief merits of this technique are the much lower temperature required and the low cost of the equipment. The process is not, however, particularly suitable for large-scale work as the press is not automatic. Nor is it suitable for conditions in tropical countries. The synthetic resin used on the plastic film also shows signs of discolouration with time.

Mipofolic process

In this process, a polyvinyl chloride film coated on one side with an adhesive is used for laminating the document, which is placed between two sheets of the film and pressed manually at room temperature in a press. This process was used extensively by the German Army during the Second World War for the lamination of maps, and has been used for lamination of archive documents at Munich, Düsseldorf and Oldenberg, in the Federal Republic of Germany, although neither the polyvinyl chloride film, nor the adhesive, are at all suitable for such documents.

Genotherm process

Polyvinyl chloride film is also used in this process, which involves lamination by heating at 70° C in an Eichner Thermofilmer press. This machine is fully automatic and can handle documents up to 30 cm in width. The process has been found useful for large documents such as newspapers, but as already pointed out, polyvinyl chloride film is not suitable for archive documents.

Hennecke process

This process is based on the use of a cellulose acetate film produced by Louzawuke, Weil (Federal Republic of Germany), under the trade name Ultraphan HK, applied at about 80° C for 20 sec under a pressure of 30 kg/cm^2. This film meets the specifications drawn up by the United States National Bureau of Standards for a suitable laminating film. For archive purposes a special matt type is available, so that no reflections from its surface disturb the reader or photographer.

Lamination by this process is carried out in a Kaschiermaschine Type K42 rotary laminator, manufactured by the firm of Karl Hennecke, Birlinghoven/Siegkreis (Federal Republic of Germany), and costing about DM. 5,000. The machine is capable of laminating documents continuously at a speed ranging from 1 to 2.5 metres per minute, corresponding to 1,500–3,000 sheets per day. Documents treated by this process are very neat and clean and properly laminated. The lamination can also be carried out in any type of flat-bed press capable of applying the required temperature and pressure.

The process has been used at the Koblenz archives, which praise it highly, and also at the Hague, Düsseldorf and Marburg. Unfortunately the firm of Karl Hennecke has discontinued manufacture of the machine, but is willing to take up its manufacture again in response to demands.

The Hennecke process certainly accelerates the process of restoration of archive documents and is suitable for the lamination of large quantities of records which must be preserved with the utmost rapidity and the greatest degree of safety against further deterioration.

Postlip Duplex process

This process was developed by Langwell and has been tested at the Public Record Office, London. According to a survey conducted by the United Kingdom Society of Archivists, twenty-one archive centres in that country are using this process of lamination, which involves the use of a special strong fibrous tissue paper—alpha-cellulose tissue of weight 15 grammes per square metre—impregnated with a polyvinyl acetate adhesive and acid-neutralizing chemical magnesium acetate. This impregnated tissue paper is applied to the document at 85° C and under a pressure of 9 kg/cm² provided by a screw-operated photographic dry-mounting press. Because it incorporates an acid acceptor, magnesium acetate, this process is claimed to achieve deacidification and lamination in a single operation. Smith in his work on deacidification has stated, however, that magnesium acetate releases acetic acid as a process of neutralization and that the pH value gradually falls from pH 8 to pH 6. Moreover, documents treated with magnesium acetate darken after lamination. These undesirable effects may be intensified in tropical conditions, so that the process is not considered suitable for adoption in tropical countries.

Lamination with Postlip tissue can also be carried out at room temperature. In this case, the document is sandwiched between the tissue paper and placed in a flat-bed press at full pressure for about five minutes. It is then removed from the press and lightly rubbed with a swab of cotton wool moistened with a solvent such as acetone, methylated spirit, isopropyl alcohol or trichlorethene. The Duplex tissue tends to retain the solvent and therefore should be left to dry for some time prior to stitching or binding. It has been observed that sheets repaired by this process stick together or block, but this problem may be easily overcome by dusting the sheets with French chalk prior to binding or storing them together. Postlip Duplex tissue has recently been replaced by a tissue of the 'glassive' type coated on one side only with a polyvinyl acetate adhesive incorporating magnesium acetate. The tissue is applied in a photographic dry-mounting press. There is no danger of blocking with this tissue. A similar laminating material which does not contain magnesium acetate is also available.

Dispro process

A laminator using Dispro tissue backed with an acrylate resin adhesive has been used at the British Museum, London, for the lamination of books. Lamination is carried out in cold, i.e. without heat, under pressure. The machine, known as the Ronosealer, exists in two types, manually operated and automatic. Originally inexpensive, costing only about $200, it is unfortunately no longer produced. The British Museum has reported that the tissue employed gives a satisfactory finish and that documents up to twenty inches wide can be treated in the machine.

In addition to the above equipment, mention may be made of the specially constructed hydraulic press designed by Ruggiero and used for lamination of printed matter, documents and parchment at the Istituto di Patologia del Libro in Rome since 1954 with films of either polyvinyl chloride or cellulose acetate. In the U.S.S.R., the Laboratory of Preservation and Restoration of Documents has developed a hydraulic type laminator similar to the one at Zagreb for the hot sealing of documents with a polyethylene film. Lamination is carried out at a temperature of 100–115° C and under a pressure of 4.5 kg/cm². The process takes between 30 sec and 1 min for completion. Research at Zagreb has shown that polyethylene laminated documents may be delaminated without risk.

Table 2 below shows the mode of adhesion and the type of film used in various lamination processes in use or developed.

TABLE 2

Method	Nature of the plastic film	Mode of adhesion
Hydraulic flat-bed lamination (United States)	Cellulose acetate film	Heat 140–150° C; pressure 22–36 kg/cm²
Mašino-Impex flat-bed lamination (Yugoslavia)	Moviphan (methacrylate film), polymethacrylate film or polyethylene film or cellulose acetate film	Heat; pressure
Hydraulic flat-bed lamination(U.S.S.R.)	Polyethylene film	Heat 110–115° C; pressure 4.5 kg/cm²
Hydraulic flat-bed lamination (Italy)	(a) polyvinyl chloride	Heat 80° C; pressure 30 kg/cm²
	(b) cellulose acetate film	Heat 140–150° C; pressure 25–35 kg/cm²
Rotary lamination (Barrow)	Cellulose acetate film	Heat 140–160° C; pressure 25–40 kg/cm²
Rotary lamination (Arbee & Co.)	Cellulose acetate film	Heat 140–150° C; pressure 22–36 kg/cm²
Rotary lamination (Kaschiermaschine)	Cellulose acetate film with adhesive	Heat 80° C; pressure 30 kg/cm²
Rotary lamination automatic (Genotherm)	Polyvinyl chloride with adhesive	Heat 70° C; pressure 4.5 kg/cm²
Dry-mounting photographic press (Morane)	(a) Cellulose diacetate with adhesive	Heat 80° C; slight pressure
	(b) Cellulose triacetate with adhesive	Heat 80° C; slight pressure

Method	Nature of the plastic film	Mode of adhesion
Dry-mounting photo-graphic press (Mipofolic)	Polyvinyl chloride with adhesive	Room temperature; pressure 6 kg/cm²
Dry-mounting photo-graphic press (Postlip)	Strong fibrous tissue with polyvinyl acetate adhesive and magnesium acetate (acid acceptor)	Heat 85° C; pressure 9 kg/cm²
Rotary lamination (Dispro)	Tissue; adhesive acrylate resin	No heat; pressure 9 kg/cm²

SOLVENT LAMINATION

The processes of lamination described require relatively expensive equipment which is beyond the financial resources of small archive centres and repair shops. Some archive institutions also hesitate to use high temperature and pressure for the restoration of their holdings. Such repair centres could employ the manual process of lamination in which an organic solvent is used to soften the plastic film. This process was developed at the National Archives, New Delhi, and is popularly known as the Indian Process of Lamination.

This is a simple, cheap and an effective process for restoring brittle and fragile documents. The document is prepared in a five-ply sandwich with cellulose acetate film and tissue paper. Using a non-linting cloth, acetone is applied to the centre of the surface of the sandwich and wiped towards the edges. The procedure is repeated on the other side of the sandwich, and the laminate is then pressed in an ordinary binder's press. The process may be employed by large and small archive repair centres alike without difficulty and, like the classical methods, permits the individual treatment of documents. All types of paper, irrespective of their thickness, may be repaired by this process. Chiffon may be used instead of tissue paper.

The technique is simple. The materials are all cut to the required size and a sandwich of the document is prepared thus: tissue paper or chiffon; cellulose acetate film; document; cellulose acetate film; tissue paper or chiffon. The sandwich is placed on a glass-topped table and its surface smoothed. A moderate amount of acetone is then applied by means of surgical cotton or non-linting cloth to the top surface of the sandwich, slowly and evenly and with a little pressure, from the centre towards the edges. The acetone soaks through the tissue paper and converts the cellulose acetate film into a gel form. The swab, which is now free of excess acetone, is quickly passed again with a little more pressure over the surface of the document. This operation takes fifteen to twenty seconds. The sandwich is lifted and inverted so that the other surface may be similarly treated. The treated document is allowed to dry for a further five seconds and rubbed with the base of the hand to remove any air bubbles and to ensure that the tissue paper has bonded to the surface properly.

The reinforced document is then lifted from the glass plate. If, as sometimes happens, the document has become stuck to the glass plate, this is not a serious matter and merely indicates that the quantity of acetone applied is slightly excessive. When this occurs the document should be lifted at one side and peeled from the plate.

The laminated sheets thus, in batches of five, are then interleaved with waxed paper and placed in a binder press to ensure a smooth surface and to remove any creases or air gaps that may be have been caused during the process of repair.

This process eliminates the need for high temperature, high pressure and expensive equipment. It is at the same time an improvement on the classical processes of reinforcement. It gives better legibility, does not increase the likelihood of insect attack and adds little to the thickness of the document. It is suitable for the repair of documents written in water-soluble inks and colours, carbon copies and documents with seals. It is also suitable for joining torn pieces of documents and for every type of repair, i.e. backing or mounting, guarding and reinforcement of documents on one side or both sides, and for all types of paper. Apart from the advantages of the process itself, the lamination so formed is much lighter than that produced by machine, for the document only retains the minimum quantity of cellulose acetate necessary for bonding it to the tissue paper, whereas machine-laminated documents retain the entire cellulose acetate film. In other words, a bound volume of documents of the same size and type repaired by solvent lamination is much lighter than a similar volume repaired by machine-laminating processes. The solvent process possesses, moreover, all the advantages of heat lamination processes and yet requires no expensive technical equipment. The only equipment and materials required are a glass-topped table, cellulose acetate film, tissue paper or chiffon, acetone and cotton wool.

This process has been tested both in New Delhi and abroad. According to Gear, data from physical tests at the United States National Archives indicate that hand lamination may be substituted for machine lamination or silking. The process is particularly useful for repairing documents bearing wax seals. The degree of success obtained will, however, depend on the skill of the restorer.

Wilson and Forshee, of the United States National Bureau of Standards, point out that the solvent process compares favourably with machine lamination using heat and pressure and should be attractive to institutions which cannot justify the cost of a laminating press.

According to Plenderleith, the solvent process is simple to carry out, since it requires no special apparatus and the document is subjected neither to heat nor pressure. Papritz has reported that figures provided by Kathpalia and Gear show that the foldability of documents laminated by the Indian process is better than that of hot-sealed documents. It would thus appear that the problem of lamination in the restoration of single documents has been solved by a process which will soon spread to archives all over the world. Indeed, this process has proved its utility since its first use in 1953, and has been adopted by many archive centres in America, Europe and Asia, and in several centres in Africa.

Certain precautions are necessary when repairing documents by this process. Care should be taken to ensure that (a) there is no smoking in the room and that no naked flame whatever is allowed; and (b) there is proper air circulation and that acetone fumes are removed by means of exhaust fans.

There is no danger of toxicity and no hazard to workers when the process is carried out in premises that are fairly well ventilated. Acetone is used extensively in laboratories and industry and no ill effects as a result of using this chemical have been reported. Persons whose skin in sensitive should, however, wear surgeon's gloves while applying acetone with surgical cotton.

During the last twenty-five years, significant advances have been made in the field of restoration. Several conclusions have clearly emerged: (a) films of polyvinyl chloride should not be used for the lamination of valuable documents; (b) lamination with cellulose acetate film is a safe method of restoring documents, and the Indian process of solvent lamination is proving its value as a method of laminating documents which cannot be subjected to temperature and pressure; and (c) polyethylene film used for lamination purposes can be delaminated, and is better for lamination purposes than cellulose acetate films.

Restoration is an exacting technique whose complexity is due to the use and availability of a great number of materials produced by human ingenuity and claimed to be effective and without harmful effect on paper. More often than not, these materials have, with the passage of time, harmed the documents treated rather than strengthened them. The only sure way of resolving this confusion is through investigation by chemists, similar to that carried out at the United States National Bureau of Standards on the preservation of documents by lamination and at the Archivschule, Marburg.

Binding

Documents strengthened by any of the processes detailed in preceding chapters and requiring binding are bound by the normal processes, with slight but important variations here and there. The different stages of binding, i.e. gathering and guarding, stitching, back rounding and backing, fixing boards and covering, etc., are all carried out manually. Only the best materials, from thread and tape to board and leather, should be used. In binding primarily for conservation purposes, the accent is on both durability and permanence, and it is therefore essential that the workmanship be of a high calibre.

Documents repaired as single sheets are collated and then guarded into sections. A section usually comprises eight sheets although it may consist of twelve or sixteen sheets. The two largest sheets of the lot are placed on the work table and a measure is

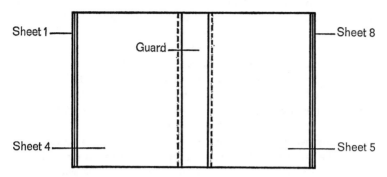

Fig. 8. Step-ladder formation of sheets.

drawn. The measure comprises two widths of the sheets plus 5 cm for the guard. Thereafter, guard strips of 8 cm width and slightly longer than the sheets to be guarded are cut. For guarding of record volumes hand-made paper should be used; bond paper (all rag) may also be used but is not as durable as good quality hand-made paper. If bond paper is used, the grain of the guard paper should run in the same direction as that of the sheets.

Each section of eight sheets is joined by means of the guard by placing the sheets in position on the work table in such a way that sheet 1 is joined to 8, 2 to 7, 3 to 6, and 4 to 5, each set of sheets being placed over the other in a step-ladder formation as shown in Figure 8.

The width of the guard decreases progressively to permit even folding of the sheets; if this is not done, the inner set of sheets will protrude outwards. Each successive section of sheets is guarded similarly.

Such guarding, if properly carried out: (a) enables stitching of the volume to be done on new paper, i.e. guards and saves the original weak paper from the stress and strain of stitching and hence tearing during use; (b) leaves any marginal inscriptions clear, thus permitting easy handling of bound sheets and easy deciphering of such inscriptions; (c) facilitates the microfilming of bound records; and (d) permits the formation of a compact volume, as sheets of unequal dimensions can be made up into sections of uniform size for binding.

In some archive centres a strip of tissue paper 20 mm wide is pasted as a guard on the folds of the sheets forming a section. In the inner set of sheets the guard strip is pasted inside the fold, while on the outer set of sheets, the strip is pasted outside.

As a result of guarding the thickness where the guard paper has been edged on the document is greater than that at the back, i.e. at the folded guard. To achieve uniform thickness, slips of paper 4–5 cm wide, i.e. slightly less than the width of the guard, are folded and placed between the folds in each section. These extra slips, called the 'get-in' paper, are placed inside each section and not on the outermost side. After completion of this stage, the sections are given a nip in a nipping press to reduce the swell at the back. Excess guard and 'get-in' paper at the tail end is then trimmed off and the volume stitched on tapes. The stitching is flexible stitching all along, i.e. the thread is passed through the inner folds of each section, to ensure flexible opening of the volume. After the sections have been stitched, end papers, usually of handmade paper thicker than that of the volume itself, are prepared and stitched in the same manner as the sections.

The back of the stitched volume is rounded and lined. The boards are cut square and laced on to the tapes and then covered. Volumes containing laminated paper are bound in half leather and have hollow backs. In other volumes, the leather is fixed directly to the back, so that they have tight backs.

Binding work is carried out in accordance with the specifications drawn up and existing in almost all countries for 'A' class binding by hand.

7 Special problems in the restoration of documents

The restoration of maps and charts, charred, water-soaked or damaged documents, parchment and vellum, birch bark, palm leaves and seals poses special problems. Such documents not only require careful attention and individual treatment to arrest deterioration, but also tax the ingenuity, dexterity, experience and patience of the restorer.

Maps and charts

Maps very in size and are on different kinds of materials, like paper and tracing cloth. They are drawn accurately to scale. Most maps are relatively large documents and are subjected to more strain in use than ordinary papers. To withstand such strain, they are drawn on an excellent grade of paper or cloth, and any method of repair should provide strong reinforcement which will resist normal wear and tear. Repairs should not cause any distortion in the sheets.

MOUNTING

One current process of reinforcement that has withstood the test of time is mounting. Other processes like machine and solvent lamination developed for the restoration of paper can safely be, and have been, used for the restoration of maps.

Mounting on cloth provides the maps with life and strength which help them to resist deterioration. Any map worth preserving, maps on thin or poor paper, torn maps which are irreplaceable and maps subjected to hard use or consulted frequently should be mounted. Each map, because of the variety of problems involved, poses a challenge to the skill and ingenuity of the restorer. If the work is properly carried out there is hardly any distortion in the restored sheet. All large maps which have to be kept folded should be cut into sections before mounting.

The process of mounting is costly and time-consuming, especially when the maps are brittle and in pieces. It is therefore advisable and economical to mount important and rare maps while they are still in one piece rather than waiting until they have broken or fallen to pieces.

MAPS ON PAPER

Maps on paper are mounted on materials such as muslin, fine long cloth or linen. The cloth is cut to a size slightly larger than the map, stretched taut and tacked closely on a map-mounting table. The surface of the table should be smooth, and covered with linoleum or soft rubber. If these facilities are not available, the cloth should be stretched on any firm surface which has first been covered with blotting papers and then with waxed paper.

The map is cleaned and if the colours are fast it is wetted with water by means of a sponge. All traces of earlier repair together with the materials used are then removed. The washed and cleaned map is then flattened and placed face down on waxed paper. Freshly prepared paste (Appendix 3) to which glycerine and fungicide 'Topane' have been added, is applied to the unwritten surface. The pasted side of the map is then laid on the backing cloth and smoothed down very carefully, first by hand and then by rubbing with a cloth and a bone folder from the centre towards the edges. If the map is brittle, paste is applied to the cloth itself and all the broken pieces are fitted into place with care. The map is then covered with waxed paper and pressed from the top to ensure proper adhesion with the backing cloth and to remove any air bubles or crease left in the map. It is then allowed to dry. When dry, the excess backing cloth is trimmed off, leaving a margin all around for turning a straight edge. Any writing on the back of the map is strengthened with chiffon and paste. The strengthened portion is covered with a patch of waxed paper cut to the size of the writing, before the map is mounted on cloth in the manner described above. After mounting and drying, the cloth over the writing is cut out, the wax paper patch removed and the cut edges are pasted down.

Maps which are to be stored flat and which are of the required size are mounted as described above. Those which are of bigger dimensions and must be kept folded are cut into sections and then mounted on a single large piece of cloth, leaving a space of 2–4 mm, depending on the thickness of the paper of the map and the number of folds required for storing it flat, between each section. If the map is very large, each section may be mounted on a separate piece of cloth. These pieces are later hinged together with polyvinyl alcohol adhesives and strips of cloth.

Cross-folding of the map should be avoided, as the material will tend to give way at the weakest point, i.e. where the folds intersect. Maps given a single fold last very well.

Care should be taken to paste the map on the cloth in such a way that the grain of the paper and the grain of cloth (the warp) lie in the same direction. Such an arrangement helps the paper of the map and the cloth on which it is mounted to expand and contract together. Maps mounted in this manner are usually stored flat, although maps mounted in one piece may be kept rolled and are so kept in many repositories.

Care should also be taken in the preparation and application of the flour paste, which should be thicker than cream but thin enough to apply easily with a brush. If it is too thick, a little water should be added to bring it to the required consistency. The paste must be free from lumps, for even a small lump left on the map shows as a bulge on its face. To prevent this happening, the paste should be strained through cloth before use.

Maps printed on poor paper and broken here and there do not have enough strength to withstand wear and tear if mounted on cloth alone. Such maps are first backed with hand-made or any other good quality paper in such a way that the grains of the backing paper and of the map paper lie in the same direction. The backed map is then mounted on cloth in the manner described above.

If the surface, i.e. face of the map, is cracked or broken, it is protected with a piece of chiffon cut to size, laid over the map and pasted with the help of a brush from the centre towards the edges. The map is then covered with waxed paper and rubbed from the top to ensure proper adhesion of the chiffon. The waxed paper sheets are removed and replaced with new sheets. Finally the map is allowed to dry under light pressure. When dry, the chiffon is trimmed to leave a narrow margin which is pasted down to form an edge all around the map.

LAMINATION

Maps which can be fed into the laminating machine may be repaired by the lamination process. The maps are first deacidified, dried and flattened. For lamination a sandwich of the map is prepared as follows: blotting papers; tafflon; cloth (muslin, long cloth or linen); cellulose acetate film (two sheets); map; cellulose acetate film (two sheets, if the face is not to be covered with chiffon, etc.); chiffon (if required to cover the face); tafflon; blotting papers.

Lamination is then carried out as described in Chapter 6, but at a slightly higher pressure, i.e. 27–40 kg/cm². The reinforced map is trimmed and placed under pressure to eliminate any tendency to curl. If, however, the map is printed or drawn on both sides, chiffon is placed on both sides of the map in the laminate instead of cloth on the back and chiffon on the face.

Lamination does not cause distortion of the map or any measurable change in its dimensions. Care should, however, be taken to ensure that colours do not run. This may be achieved by controlling the temperature and pressure. Blueprints and photostats can also be laminated as above. In the case of photostats, however, the face is not covered at all, and the document is merely backed with cloth or acetate film.

MAPS ON CLOTH

A number of maps either on tracing paper or cloth, or photographs of maps come to the restorer for treatment. Such maps cannot be reinforced by the lamination process. The most suitable method for reinforcing them is mounting on cloth with the use of cellulose acetate-propionate lacquer or polyvinyl alcohol adhesives. Maps on these materials are extremely sensitive to moisture and to changes in humidity, and require careful processing. Tracing paper which is too wet blisters during the process of flattening with electric irons, while maps on cloth are stretched too much and lose their finish. Maps on these materials are flattened by minimum damping followed by ironing. However, wrinkles cannot be removed completely from tracing cloth. Therefore, maps on such material should be stored flat after repair and not rolled.

Rolled maps are subjected to considerable strain when they are opened for use and rolled again. Such maps eventually require flattening and surface protection to preserve them. The surface of such maps may be treated with cellulose acetate lacquer, which imparts a high gloss to the surface and does not damage the paper of the map. Another varnish which gives good protection and finish without imparting high gloss to the map is a 15 per cent solution of 'Bedacryl' (methylmetacrylate) in benzene.

If gloss is not desired, a dull, 'antique' surface may be simulated by applying a mixture of a small quantity of burnt umber in oil, usually in the ratio of 1 : 3 umber to 2 : 3 turpentine oil, with a soft brush over the varnished surface and wiping it off with a lintless cloth. Such treatment is sometimes accorded to maps destined for decorative use.

These varnishes protect the surface from dust and dirt but if not applied in correct formulation have a harmful effect after a period of time when the paper turns brown and becomes brittle.

Charred documents

Burnt documents are not often encountered under normal storage conditions. Documents may, however, become badly charred or partially burnt as a result either of sabotage or accidental fire. Such documents are salvaged by carefully separating the sheets with a spatula, piecing the fragments together and then laminating them between cellulose acetate film only under slight pressure. Such lamination does not interfere with photographic reproduction, and permits normal handling and deciphering of the writing.

In cases where the covers of books damaged by fire are charred but the boards remain intact, the charred portion is scraped off and a new cover pasted over the boards. In cases of severe damage, the old cloth is completely removed and the volume recased. If the edges of the paper have also charred, the charred portion is scraped off and the sheets are inlaid to make them of uniform size, after which they are collated, resewn and rebound.

DECIPHERING CHARRED DOCUMENTS

In order to decipher a charred document, it is necessary to understand the effects of fire and heat on ink. Different types of ink are affected in different ways. Aniline inks are decomposed and leave no trace on the paper. Carbonaceous inks and iron-gall inks, on the other hand, leave sufficient residues to render the writing legible on suitable treatment.

Photographic process

A photographic reproduction of the charred document is made with infra-red sensitive plates. The writing on the print obtained generally appears black on a light background, and may be read without difficulty.

Devies method. In this method, the charred document is placed in contact with a rapid photographic plate in a dark-room. After a fortnight an image of the writing is reproduced on the plate which is affected by the paper but not by the ink. If film is used instead, the opposite effect is obtained.

Cherril's method. This method is applicable to documents written with inks which leave a metallic residue on paper. The carbonized sheet is placed on a glass plate at the bottom of a photographic dish containing 5 per cent aqueous silver nitrate solution. A second glass plate is lowered over it. If the sheet is distorted or fragile, it is protected from the weight of the second (i.e. top) glass plate by two glass rods placed parallel to the sides of the sheet. The dish is protected from direct sunlight. After three hours the writing becomes visible as a black image on a dull background. It is photographed when the sheet is still in solution.

In addition to the above processes, the use of ammonium sulphide, polarizing screen and chloral hydrate has been recommended in the relevant literature.

Water-soaked documents

Documents which have been exposed to water either during floods or during fire-fighting operations should be treated as soon as possible in order to prevent attack by mildew and sticking together of wet papers on drying. Most papers allowed to dry out in masses stick together and become difficult to separate without damage. The size, softened by water, causes the pages to stick to one another and if allowed to dry in this state, they become a solid mass.

Wet papers should therefore be carefully lifted from one another and placed individually between white blotters and pressed. When fairly dry, they are ironed to complete the process.

Papers which have dried in a mass and become mildewed are first fumigated. They are then carefully separated by manipulating a thin steel spatula between the adhering sheets. Any mildew residue noticed is dusted off with a soft cloth. The separated sheets are then humidified and flattened by ironing. Material which has been weakened by mildew is strengthened by resizing or if in a very bad state by lamination techniques.

Books made of better paper submit to wetting with less serious damage, although the pages invariably wrinkle and swell. To remove wrinkles, a few sheets at a time are damped with a moist sponge, and smoothed. They are then interleaved with blotters and allowed to dry under pressure. The process is repeated with the next batch of sheets and so on till the whole document has been treated.

If the book has been thoroughly soaked, it is best to take it apart, smooth the sheets and dry them under pressure. When this is properly done, the only treatment the paper will probably need after drying is resizing. If the book has been only slightly wetted, it is interleaved with blotting paper and placed under a weight. The blotting papers should be changed frequently, first after fifteen minutes, again after an hour or so, and again if necessary until the book becomes dry. Special attention must be given to books containing art papers, as the sheets after a time stick together and become impossible to separate without damage.

If the number of books and documents which have been soaked is large, there may be no time to attend to them individually, nor may enough blotting papers be available for the purpose. In such cases, the documents are usually spread out in the open in a shaded place, and exposed to the air. Electric driers and hot-air blowers have proved to be very useful for drying wet volumes and documents.

A near-catastrophe occurred at Florence and Venice in 1966, when more than 100,000 volumes were damaged by floods. Fortunately most of these were salvaged by ingenious techniques.

At Florence documents on nearly six kilometres of shelf space were submerged by flood water when the shelves swelled and burst. Many of them fell into the mud left by the flood water up to a depth of about thirty centimetres. Since it was not practicable to treat this huge amount of documents by the usual processes, new techniques had to be adopted.

At first, as an experiment, soaked volumes were treated with jets of hot steam (about 110° C). This helped to destroy the bacteria causing putrefaction and also spread the leaves of the volumes, thus helping considerably to prepare them for subsequent drying in hot air. However, this technique was abandoned in favour of treating the entire collection in tobacco barns, because of enormous number of volumes that could be treated there and the urgency of the task of salvage and protection from deterioration.

In the tobacco barns the work of washing and drying was entrusted to about one hundred women workers, experienced in the handling of tobacco leaves and thus accustomed to the most delicate work. The documents are first washed with sponges in running water in a properly equipped and heated room. During this process the volumes were separated according to size to facilitate their feeding into the drying furnaces, the idea being to feed volumes of the same thickness into the furnace at the same time in order that they might become dry as simultaneously as possible. The drying furnaces are rooms about eight metres long, six metres wide and four metres high, heated by steam from a boiler circulated through spiral coils. In these rooms the volumes were spread open on specially constructed wooden frames or suspended from poles placed side by side, the frames or poles resting on wooden scaffolding. Exhaust fans expelled the damp air which collected and fresh air was continually drawn into the room, with the result that only hot dry air circulated in the drying furnace. The drying was carried out gradually over a period ranging from twelve to fourteen days, at an initial temperature of 30° C which was gradually increased to 40° C and finally to 45° C during the last two days. The volumes were then gradually cooled, first at 40° C, then at 35° C and at decreasing temperatures until the cooling was completed at 20° C. Some 15,000 volumes could be treated in a single operation. Since there were seven such furnaces, the work of washing and drying was completed rapidly.

At Venice, where the damage was considerably less, all the documents were salvaged by spreading and drying them in every conceivable place where there was a draught of air. After drying, the sheets were sprinkled with ordinary talcum powder and placed between blotting papers for drying. It was observed that sheets treated in this way dried smoothly and required no further treatment.

Dusting with ordinary talcum powder prior to drying in blotters under pressure would thus appear advisable in the case of small collections of water-soaked documents.

Damp books and documents which cannot be attended to at once should be kept in a cool place until they can be processed, to reduce the danger and inhibit the growth of mildew. The storing of damp records in a centrally heated room or any room without ventilation should be avoided, as this helps to spread the dampness and encourages the growth of mildew on the paper and glue or paste.

Where, as a result of soaking, writing has smudged or been erased, it may be deciphered with the help of ultra-violet photography.

Vellum and parchment documents

Documents on vellum and parchment present a number of problems in handling. They are affected more than paper by heat and moisture. They stretch, shrink, wrinkle, cockle, warp and become stiff and brittle as the surrounding air becomes humid, moist or dry, and are thus more difficult to repair than documents on paper. It is only after much experience and practice that work on them may be undertaken.

FUMIGATION

Vellum and parchment documents, if affected by fungus growth, are sterilized by exposure to thymol vapours in a fumigation chamber, after which the dead spores are removed by brushing. Any mildew stain is removed with alcohol or benzene, while undesirable ink stains are removed by painting with a 5 per cent solution of chloramine-T.

CLEANING

Old vellum and parchment generally have a yellow or creamish colour, although some documents on these materials become so brown that they are difficult to read. Such documents may be bleached, but this should be done carefully; even with the mildest of bleaches like chloramine-T, there is every possibility that the ink or colours will run. Another method is to clean them with a lather made from a good, alkali-free soap. The skin is then wiped dry, placed between blotters and dried under slight pressure, the blotters being changed at intervals. During drying, the document sheet is held taut by weight at the edges or by clips to prevent shrinkage and cockling.

After this treatment, vellum and parchment become somewhat soft. To prevent them from becoming brittle and hard on drying, documents are treated with a good leather dressing, usually containing Neat's foot oil and lanolin or a mixture of cedarwood oil, beeswax and hexane. This treatment, which is easy to apply, keeps the skin in good condition. The dressing is first rubbed lightly into the skin. The excess is then wiped off with a clean cloth, and finally the surface is cleaned with a soft new cloth. In some cases, rubbing with cedarwood oil alone helps to clean the skin.

Other methods of cleaning involve the use of a soft rubber eraser, alcohol and benzene. The use of organic solvents to clean parchment is not advisable as these stiffen the skin and make it brittle. In Vienna, damp documents are dehydrated by dipping them in a bath of either acetone or ethyl alcohol containing a small amount of lanolin, which is deposited on the skin after the solvent has evaporated and prevents it from becoming hard and brittle. The same technique may be employed for cleaning yellowed or browned skins. However, these organic chemicals should be used with great care and the work carried out in fume cupboards.

FLATTENING

The flattening of parchment and vellum documents is an easy but at the same time tiresome and lengthy process, as these documents cannot be damped directly by applying water to the surface, dampness being fatal to the colour and to the adhesion of gold on illumination.

Twisted, bent or cockled skin or skin which has been folded is first moistened with damp blotters or by keeping it in a humidification room until it has absorbed sufficient moisture to become soft and pliable. It is then stretched taut in a frame by means of clips or by strings attached to weights ajusted so that the pull is equal in all directions. The moisture absorbed by the skin permits even flattening, and the skin is left to dry in this position. During the drying process, it is covered with dry blotting papers and kept under boards to give a slight pressure. It usually takes twenty-four hours for the parchment to dry out completely. If the clips are removed before the parchment is completely dry, warping and cockling occur again. Heat must never be used on parchment to accelerate the drying process, as even in moderation it causes considerable permanent shrinkage.

Creases and wrinkles may be removed by flattening the skins between damp blotters under moderate pressure for a week or two.

Scrolls or rolled vellum or parchment are covered with blotters damped with a 0.25 per cent solution of sodium pentachloro phenol. When the skin has relaxed, it is stretched slowly to remove the folds and wrinkles, and dried on a stretcher, i.e. with strings and weights. Alternatively, the stretched parchment may be placed on a clean board or glass plate, and the edges weighed down by strips of lead. As it dries, the wrinkles and creases are satisfactorily removed.

REPAIR

Parchment or vellum which is badly torn is repaired after flattening, but while still damp, by mounting on new parchment. The surface of the new parchment is first roughened with the help of sandpaper, and then pasted on terylene (polyester) cloth spread taut on a wooden board. Paste is applied to the roughened side and the document is laid over it and smoothed. Holes or missing portions are filled with parchment patches. A patch slightly larger than the hole is pared at the edges, which are then roughened with sandpaper. The patch is pasted over the hole, filling it exactly and making the whole surface of the document even. The repaired skin is then allowed to dry. When dry, it is lifted and separated from the terylene base by pulling the two apart. It is then placed between blotters and dried under slight pressure. The adhesive used is a flour paste containing a small quantity of glycerine which, in contrast with its use for repairs on paper, is not thinned before application.

The repair of parchment documents requires great skill and is expensive, because only the best materials must be used. Repair work is therefore confined to fragile or very important documents.

Tears in the skin are mended by pasting the overlapping edges and holding them together with weights until dry. The repair of tears and cuts in which the edges do not overlap requires great skill. The technique is similar to that employed for filling holes in the parchment. For minor repairs, gelatine containing a drop of glacial acetic acid is used instead of paste to fix the edges or joints. The acetic acid pits the skin and permits the gelatine to bite in and form a strong bond.

Faded inks on parchment cannot be restored by chemical means to examine and if necessary to photograph the document under ultra-violet light. The ink residue appears dark and the contrast with the parchment is enough to render the writing fairly distinct.

Manuscripts on birch bark

Manuscripts on birch bark are mostly written in carbon inks. These may be cleaned with a swab of cotton dipped in acetone. The solvent is applied all over the surface to remove dirt or any resinous material. In place of acetone, carbon tetrachloride can be used. But care must be exercised in its use and handling. In some cases, birch-bark sheets are cleaned with a mixture of alcohol and glycerine in equal proportions.

Sheets which have stuck together may be separated by placing them in a humidification room or exposing them to steam. When they have become sufficiently moist, each sheet is separated carefully by means of a blunt spatula. Alternatively, the sheets may be separated by immersion in a bath of hot (70–80° C) liquid paraffin. The separated sheets are then cleaned with acetone or carbon tetrachloride. This treatment requires care and skill, and should not therefore be attempted in the absence of proper facilities and trained personnel.

The cleaned sheets, if torn or brittle, are repaired either with chiffon using flour paste or by the solvent lamination technique described earlier. If the latter is adopted, chiffon is used instead of tissue paper in the laminate. The reinforced sheets may then be guarded and bound into volume form.

Manuscripts on palm leaf

Palm leaf has good keeping qualities, but manuscripts exposed to a dry climate for a considerable time break at the holes made in the centre for tying the leaves together with thread, become brittle at the edges or dry out and break into pieces. Sometimes, as a result of exposure to rain water or storage in humid conditions, the palm leaves stick together.

There are two types of inscriptions on palm leaf. One involves the use of carbon ink and the other the use of a stylus. As a result of handling or for other reasons, stylus inscriptions may be rubbed off or become indistinct and must be reinked to make them legible.

As a first step in their restoration, palm leaves are cleaned with mixture of glycerine and alcohol, which removes dirt or any other foreign material from the leaf and makes it supple. It can then be handled without risk of breaking or damaging it. Some carbon ink writings have a tendency to smudge. These are cleaned with acetone or benzene and then fixed by the application of a 5 per cent solution of cellulose acetate in acetone.

Leaves which have stuck together or become a solid mass are separated by humidification and separation in the manner described for birch bark. In some cases, leaves may be separated by placing them in a bath of hot water (60° C) containing 5–10 cc of glycerine. The water in the bath is changed every half hour. After soaking for one hour, individual layers of leaf are lifted by means of a metallic spatula. During this process, water is poured continuously into the space between the detached leaf and the solidified mass to facilitate separation. Leaves thus separated are dried over blotters and then cleaned with a mixture of alcohol and glycerine in equal proportions. It has been observed that after this treatment the leaves become soft and regain their original flexibility.

Even leaves written with carbon inks may be separated by this process if care is taken in handling and during the process of separating individual leaves from the mass. This is possible because the writing becomes fixed to the leaf because of the mud and other materials present during the process of wetting and subsequently drying as a mass. Alternatively, the leaves may be separated by immersion in a bath of hot (70–80° C) liquid paraffin. The separated leaves are cleaned with acetone to remove the paraffin. Leaves treated in this way tend, however, to become fragile as soon as they become dry and require exceptional care in handling during separation and subsequent treatment.

REPAIR

Palm-leaf manuscripts in carbon inks are repaired with chiffon pasted on both sides by means of flour paste suitability thinned for the purpose. During the process of chiffoning or silking, the edges of chiffon, which usually fray on drying and handling, are protected by inlaying the leaf with hand-made paper.

Repairs may also be effected by first inlaying the leaf with hand-made paper and then covering leaf and paper with a 5–10 per cent solution of polyvinyl acetate in benzene. The solution is applied with a brush, like ordinary flour paste, all over the surface. Cellulose acetate film larger in size than the leaf and frame combined is then placed over one side and pressed to achieve bonding. The other side is treated in the same way. The treated leaf is given a slight nip to ensure uniform adhesion.

Crowley of the British Museum has developed a method of reinforcing palm leaves with acrylic emulsion adhesive and tissue paper coated on one side with adhesive acrylic rubber and protected by a layer of silicone paper. The process is as follows:

Holes or missing portions are filled with paper-backed wood veneer of birch prepared by placing two layers of veneer back to back with a layer of *kozo-shi* paper between them, sticking them together with an adhesive and finally pressing them in a small hand press. Pieces of veneer of the required size are then cut from this sheet.

The palm leaf is laminated with special tissue paper coated on one side with adhesive acrylic rubber which, in turn, is covered with a layer of protective silicone paper. This tissue is cut slightly larger (3 mm) all around than the palm leaf. The silicone paper is removed and the tissue paper is then firmly pressed against the leaf to remove any air bubbles. The leaf is then turned over, the cut veneer is placed in position and the leaf covered with another sheet of tissue paper. Acrylic emulsion adhesive is then applied to both sides of the leaf, to fill the tissue fibres and prevent light refraction during photography. The treated leaf is placed between release-coated papers and introduced into the press. Speed is most important at this stage, because if the acrylic emulsion adhesive is allowed to dry before the leaves are pressed it is not absorbed by the interstices of the tissue paper. After five minutes the laminated leaf is removed from the press and treated with dilute paraffin wax emulsion, applied to both sides with cotton wool. This prevents the repaired leaves from blocking or sticking together. The leaf is again placed between release-coated paper and set under the press for another five minutes. It is then removed and the paper is pulled away from the surface of the leaf. Finally, the leaf is rubbed with a dry cloth to spread any excess wax evenly. The tissue paper is then trimmed, leaving a small margin all around. The repaired leaf is flexible and safe to handle. Under the action of the acrylic emulsion adhesive the tissue paper becomes transparent and the writing thus remains legible. This process is reversible; if it is desired to recover the leaf, the tissue paper may be removed with chloroform without causing any damage. Since no heat is required during the process, there is no danger of heat damage to the leaf.

Another method of preserving palm leaves involves framing them between two sheets of glass.

Engraved palm-leaves

When engraved writing on a palm leaf has rubbed off, it is reinked. The cleaned leaf is rubbed with powdered graphite or lampblack by means of a cotton swab, and the engraved incisions are filled, thus making the writing legible. Excess graphite or lampblack is removed with a soft cotton cloth. The leaf is cleaned with a 1 : 1 mixture of alcohol and glycerine, and then repaired in the manner described above for palm leaves written with carbon inks.

Reinking may be effected with lampblack and oil of camphor mixed to the desired shade. The mixture is applied over the entire leaf and left overnight. The leaf is then cleaned with alcohol to remove any surplus mixture.

Repaired leaves are finally stored loose in a box or cabinet. To safeguard them against insect attack, naphthalene or camphor is put inside the box.

Seals

Seals which have become dry, cracked or broken are preserved by joining the cracks or replacing the broken pieces with a mixture of beeswax and resin. Natural wax is used to reinforce the seal and no attempt is made to match the colour. As a rule, seals are repaired with wax of the same consistency but of a different hue. This is to preserve the authenticity of whatever remains of the seal and to avoid the suggestion of faking.

A mixture of beeswax and resin is prepared by mixing the two in the ratio of 2 : 1 and heating the mixture to ensure thorough blending. The more the mixture is heated, the darker it becomes. The heated wax mixture is inserted in the cracks with the help of a knife. When it is set, hot pins are slowly inserted from one side to the other to hold the cracks together. The sides of the seal are then touched with a hot knife to even the edges. In the case of a seal with a tape which is broken, the surrounding wax, approximately 1 mm, is softened, and a new tape is attached.

Broken seals are joined in a similar manner. Missing portions are filled to the shape of the seal with the wax mixture, which is pressed just sufficiently to cover the entire broken portion. A hot knife is then applied to smooth the surface and to join the new wax to the seal. The edges are finally rounded off to the required shape with the help of the hot knife.

The repaired seal is left for a day or so to allow the wax to harden. The new wax is then scraped carefully with a knife, and the entire portion is rubbed with beeswax paste to introduce natural oil into the seal.

Brittle seals may to some extent be repaired in the manner described above. Their surface is then covered with a paste made from beeswax and turpentine oil, which helps to introduce some natural oily matter into the seals. It also helps to clean dirty seals and polish them.

If the seal is on paper which is in a poor state, the latter is first reinforced. This poses no problems if the reinforcement is carried out by any of the traditional processes or by solvent lamination. Reinforcement with the use of tissue or chiffon or by mounting processes is best effected on a perspex sheet using terylene cloth as support. The repaired document is left to dry on the support. If lamination by machine is desired, the sandwich of the document prepared in the usual way is covered before introduction into the press with blotters cut with a hole equal to the size of the seal, till the thickness of the blotters is slightly greater than the thickness of the seal, which is thus protected from pressure or damage during the lamination of the document. Parts of broken seals are carefully fitted together and held in place with a solution of Canada balsam in a mixture of benzene and toluene as an adhesive. When the solvents have evaporated the various fragments are joined together firmly and invisibly.

Seals which are in good condition require no treatment, and should merely be cleaned. For this purpose, a mixture of beeswax and turpentine made into a paste is applied to soak in for some time. The surface of the seal is then cleaned first with cotton wool and then with a jeweller's brush to remove as much of the dirt and wax paste as possible. The seal is finally polished by treatment in a solution of equal weights of white beeswax and turpentine dissolved in benzol until the mixture has the consistency of treacle. When this has dried, the seal is polished with a very soft silk rag.

For protection, seals are placed inside pads which may be easily made from bank paper, waxed paper and cotton wool. Waxed paper cut to a slightly larger size is placed on the bank paper, with a layer of cotton wool between them. The inner side of the pad so formed is of waxed paper, and the bank paper is at the top. For storage, seals are placed in boxes padded with cotton wool over which waxed paper has been stretched. This prevents the seals from flaking and powdering. On no account should they be allowed to come in contact with the cotton wool itself, which will absorb moisture from the wax and cause it to deteriorate. Seals may also be covered with pads and stored, if desired, inside envelopes. Treated seals are stored on the edges and not flat. Seals with tapes or ribbons must carefully be supported during both storage and display to prevent strain on the ribbon or tape and on the document paper to which they are attached.

MOULDS

For exhibition and also for conservation purposes, copies of seals are made by casting in moulds of plaster of Paris or latex or in materials such as calestone or an ordinary dental plaster.

For preparing temporary moulds and also for small seals on paper, 'Duplit' and 'Zelex' synthetic plastic materials may be used.

Method

Waxed paper is placed round the seal and edged with aloplast—a non-sticky substance similar to plasticine. Oil, preferably olive oil, is then applied to the surface of the seal. Calestone is then mixed with water in the ratio of 100 parts to 30 parts of water in a rubber vessel and stirred with a spatula to ensure thorough mixing. The pasty mixture so formed is first applied evenly by means of a brush to every corner of the seal, and then it is slowly poured into the mould. Throughout the entire period of pouring, the mixture is stirred continuously to spread the paste evenly and to remove any air gaps that may be present. The paste is then allowed to set.

Care should be taken to clean the rubber vessel and the brush of any of the pasty mixture sticking to them at the end of this operation, otherwise they cannot be used again.

Calestone is quicker to set and is used only for small seals. For large seals, i.e. of 70 cm diameter or above, ordinary dental plaster is used. This is prepared and applied in the same manner. It takes two weeks to set, after which it is hardened by means of varnish —shellac in methylated spirit which is allowed to soak in for four to five hours.

To obtain a plastic impression from the mould prepared as above soapy water is applied over the surface and the plaster is poured in the same way. Wax impressions from the mould can also be made in a similar manner. During the process, the wax will not stick to the hands of the worker if he wets them in advance. Wax impressions are cheaper and better than plaster casts. 'Zelex' dries quickly. It is prepared in the ratio of one part to one part of water and poured as above. The mould so formed is very good. An impression of the seal may be obtained immediately by means of 'Calaspar'. In the case of moulds made from Duplit or Zelex, there is no need to use either soap or any other material as a separating agent.

Success in the preparation of moulds and impressions depends on the experience of the worker.

Care of bound volumes

Many bound volumes in archive institutions show signs of decay. Some are in an advanced stage of deterioration while in others the process of degradation has just begun. Such deterioration may be counteracted by remedial measures.

As a result of poor binding or improper use and storage conditions, the centre of a volume either sags within the covers or becomes separated from the cover. When the covers have become loose or separated, the stitched sheets are glued back into the original covers after stitching in new end papers. In the case of volumes which have sagged and assumed a V shape in place of the convex curve which exists in properly bound volumes, the thread breaks as a result of strain and the sections become separated entirely. In such cases there is every danger of loose sheets being damaged or lost. The disappearance of the roundness at the back of a volume may be attributed to faulty backing, cheap glue and lightness of backing material. Such volumes should be rebound to prevent further damage.

Poor binding is not always a direct cause of the above conditions, for such damage may also be observed in well-bound books which have been subjected to improper or rough treatment and storage on the shelves. It is not uncommon to see shelves so tightly packed that it is literally impossible to remove a volume out without tearing its covers apart. The piling of volumes on top of each other causes the lower volumes to be crushed out of shape. To prevent damage due to faulty stacking, bound volumes should be placed on the shelves in such a way that they do not rest on the fore-edges of the cover, i.e. they should be kept either lying flat or resting on the tail edges.

Damage to bound volumes may also be prevented by proper handling in use. A bound volume should be properly opened before it is read. For this purpose, it should be placed on a horizontal table and opened in the middle. A few sheets at a time are turned over and rubbed at the inner margin, until the beginning of the volume is reached. The process is repeated on the other side of the centre, i.e. until the end of the volume is reached. This technique of opening a newly bound volume tends to lessen the strain at the point where the sections are sewed and glued and permits the leaves to lie open more freely. It also enables the back to bend evenly at all points and prevents premature 'breaking'.

Another enemy of bound volumes is dust, which causes discolouration of the covering material and provokes other forms of degradation. All bound volumes should therefore be cleaned and the leather given a protective treatment. As a general rule, the leather used for binding record volumes is very stable. But if it is not treated with a protective oil dressing, it may begin to rot and turn powdery. This happens because the oil in the leather dries up, the fibres become dry and stiff and develop cracks. This process is accelerated by atmospheric contaminants, mainly sulphur dioxide gas, and by adverse storage conditions. The application of a good oil dressing prevents the leather from decaying and becoming powdery. Care

Drying of flood-damaged volumes in tobacco barns.
[*Photo:* Florence State Archives].

A view of flood-damaged volumes.
[*Photo:* Florence State Archives].

Medium-size room for equipment and machinery.
[*Photo:* Florence State Archives].

Repair room
[*Photo:* Florence State Archives].

Records received for repair.
[*Photo:* Florence State Archives].

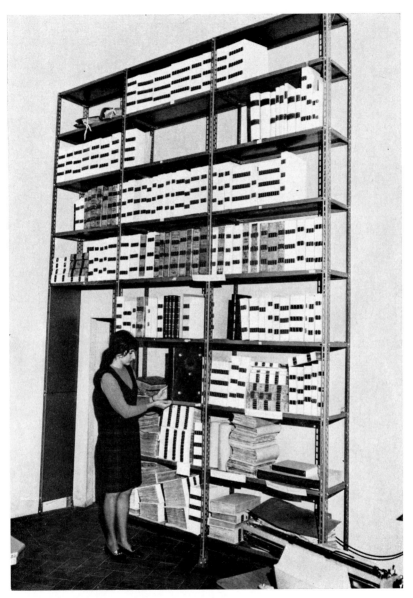

Storage of properly bound and improperly bound volumes.
[*Photo:* Florence State Archives].

Storage of document boxes on shelves
[*Photo:* United States National Archives].

should be taken to ensure that volumes so treated have dried completely before being replaced on the shelf.

One simple leather dressing is petroleum jelly. This is rubbed over the leather and allowed to soak in, and the leather is finally polished with a soft clean cloth. Other leather dressings are used in various archive institutions for this purpose. Practically all of them contain Neat's foot oil as a base. One simple dressing consists of equal parts of pure Neat's foot oil and castor oil, mixed together, heated and allowed to cool before applying. Another dressing which has proved useful consists of: lanolin anhydrous, 300 grammes; beeswax, 15 grammes; cedar-wood oil, 30 ml; benzene or hexane, 350 ml. To prepare the mixture, the beeswax is dissolved in hot benzene or hexane. Cedar-wood oil is added to the mixture, and thoroughly mixed. Finally, the lanolin is slightly warmed and softened, and added to the mixture, which is thoroughly shaken to ensure the blending of the ingredients. This mixture is highly inflammable and should be kept away from naked flames.

Lanolin is an animal fat and is easily absorbed by leather. It does not become rancid. The beeswax fills the cracks in the leather and assists by imparting a thin film to the leather while polishing. Cedar-wood oil is a preservative and is good for leather. Benzene or hexane are the media in which these ingredients are dissolved so that they may be applied evenly over the surface.

Other formulae of leather dressings which are in use and have proved useful are provided in Appendix 4.

For the application of a leather dressing, a sheet of waxed paper is placed between the cover of the book and its contents to protect the latter. The volume is cleaned with a cotton cloth to remove particles of dust, etc., for if these are not removed they have an abrasive effect on the leather surface during the application of the dressing. Before applying the dressing, the leather is protected against acidic contaminants in the atmosphere by applying a solution of a buffer salt such as sodium benzoate or sodium stearate. A 1–2 per cent solution of the buffer salt is applied to the leather, which is then allowed to dry. A small quantity of the dressing is then applied with a cotton or flannel cloth or with a brush. The treated volume is allowed to dry. When the dressing has soaked in, the leather is polished with a soft cloth or a sheepskin shoe polisher.

The treatment of bound volumes with leather dressing should be carried out once every two or three years. Care should be taken to ensure that water is not allowed to come in contact with the leather during the application of the dressing as it has a tendency to blacken or darken the colour of old leather.

8 Special problems concerning work rooms and restoration materials

The conservation and restoration of archive documents require agreeable working conditions and materials of quality which have proved their usefulness, either by use over a long period of time or on the basis of laboratory tests. The use of a great variety of materials without first ascertaining that they are effective may result in more harm than good to the document for such materials may not only be unstable but also contain chemicals potentially harmful to the materials on which they are used. Even restoration with good materials may result in damage to the original document if it is not carried out properly. In addition to the use of good materials, the quality of the work produced also depends upon the intelligence and skill of the restorer.

Conservation and restoration unit

Every institution concerned with the preservation of its archive holdings should have a repair unit, housed in well-ventilated and lighted premises, together with facilities for verifying the utility of the materials to be employed. In the absence of a laboratory of its own, the institution should not hesitate to seek advice from government or university laboratories or from commercial establishments with facilities for testing. Such facilities are available in at least one or two government institutions in every country and a number of archive centres are in close contact with these laboratories or test centres.

REPAIR ROOM

The repair room should be well lighted and well ventilated, and spacious enough to permit free movement for work and materials. It may be in the basement of the building, as in the United States and elsewhere or on the ground floor as in New Delhi and other countries in Europe. If in the basement, it must have good artificial lighting and an arrangement for the circulation of fresh air in the room and for the removal of stale air.[1] If the repair room is located on the ground floor, the windows should preferably face north to obtain maximum natural lighting but not direct sunlight. In addition, the room should have running hot and cold water and be fitted with a sink.

Requirements

A restoration unit with a staff of ten should comprise at least one large-sized room (100 m²), one medium-sized room (40 m²), and three or four small rooms, or a large hall of approximately 200 m² which may be partitioned into rooms of the required size. These premises should suffice to house the staff, machinery and equipment required for conservation work.

The large-sized room should be used for preservation work, i.e. repair and binding work of all types. It should have arrangements for storing (a) various types of paper and other repair materials flat; (b) records admitted for repairs; and (c) treated records pending their return to the storage rooms. It should also be equipped with running water. Repair materials and all important documents should be kept under lock and key, and the room should therefore be provided with several almirahs, either of wood or steel.

The room should be furnished with glass-topped tables, illumi-rated from below, for repair work; and a large, rubber-surfaced table for map-mounting purposes and the repair of outsize or

1. The environmental conditions of the repair room should conform to the health standards established in each country. Three changes of air per hour in a room where work with volatile chemicals is being conducted or is contemplated should normally suffice. However it would be advisable to consult local authorities on explosives and pollution and other authorities responsible for safety regulations. In addition, all work with volatile chemicals such as acetone, etc., should be carried out under a fume cupboard.

large sheets if the institution has holdings of this type. It should have a work-space for tooling bound volumes, and all the equipment necessary for work such as the deacidification and drying of documents, the trimming of repaired documents and binding work. In addition, the room should be spacious enough to permit the free movement of records and personnel. It is most important for the various materials and equipment of the repair shop to be kept in good order, and for the premises to be comfortable, warm and clean, and equipped with good, preferably adjustable artificial lighting. The amounts and types of equipment required for restoration work by one, four or ten restorers respectively are listed in Appendix 5.

The medium-sized room should be fitted with the equipment required for conservation work, such as vacuum fumigation and air-cleaning units, thymol and paradichlorobenzene fumigators. The nature of such equipment will depend on the resources and requirements of each institution. Thymol and paradichlorobenzene fumigators will meet the requirements of institutions with small holdings. Cleaning, i.e. the removal of dust, can be effected in such institutions with the help of vacuum cleaners. If, however, the holdings are large and insect infestation serious, the installation of vacuum fumigation and air-cleaning units is absolutely essential.

Of the small rooms, one should be used for humidification. It should be fitted with a humidifier of the 'Pettifoger' or any other type, and with racks of plastic-net frames for spreading folded documents. Another room should have facilities for cleaning documents with chemicals and determining acidity in paper, with, if desired, a small laboratory for testing paper and other materials. The third room should have space for preparing paste, size and solutions for processes such as deacidification, and facilities for the washing, deacidification and drying of documents so treated. A fourth room should house the laminator, where its use is justified by the large number of documents requiring treatment, and the other equipment necessary for lamination work, such as a nipping press, trimmers and a work table.

No preservation unit can be complete without facilities for microfilming, which should be housed separately, though in the vicinity. The photographic department, including the developing, printing and microfilm storage sections, should preferably be air-conditioned.

The suggested staff of ten restorers may be employed as shown in Table 3.

TABLE 3

Work	Staff required	Work	Staff required
Deacidification, washing, resizing, etc.	1[1]	Gathering and guarding	1[1]
		Stitching and binding	1
Restoration	3[1]	Tooling	1[2]
Minor repairs and map repair, etc.	1[1]	Supervisor	1
Repair of parchment documents, seals, and conservation work	1[1]		

1. All interchangeable.
2. To undertake repair or binding work when free or required.

The supervisor should be fully trained and familiar with the operation of the different equipment, such as pH meter and fumigation chamber, and with the various processes of repair. He should be responsible for keeping records of the consumption of materials and concerning other aspects of the work. The restorers should be experienced and skilled and should have a thorough knowledge of restoration work. The preparation of paste and other solutions may be entrusted to one of the restorers or shared between them. If a laboratory is to be installed, a chemist must be recruited. The selection of documents for repair and their numbering in sequence should be the responsibility of the archivist or staff in charge of the muniment rooms.

The staff suggested above should be capable of washing, deacidifying, resizing, repairing, guarding and binding a minimum of 8,000 sheets a month by the classical process of repair, in addition to attending to other conservation work such as the repair of seals, parchment documents, etc. The output is likely to be in the region of 12,000 sheets per month if mechanical processes or processes like solvent lamination are adopted. The figures quoted refer to work on brittle papers or papers which have broken and require special attention. Most of the institutions visited by the author in Asia, Europe and the American continent have norms of output based on experience and adapted to their particular conditions. An idea of the norms applied in archive centres in Europe may be obtained from Appendix 6. In these institutions, if only deacidification and lamination, either by machine or with the use of solvents, is required, the output from the same staff will amount to approximately 16,000 sheets per month.

Materials

Of the different repair and binding materials required for conservation work, some have been in use over a number of years and have proved their usefulness, while others are new materials which have recently come on to the market. Of the latter, those whose value has been proved on the basis of laboratory tests are being used. Their practical utility under actual conditions of utilization and storage throughout the world is being observed.

For conservation and preservation work, it is essential to use only the best materials. Specifications of those which have proved useful and are currently employed are set out below. These specifications were drawn up some time ago, and the knowledge acquired since then as a result of studies of the mechanisms of deteriorative processes call for reappraisal of these specifications. Some work in this direction has already begun in the United States.

REPAIR MATERIALS

Tissue paper

This is a thin strong paper with long fibres. For repair work, it may be used either alone with flour or dextrine paste or synthetic adhesives, or combined with cellulose acetate film in the mechanical and solvent lamination processes. Tissue paper is also used for strengthening torn edges or filling missing portions with polyvinyl acetate adhesive.

Tissue paper for repair purposes should meet the following specifications:
Stock: 100 per cent bleached pulp free from groundwood.

Acidity: pH value not less than 6.0.

Size and weight: 61 cm by 91.5 cm; 5.9 kg (13 lbs) per 1,000 sheets.

Bursting strength: average of 5 sheets together, not less than 18.

Opacity: not more than 30 per cent; free from oil and waxy constituents.

Ash content: 0.5 per cent maximum.

When subjected to the accelerated ageing test, i.e. heating at 100° C for seventy-two hours, the paper should show no change in colour or opacity; the alpha cellulose content should not decrease by more than 1 per cent; it should not be less than 88 per cent after ageing. A special highly transparent, viscose-sized tissue paper known as 'Renova Paper' is produced in Holland for the repair of documents by traditional processes of repair with tissue paper. Because of its high wet strength, this paper is claimed to be easier to apply.

Hand-made paper

This paper is used for backing documents written on one side, mounting maps, and also for guarding loose sheets into gathers for binding purposes. It should be of extra strong quality and meet the following specifications:

Stock: all rag.

Colour: white or cream toned; if cream toned, the dyes used should be fast to light.

Size and weight: 51 by 71 cm; 9.1–9.9 kg (20–22 lbs) per 500 sheets.

Folding endurance: 500 double folds in weak direction under ½ kg tension MIT, or 500 double folds under 1 kg tension—TAPPI.

Acidity: pH value not less than 6.

Chiffon or silk gauze

Chiffon is used for the repair of brittle records and for covering the surface of maps. It should have the following characteristics:

Stock: 100 per cent pure silk.

Warp: not less than 75.

Filling: not less than 75.

Sizing: less than 1 per cent.

Acidity: pH 6 minimum.

Width: 101.5 cm (40 in).
Thickness: 0.0086 cm (0.0034 in) maximum.
Colour: white or slightly creamy.
This material should be pre-shrunk, have a plain weave and be treated against fungus growth.

Muslin

Muslin is used for mounting maps, both by the lamination processes and by the classical processes of repair. Muslin used for the purpose has plain weave. Other characteristics are:
Quality: fine and bleached.
Thickness: 0.1 mm (0.004 in).
Sizing: nil.
Warp: 76.
Filling: 70.

Linen cloth

For mounting large maps with paste, linen cloth is generally used. It has even, plain weave and like muslin is bleached and of fine quality. Other characteristics are:
Thickness: 0.15 mm (0.006 in).
Sizing: nil.
Warp: 76.
Filling: 70.

Oiled paper and waxed paper

These papers do not adhere with starch or flour paste or other adhesives, and are used as a base for repairing documents and for covering and interleaving documents. They should be of very good quality and the oily and waxy constituents should not stain the documents.

Size and weight: 46 by 61 cm; 22–23 kg per 500 sheets.

Cellulose acetate film

This is used for the reinforcement of documents by lamination under heat and pressure either in flat-bed or rotary type machines or by the solvent lamination process. A complete study and reappraisal of the machine lamination process was carried out by the United States National Bureau of Standards between 1954 and 1957, as a result of which the following specifications were laid down for cellulose acetate film for use on archive documents:

Folding endurance: 1,000 double folds at 1 kg tension MIT.

Thickness: 23 microns (0.00088 in).

Heat softening temperature (Moelter-Schwizer): 114.5° C and 2.5° C.

Tensile strength at break (15 mm width): 1.8 kg minimum.

Tensile strength at yield point (15 mm width): 1.8 kg minimum.

Elongation at break: 15.0 per cent minimum.

Elongation at yield point: 3.5–0.5.

Cellulose acetate film should contain plasticizers and an acid acceptor, an ultra-violet absorber and an anti-oxidant. It should be free from nitrate. On accelerated ageing it should show no change in colour. Of the various types tested, the P–9 11 film manufactured by the Celanese Corporation of America was found to meet these specifications. Another film found suitable is 88 CA 148, manufactured by E. I. DuPont de Nemours & Co. of America. Cellulose acetate films manufactured in other countries such as France, the United Kingdom, Federal Republic of Germany, etc., have also been found to conform to the above specifications. Cellulose acetate film is available in roll form and may be cut to the desired size. The dimensions commonly employed are 61 by 81.5 cm, 51 by 76 cm and 25.5 by 38 cm. Cellulose acetate film in roll form is cheaper than in cut form.

In 1960, the Fourth Congress of the International Council of Archives, at Stockholm (Sweden), stressed that an ideal film for restoration purposes should be: (a) impermeable to water, air and light; (b) immune to attack by plant and animal pests and preferably insecticidal; (c) non-inflammable and heat-resistant; (d) inert to acids and probably also to alkalis; and (e) capable of absorbing ultra-violet radiation.

Werner has clearly enunciated the various properties required of film for restoration purposes, stating that it should: (a) be inherently stable, i.e. show long term resistance to degradation when exposed to environmental conditions under normal conditions of storage and use; (b) be flexible and resistant to abrasion, so that it can withstand the normal handling that documents receive in use; (c) confer considerable increase in strength on the document it is meant to protect, and at the same time be as thin as possible; (d) be attachable to the document with the minimum of effort; and (e) be removable, if necessary, by a simple method which will not damage the document.

In addition, the film should not contain any additive that might leach out and have a harmful effect on paper; or interfere with the legibility of the document on which it is used.

As yet no plastic film exists which can be said to meet every one of these requirements. Properly formulated cellulose acetate films, as indicated earlier, have proved satisfactory in most respects and have been put to practical use over a number of years. Other films which may be considered to offer possibilities for laminating purposes are polyethylene and polyethylene terphthalate films, whose chemical and physical properties are superior to those of cellulose acetate film. The difficulty of removing such film has been overcome by using benzene or decalyne for delaminating purposes. Polyethylene film is in use in the U.S.S.R., Yugoslavia and many other countries. Kathpalia has experimented with polyester films. Terylene tissue (textryl), a non-woven fabric, has been found to be suitable for the lamination of documents. Documents repaired with this material may be delaminated without difficulty if it is used in combination with cellulose acetate film, as demonstrated by Kathpalia, who has suggested the use of polyester tissue treated with cellulose acetate on one side in place of tissue paper and cellulose acetate film in a laminate, as a means of accelerating the process of restoration. The thickness of documents so laminated is also less than that of documents laminated with tissue paper and cellulose acetate film.

BINDING MATERIALS

Thread

A prerequisite of good binding is the use of strong thread of the right type. Unbleached linen thread is the most suitable. Durable and stronger than cotton, it is used in hand-bound volumes. Terylene thread is, however, stronger than linen thread and may well replace the latter in due course.

Tape

Tapes commonly used are made of linen. Other materials in use include flat strips of leather and hemp cords. Linen tapes are better than cotton tapes, and hemp cords are more durable than leather strips. As in the case of thread, terylene tapes may eventually replace the materials used at present.

Leather

Leather is a natural product obtained from a large variety of animals. Its fibrous structure gives it a very desirable softness and strength. When applied with paste, it adheres well to paper, boards, linen and cellulosic materials in general. Real leather is superior to synthetic leather and leather cloth and is durable. It has been used for binding for a number of centuries.

However, there have been cases where the leather used has rotted and given way after only a few years. For binding archive documents, it is essential to use leather which has been properly tanned and which meets the requirements of the PIRA test of the standards for durable leather drawn up in various countries. Most countries have formulated standards and specifications for book-binding leather.

Goat skin, uniform in thickness and vegetable tanned, chrome tanned or tanned by a combination of the two techniques, makes a good leather for binding purposes. Such leather is usually dyed in a variety of colours which are fast to light and water. One variety of leather commonly used is Morocco leather.

Morocco leather

This is made from goat skins and has closed or small grains. Its uniform thickness enables the entire skin to be used for binding purposes with minimum of paring along the joints and at the turn-in over the boards. Morocco leather is strong and fibrous in nature and is appreciated throughout the world for binding purposes. It has a fine appearance after polishing. Skins vary in size from 150 cm to 210 cm, although larger skins may also be obtained.

Levant Morocco

One variety of Morocco leather is known as Levant Morocco. This is made from South African or Cape goat skin, which is thicker than the Morocco and has a much heavier and bolder grain. Tough, hard wearing and durable, beautifully finished and available in many colours, Levant Morocco is suitable for large books and volumes. The size varies from 270 cm to 360 cm.

Natural and dyed calf

Natural-coloured calf is biscuit coloured. It has been used since the sixteenth century for binding purposes, and a number of old bindings are still intact. Well prepared calf skin is a good and durable material. If, however, it is not properly prepared, it deteriorates, rots and becomes powdery.

Natural-coloured calf after many years takes on a pleasing brown colour. This tanned look was later obtained by staining calf with salts of tartar, a practice which has continued up to the present day.

Calf leather may now be obtained in many colours and in a number of shades. It is a soft leather, very porous but pleasing both to look at and to handle. Its main disadvantages are its soft nature and its tendency to mark very easily.

Calf leather is thicker than Morocco leather, and is, therefore, unsuitable for binding thin books because the skin has to be excessively pared down in order to permit opening of the book. A thick skin which has been pared down is not as strong as a naturally thin skin. Excessive paring combined with faulty preparation of the leather are responsible for the early deterioration of many calf-bound books.

Other varieties of leather exist, but are unsuitable for binding archive documents. Sheep skin, for example, is a soft skin which cracks easily on the surface, and is not at all suitable for quality binding.

Binding cloth

Various materials, such as calico binding cloth, art canvas and linen buckram have been used for binding purposes. These materials are cheaper than leather, and books bound with them remain in good condition while leather used at the same time has rotted and crumbled to pieces. Buckram and art canvas have proved to be lasting materials suitable for heavy books, and have replaced leather in some institutions. Cotton buckram is not as hard wearing as the linen variety.

A good binding cloth should be soft and pliable, and should not crack on the surface when bent sharply; it should also permit finishing and tooling. Some binding cloths of heavy volumes have a tendency to crack at the back with use, but if they are used in combination with leather, the result is often a durable binding.

Because of its suppleness and the close interweaving of fibres throughout its entire thickness, leather is an ideal material for covering the spine of the volume, while buckram and art canvas are ideal for covering the boards, edges and binding of volumes which are not too heavy. A quarter-bound volume is the most durable provided that good quality leather has been used on the back.

Rexine and PVC cloth are other materials which have been used for binding. The base of both these materials is fabric cloth. Nitro-cellulose is the covering or filling material in Rexine, whereas poly-vinyl chloride is used in PVC cloth. Rexine suffers from all the defects of nitrocellulose, while the high chlorine content of PVC cloth leads to the formation of hydrochloric acid, which is harmful. Neither of these materials is therefore recommended for binding archive materials.

ADHESIVES

The use of adhesives in archive conservation work is very important from the point of view of permanence. In the broadest definition, an adhesive is a material which bonds together two other materials by adhering strongly to their surface. The adhesive bond so formed should be internally strong, otherwise the bonding is ineffective. Adhesives, whether natural or synthetic, are usually applied in the form of solutions, emulsions or soft gels.

The two most commonly used adhesives, both in the past and at the present time, are flour or starch paste and glue. These adhesives, when properly made and used, are suitable for permanent archive work and have withstood the test of time. During the last decade or so, a number of ready-made pastes, different from the traditional flour paste and glue and claimed to be effective have been marketed. The variety of newer, i.e. synthetic pastes now at the disposal of the conservator is so large that the selection of the most suitable type for the work in hand is a confusing business. Moreover, a large number of trade names have been used to describe material of the same type. Many of these synthetic pastes possess physical and chemical properties which are not to be found in natural pastes and glue. The enterprising conservator will be careful in the selection of the material best suited to the task. It must, however, be emphasized that no synthetic material should be used for conservation work unless its properties and permanence are reasonably well known and can be accurately assessed.

In choosing an adhesive, it is not sufficient to rely on the class of polymer, e.g. polyacrylate or polyvinyl, or even on the type, e.g. polymethyl methacrylate, because other unspecified ingredients, potentially undesirable from the point of view of conservation may have been added to the product. The position in this respect is, however, improving and most manufacturers now provide sufficient details concerning the composition of their products, and are in fact prepared to disclose in confidence the composition of their adhesives to institutions concerned with the restoration of archive documents, so that only those which are of proven quality may be selected.

A good adhesive for archive work should have the following properties:

It should allow time for working and manipulation. For this purpose, it should be fluid or plastic at the time of application and should wet the joint for manipulation, i.e. fixing or covering the joint, etc., without drying quickly. If, for example, the glue in a joint is allowed to cool and set before the joint is made, it loses most of its adhesiveness, and the joint thus formed will be weak. On the other hand, paste is convenient for working. It does not dry quickly and permits manipulation.

If, on the other hand, the adhesive makes the paper to which it is applied too wet, the result is severe cockling due to uneven or excessive expansion, which gives trouble on drying.

It should have a quick initial set followed by a final set to reach maximum strength.

The initial set takes place by cooling, as in the case of glue. Once the joints have been brought together, the quicker the glue sets, the sooner the joint can be handled without damage or distortion. With continued drying, the joint becomes stronger and stronger until it reaches its final strength when drying is complete.

Initial set may also take place by evaporation, e.g. by evaporation of water in the case of paste. The quicker the water evaporates, the quicker is the joint formed.

The final set with paste and glue and many other adhesives takes place by evaporation. If shrinkage is excessive, the joint formed is defective.

The adhesive should itself be strong. For example, wax when melted and applied can join two sheets, but such a joint is weak and gives way easily. Similarly, an adhesive paste which is too thin does not have enough strength to hold the joint, which thus gives way.

In the case of synthetic materials, the adhesive must possess a certain minimum strength and must be able to stretch to a certain extent without cracking on drying.

The adhesive should be reversible. This is an important characteristic when dealing with the repair of documents, since it ensures that mistakes may be corrected and the document re-repaired if necessary. For example, flour paste and glue can be re-dissolved in water after they have set, while this is not so in the case of many synthetic adhesives.

Paste

Paste has been used for centuries. It satisfactorily meets the many practical requirements for an adhesive, and at low cost. It allows working time and is convenient to prepare and apply. The formulae of certain pastes which have proved their usefulness are provided in Appendix 3. To improve flow and preserve the various pastes against mouldiness and putrefaction, and also to increase their resistance to moisture on drying, thus increasing the usefulness of the paste, chemicals have in some cases been added.

Properties such as tackiness, initial set, water sensitivity and spreading power may all be varied to suit requirements. Institutions which do not wish to prepare their own adhesives can obtain suitable ready-made pastes, but these are poor substitutes for freshly prepared paste in conservation work. There is no means of determining whether ready-made paste contains excess acid or alkali or oxidizing agents which have a deteriorative effect on paper, or whether it contains any of the many antiseptics and fungicides required in a paste for conservation work. In some cases, ready-made pastes tend to stain document paper. It must be admitted, however, that the moderate cost of ready-made pastes is an important consideration for any archive institution whether in a developing or a developed country.

Paste differs from glue in (a) having a greater moisture content, and (b) drying more slowly. It does not stain the paper but, like glue, attracts insects. Paste is used for mending and repair work, fixing end papers and for covering and fixing soft cloth such as cambric, silk, etc. It is not used for fixing book-binding cloth as it softens the cloth and removes its colour, size and grain. Paste is used for fixing leather to volumes which require binding, because it dries slowly and allows the binder more time to handle the whole process, while glue dries quickly and does not permit enough time to pull and form the leather into shape.

Another paste which has been used with success at the Florence Archives and also at the National Library in the same city is a mixture of 15 per cent polyvinyl acetate emulsion and 85 per cent rice starch.

In applying paste, a thin coat is more useful and imparts better joining. In fact, the less paste used, i.e. the minimum required for proper adhesion, the better the result. The normal tendency is to use too much paste, which on drying begins to crack. Excess paste also squeezes out of the sheet or joint when pressed, which either causes other pages to stick or stains portions which become difficult to clean.

Skill at thinning paste with water comes with experience. The amount of thinning depends on the moisture required for the particular task in hand. For example, a thin paste is required for mending work with either tissue paper or chiffon, whereas for map mounting work a thick paste is necessary. In general, it may be said that the drier the paste the less chance there is of wrinkling of the repaired sheet.

Paste is usually applied by means of a brush, although some binders find it easier to apply paste with the thumb or fingers.

Practical book binders often use a mixture of paste and glue for certain purposes, chiefly because the paste slows down the initial set of the glue, while the glue imparts tack and quicker set to the paste. Pastes containing a small amount of glue revert much more slowly. Certain synthetic materials such as carboxy methyl cellulose (CMC) and methyl cellulose are superior to glue in this respect. A paste made of CMC alone (2.5 per cent) is used at the National Archives, New Delhi, for repair work with tissue paper and chiffon.

Glue

Glue is an organic substance prepared from hides and bones of animals such as cattle, sheep and horses. It has been used in book binding for centuries for attaching the spine, fixing cloth to the boards and in making split boards. Glue differs from paste in that it remains flexible at normal temperatures on drying, whereas paste dries to a brittle consistency. It has a rapid initial set and high solid/water ratio. It dries quickly and enables faster working, and its use reduces cockling to a minimum.

Glue is of special value in the rounding and backing of volumes. After the initial set it permits rounding of the volume without causing damage to the spine. It penetrates between the various sections when hot and ensures a better mechanical hold. It must be applied hot, but should not be heated beyond 55° C (130° F). For this reason, it is heated in a thermostatically controlled glue pot or if this is not available, in a double boiler. The danger of burning is thus avoided and the hot water heats the glue uniformly. Glue is soaked in water before heating. During lengthy operations, the strength of the glue in the pot should be maintained by adding fresh glue and water.

If the glue is allowed to chill and set before the materials are joined together, the result is a weak joint. Therefore, the room should be warm, and the glue should be applied as soon as it is ready. Excessively thick application leads to difficulties.

The repeated heating of glue should be avoided, as it degrades the quality and affects the initial set. The glue pot should be frequently cleaned.

A satisfactory glue for bookbinding should be clean, translucent and light amber in colour. It is available in the form of sheets, flakes and cake, or in a pulverized form. For protection against insect or other pests, 1 per cent phenol is added to the glue during heating. Phenol also helps to prevent the glue from setting too rapidly. The addition of a small quantity of glycerine helps it to dry flexible, but too much glycerine can result in a greater absorption of moisture and a risk of mould growth unless sufficient antiseptic has also been added to prevent the latter.

Liquid glues marketed for binding work usually contain additives such as cresol or acetic acid. These glues tend to affect the colour of certain papers and cloth, and their effect should therefore be tested before use. Moreover, the exact composition of such glues is unknown. Their use is not recommended for institutions which do not possess facilities for testing the effect of the various materials and chemicals used for the conservation of paper or which are unable to have such materials tested by suitable laboratories or establishments.

Synthetic adhesives

Thermoplastic polymers of good general durability which have been utilized in conservation work as adhesives and also for such purposes as varnishing include polyvinyl acetate and polymethacrylates.

Polyvinyl acetate in the form of an emulsion has been used in place of traditional glue for a number of binding operations. For example, as an adhesive for the spine of the book it has remarkable adhesive properties and can be used cold. It is a good adhesive for silk, nylon and terylene, where glue and paste are not very satisfactory. It is also less liable to attack by insects and mould growth.

Polyvinyl acetate emulsion is marketed under various trade names. These products contain various additives which influence their ultimate use, and care must therefore be exercised in choosing such a product for conservation work. Particular attention should be paid to the following features: (a) the nature of the material added to stabilize the emulsion; (b) the pH of the emulsion; and (c) the possible presence of a thickening agent used to increase the viscosity of the emulsion. Any emulsion containing a thickening agent should be viewed with reserve by the conservator.

For binding purposes, polyvinyl acetate emulsion, which is internally plasticized, should be selected. If the commercial product chosen is of a consistency unsuitable for the particular task in hand, it can be thinned by the addition of water.

Polyvinyl acetate emulsion, unlike glue, is difficult to remove once it has set. This is a disadvantage from the archivist's point of view, as it hampers the removal of repairs from valuable documents. Errors are always possible, and may result in serious damage if they cannot be corrected. This emulsion should therefore not be used for archive repair work.

Langwell in his book, *Conservation of Books and Documents* states that the objection to modern synthetic adhesives is

... that they require dangerously high acidity to set them at low temperature in a reasonable time. Unless considerable changes are made in their properties these plastics should not be used for archive work.

Cunha in *Conservation of Library Materials* points out that:

... extravagant claims have been made by some manufacturers of polyvinyl acetate (any other synthetic resins) regarding the alleged capability of these materials to make old books like new. These white emulsions, generously painted on worn-out books, are claimed to fasten separated covers, consolidate rotted leather and rejuvenate cloth. Large numbers of fine volumes have been ruined by the improper use of these products. What must be remembered is that polyvinyl acetate emulsions are good adhesives and nothing more. When used as one should use paste or glue, they make very strong bonds which can rarely be separated without damaging the fastened materials. Since one of the basic principles of rare books and archive restoration is that nothing shall be done in the restoration that cannot be undone if necessary, these irreversible adhesives should be avoided for all except general library work.

It is not known how the plastic adhesives will behave over the years or what will be their durability in terms of hundreds of years. Old adhesives like glue and paste can be re-dissolved by damping with water and the parts of a binding or repaired sheets can be separated without damage to the text, if re-repair is necessary. But this cannot be done easily with plastic adhesives. There is always a danger of the document being damaged in the process. This danger is all the greater if the future restorer does not know which adhesive has been used or in which material it is soluble. Books and documents require repair from time to time, and it is therefore essential to insert a note inside the book or document identifying the adhesive used and stating how it may be dissolved. Moreover, the bond formed by synthetic adhesives is a strong one. The use of such adhesives on weak paper may result in breaking of the paper at the joint.

The choice of synthetic adhesives for conservation work should, therefore, be limited to those which are soluble in water or solvents like alcohol, acetone and benzene. Such adhesives may be used either alone or in combination with the traditional pastes and glues. As we have already seen, the synthetic adhesives currently used as pastes are carboxy methyl cellulose (CMC) and methyl cellulose, polyvinyl acetate emulsion mixed with starch paste also being used with success.

9   Aids to preservation

Archive institutions concerned with the preservation of their holdings are coming to realize the importance of a scientific approach to the problem, stress being laid on the need to prevent and avoid costly repair and restoration. No institution in the world has sufficient staff and funds to keep its collection in perfect repair. The problem is accentuated in tropical countries where, unless the environment is controlled, the degree of light, temperature, humidity and other conditions may often be outside the normal safety margins for adequate preservation. Even in temperate regions, no document can last for long if it is not stored under proper environmental conditions and suitably housed. Whether it is on good durable paper or restored by a method that ensures maximum longevity is immaterial.

The conservation of documents comprises their display, storage and handling in conditions likely to inhibit further deterioration. Contributory factors include: (a) the location and design of the repository; (b) the equipment available for and manner of storage; (c) air-conditioning; (d) the manner of handling and servicing the materials; and (e) the steps taken to safeguard archive materials against natural calamities like flood and fire, and man-made disasters like wars or other acts of violence.

Great advances have been made in the design and air-conditioning of buildings and in the provision of other prerequisites of proper storage and servicing of archive materials. Guidelines for this purpose have also been drawn up by bodies such as the International Council of Archives and other societies interested in conservation, and presented in various publications, for example, the

American Archivist, the *Journal of Society of Archivists* in the United Kingdom, the *Unesco Bulletin for Libraries*, *Archivum*, etc.

When designing or commissioning a building, the custodians of archive materials should decide upon the essential features which will have a direct bearing on the safety of their collection, and explain their requirements to the specialists entrusted with the task. In general terms, a building should have an attractive exterior and a pleasant interior. It should combine maximum structural stability with utility and an economy of space. At the same time it should have all the essential features of any good building, with adequate light, warmth and fresh air. It should include a stack area for the permanent storage of documents; an office space for use by staff engaged for conservation work; a repair and binding unit for the treatment of documents requiring attention; a photographic unit, for preparing security copies of all the items held and for reproducing copies of documents for scholars and searchers; a reference or reading room, where documents may be consulted by scholars and other interested persons; an exhibition room, where documents may be displayed or which could be used for exhibitions on various topics for general educational purposes; a reception area where documents may be quarantined and sterilized prior to storage in the stack area; and a reference library for the use of staff and scholars alike.

A building for the storage of archive material must also provide adequate security against adverse environmental conditions, insects, rodents, variations of temperature and humidity and against fire, flood, theft and wanton destruction. Before, however, deciding upon the design of the building and the servicing facilities it should offer, it is desirable to carry out an assessment of the holdings and the annual rate of additional increase in load, to take account of and prepare for the expansion which is inevitable due to the constant growth of archives and also to prepare for any future emergency. In other words, the building should meet the essential and functional requirements, typical of all archive institutions. In addition, the planning and designing of a building should include consideration of the points listed below.

Climatic conditions of the region

A record of variations of temperature, the number and frequency of rainy days, atmospheric humidity and variations in humidity during the day, the length of humid and dry seasons, hours of sunshine and direction of winds should be maintained over a period of at least one year. This will help the architect, in designing the building, to take account of conditions of sunlight and rainfall which might otherwise pose problems in a well-lit and well-ventilated building.

Selection of site

This is of the greatest importance. The efficiency and utility of the building depend on careful siting. The site should be capable of providing dry foundations, good drainage to prevent the accumulation of water, and clean air, i.e. it should not be close to sources of pollution. In addition, it should allow room for expansion of the building. For the sake of convenience and to meet the needs of the majority of users of archive materials, the site should be centrally located.

Foundations

The foundations of the building should be termite proof. This may be ensured either by driving pile foundations or by treating the soil surrounding the foundations with suitable chemicals and by using metallic termite shields. Any wood employed in the construction should be treated. Wherever steel is used, it should be painted to prevent rusting.

Ventilation

The ventilation of a building is determined by the design and direction of its windows. In tropical countries, the traditional method of limiting the discomfort caused by high temperature and relative humidity involves the provision of a large number of doors and windows to allow free circulation of fresh air. Such arrangements often lead to the formation of pockets of stagnant air and sometimes to high temperatures or high humidity in the storage area. If the building is to be air-conditioned, ventilation apertures should be reduced to a minimum, for too many ventilators, windows and entrances make it impossible to obtain full advantage from air-conditioning. Ventilators, doors and windows in an air-conditioned building should be designed in such a way that the building may be hermetically sealed. In non-air-conditioned buildings, all ventilation apertures should be protected against direct sunlight and rain-water, by providing vertical fins and horizontal sun-breakers. The use of heat-resistant glass has also proved useful.

Lighting

Good natural or artificial lighting is necessary in every building. The modern lighting practice is to provide diffused lights of varying intensity in different rooms. The illumination of interior rooms can be improved by using paints which reflect light. Proper layout and planning of the building in relation to adjacent blocks can also add appreciably to daylight illumination.

Location of rooms

The location of service rooms, record reception centres, stacks, restoration and photo-copying rooms, etc., should be determined with reference to the work flow. The administration block, service block and storage areas should be interlinked in such a way that each retains its separate entity. Space for an auditorium, a conference hall, an exhibition room and a recreation room should also be provided.

Stack area

The stack area is a vital portion of any archive building where documents are permanently stored. For reasons of safety and security, the stack area should have limited entry, and should be planned in such a way that approach from outside is, as far as possible, denied. Windows opening on the exterior of the building should be fitted with metal grills and wire-mesh nets. The stack area should be situated near the restoration, photo-copying, reference and record reception rooms. Provision should be made for easy movement of record-carrying trolleys, etc., between the floors of the various storage rooms.

Water and other facilities

Binding, restoration and photo-copying rooms require running hot and cold water and also special electrical installations for equipment and machinery. These should, therefore, be properly planned.

Drainage

All sewage and drains should be waterproof and the outlets should have metal flanges. To prevent the accumulation of rain-water, the building should be sited on gently sloping ground so that all rain-water will flow past and not collect around it. Efficient drainage should be provided all round the building. Steps should be taken to ensure that no water pipes pass near, above or under the stack area, the floor level of which should be a few centimetres above the general level of other floors in the building, to prevent any inflow of water into the area as a result of blockage or accidental damage in water-pipes and drains.

Air-conditioning

The decision whether or not to install air-conditioning throughout the building must be made when the plans are being drawn up. At this stage, it is easy to provide for a central air-conditioning plant with air-ducts leading off from it and for the separate regulation of atmospheric conditions in each room. The cost of installing such a plant at a later stage is prohibitive.

In a building to be air-conditioned, the ventilation should be planned in such a way as to permit minimum leakage of the conditioned atmosphere. Passage between non-conditoned and conditioned areas should be controlled by means of vestibules. Calculations of the conditioning load should take account not only of the amount of shelving and archive material but also of the number of persons working in the building and of the traffic of material into or out of the area to be conditioned.

For proper humidity control in the conditioned area, dampness should not be allowed to permeate through walls or floors. The floor should be waterproof and the walls should be coated with waterproof oil paint.

The conditioned area should be as far as possible dust proof. Dust in the fresh air supplied to the conditioning plant must be filtered before it enters the plant, but the amount of filtration and the degree of recirculation of air will depend upon local atmospheric conditions and on the average number of persons frequenting the area. Electrostatic precipitation, although the most efficient method of filtration, must be avoided as it leads to the production of ozone, which may provoke oxidative reactions in cellulose material and cause degradation of archive materials in storage. Ordinary fabric or oil filters combined with dust separators serve the purpose well, and are also the least expensive. In view of the fact that contaminated air will enter the building every time a door or window is opened, it is pointless to insist on 100 per cent effectiveness in air filtration. Acidic gases such as sulphur dioxide, etc., may be removed from the incoming air by washing, and although pure water sprays will help to remove about half the acidic impurities, washing is best done with an alkaline water spray, of pH 8.5–9, which will do much to remove all the acidic gases present in the incoming air.

If available financial resources do not allow for complete air-conditioning, partial air-conditioning should be provided for areas where important collections are stored. Most available appliances are neither bulky nor costly and can be used successfully in small rooms; for larger rooms several units may be required. But before selecting an appliance it is desirable to estimate the rate of relative humidity in the atmosphere by taking an average of the readings made over at least a year. Humidity and temperature in conditioned rooms may easily be measured with instruments called hygrometers, of which a simple example is the hair thermo-hygrograph, which traces two graphs, one showing variations in relative humidity, and the other variations in temperature. Instruments of this type should be placed in each of the rooms to be air-conditioned to check the efficacy of the equipment installed. The hygrometer should be checked for accuracy occasionally against readings obtained from dry-bulb and wet-bulb thermometers. This is necessary to get correct readings of humidity in the room as the relative humidity in the outside atmosphere may fluctuate between 10 and 90 per cent in a very short time. Unless the relative humidity is maintained between 45 and 55 per cent, air-conditioning is pointless as far as conservation is concerned.

In the absence of air-conditioning, conservation is easier in dry tropics than in humid regions. The chief hazards in dry tropics are light, dust and sand. Light may be reduced by using opaque glass and curtains and also by keeping interior lighting at a low level, while the penetration of dust and sand may be checked by reducing apertures to a minimum and by general cleaning. If the relative humidity falls too low, i.e. to 10–20 per cent, portable humidifiers should be installed. Humidification is a much less expensive process than dehumidification and is worth attempting when required in such regions even though close control is not possible.

In humid regions, the chief deteriorating agent is mould, and this may be kept under control by adequate ventilation, regular inspection, and the use of fungicides. All materials in storage should be packed loose or kept on shelves in such a manner that they do not press against each other. The arrangement of shelves, racks and storage in the stack area should permit the free circulation of air and prevent the formation of pockets of stationary air. If infestation is detected, the area should be isolated and the contents fumigated.

High humidity can be reduced in the stack area by the use of dehumidifying machines. Two types of machine are available. One works on the principle of refrigeration. Water condensed from the surrounding atmosphere is collected in a cistern and expelled at intervals. The other employs a chemical dehydrant, usually silica gel. When such machines are employed, the atmosphere in the room must be regulated by adequate ventilation and the air circulated by electric fans or other suitable equipment.

One method for checking high relative humidity in a room involves the installation of an electric heater with a fan or hot-air circulator. This method has been used in Ceylon (now Sri Lanka), where conditions of 90 per cent relative humidity at 30° C may be encountered during much of the year, to protect stores from damage by mildew. By raising the temperature to 38° C the relative humidity is easily reduced to 70 per cent.

Fire hazards

Fire is often accidental and often due to an electrical short-circuit. The proper installation of electrical fittings is therefore of utmost importance in an archive building. All wiring should be through conduits and main control switches should be located outside the storage rooms. The entire stack area should be fire-proof and, if possible, divided into separate fire-proof compartments as in the case of the new premises of the India Office Library, London. All ducts leading from one compartment to another, such as those required for air-conditioning, should be fitted with mechanical dampers to provide complete isolation from the affected area if an emergency arises. It is desirable to provide emergency exits on all floors of the stack area so that the valuable archive material may be removed to safety in case of emergency.

To permit location of the fire and prompt action, a fire detection alarm system should be installed in the building. A number of such devices are available. The alarm is sounded either when the temperature in any part of the building reaches a predetermined height or when smoke is detected by a special sensor fitted at different locations in the building.

Adequate fire-fighting equipment should be installed at points easily accessible in an emergency. Different types of fire-extinguisher using either water, carbon dioxide gas, or chemical foam are available. All are satisfactory depending upon the place of use. For photo-copying rooms and laboratories chemical foam extinguishers are desirable, whereas carbon dioxide gas extinguishers are suitable for stack areas. To cope with a major conflagration, water pipes and hoses should also be installed at conveninent points. All fire-fighting installations and the fire-alarm system should be checked at regular intervals to ensure its readiness. Staff working in archive institutions should receive training in fire-fighting and an occasional drill.

Shelving

The shelving equipment available varies in design, strength and capacity. Shelving equipment for archives should provide maximum storage space at minimum cost. It should preferably be of the adjustable type and provide adequate safety from fire, pests, etc., together with maximum convenience for servicing. As a general rule, shelving should be so desingned and erected that no material is stored out of reach by hand from the floor. All shelves should be of the same dimensions, and should be interchangeable and adjustable at different heights.

Shelves may be fitted by means of wall supports, fixed on uprights with provision for adjustability, or movable. Adjustable steel shelving on equidistant uprights is satisfactory for archive storage. Rows of shelves should be so arranged that the central and lateral aisles provide sufficient space for servicing and the movement of records on trolleys, etc.

Shelving in archives should be functional, durable, easy to clean and simple in design and should offer maximum protection to the stored material.

If steel shelving is provided, it should be rust-proofed with a product which does not harm the documents. All steel shelves should preferably be perforated to ensure the circulation of air and to prevent the precipitation of moisture. Wooden shelves should either be pretreated against termite damage or, if already erected, treated with preservatives. Sharp edges and corners in shelves and supports may lead to physical damage, and these should therefore be avoided.

Storage

Archive collections differ in bulk, size and shape and normally consist of bound volumes, loose sheets, files, manuscripts, maps, drawings, photographs, prints, etc. Bound volumes should either be stored upright, i.e. on the tail edges with the weight resting on the binding boards, or kept flat. They should not be packed tight on the shelves. The use of book-ends helps to ensure that volumes are stored properly on the shelves. When stored flat, not more than three or four volumes should be placed on top of each other.

Loose sheets and files are provided with protective covers or folders and stored inside document boxes made of fine quality compressed boards. These document boxes are usually made of one piece, with rust-proof clips at the joints. They are light and handy, may be stored neatly on shelves and are in use in almost all the archives in the world. In some centres, such as the National Archives, New Delhi, loose papers in covers and folders are tied in bundles between stiff wooden boards of five-ply, larger in size than the covers of the bundles so that the cord used for tying does not come in contact with and thus cause damage to the documents so stored. Boards of plastic or aluminium are also suitable for this purpose.

Steel plan-filing cabinets are used for filing maps and drawings. Outsize maps are cut into sections and filed flat in these cabinets. Maps are often large and difficult to serve to readers. Map cabinets should therefore be adjacent to the tables on which the maps are examined. Large-sized maps, if so desired, may be kept rolled on specially installed brackets on the walls or hung in glass panelled almirahs.

All stored materials should be within easy reach. In certain cases, the stack height may necessitate the use of step-ladders and plat-form-type ladders for access to records stored on the top shelves. Platform ladders should be provided with swivel castors for easy movement. Servicing trolleys should be used for moving archive material from place to place, while the movement of records from one floor to another may be facilitated, and time and labour saved through the installation of electrically operated equipment.

Dusting

The most important aid to preservation during storage is a vacuum cleaner. In spite of dust-proof buildings and air-conditioning, dust does find its way to the archive materials stored in the repository. Regular dusting in the stack with the help of a vacuum cleaner is desirable to remove dust. Every archive should possess a mobile dusting unit for vacuuming all records at least once a year.

Dust is harmful to all archive materials and may lead to serious damage. Its hard particles have an abrasive effect on paper and similar materials. The presence of dust among documents makes them prone to fungus attack. Dust consists mainly of organic particles, and forms a breeding-ground for bacteria which stain documents or cause damage by their acidic excreta. It is also harmful to the health of the staff working inside the stack rooms. Staff engaged in dusting operations should be provided with dust respirators, if only in the form of a cloth bag with a surgical cotton lining which can be changed occasionally.

In storage rooms which are not air-conditioned, it is necessary to spray insecticides and preservatives on walls, beneath the shelves, behind the cabinets in corners, etc., by means of hand spray-guns, electrically operated pressure guns or any other similar equipment. Only those chemicals should be sprayed whose effect on the durability and permanence of paper and other cellulose material has beeen properly evaluated.

At the first sign of increasing humidity, preventive actions should be initiated in the manner detailed earlier. Staff responsible for dusting can be of great help in keeping a constant check on hygrometers and reporting any fungus growth.

10 Preservation of microfilms and sound recordings

Nearly every archive institution has its own collection of microfilms, photographic prints on both film and paper, negatives, and in some cases colour films, prints and sound recordings, which must be preserved with care.

Microfilms

Microfilms as a means of circulating and utilizing documentary materials and in the form of security copies of those documents have become an indispensable element of properly administered archives. Their proper care depends on knowledge of the materials employed in their manufacture and processing, and of the manner in which they should be handled and stored.

BASE

The production of microfilm base and emulsions for use in archives has been the subject of considerable technical study. Film suitable for work with archive materials is finely grained and capable of giving a high degree of resolution and contrast. Nitrogen-free safety film with cellulose acetate base is ideal for the purpose. Films with cellulose nitrate base are not acceptable for archive use. Accelerated ageing tests in various laboratories, and years of experience have demonstrated the high degree of chemical stability of acetate films. For archive use, however, all acetate films, whether composed of cellulose diacetate, cellulose triacetate or mixed esters, should conform to standards for safety film and permanent records laid down in different countries, such as the United States of America, the United Kingdom, Federal Republic of Germany, France, India, etc.

Colour films are not approved for archive use as the dyes used in their preparation are known to fade with time, although if they are processed and stored with due care and as recommended by the manufacturer, they will retain the original colours for many years.

Polyester films are now available. On the basis of tests, their permanence equals and even surpasses that of cellulose triacetate films, whilst they also meet the standards established for safety film. They are of particular interest in special cases where high dimensional stability and film strength, as well as greater resistance to extremes of temperature are required. Polyester films are not yet, however, being used for archive records.

PROCESSING

Processing comprises the development, fixation, washing and drying of exposed film. Each step is important for the stability of the final product and therefore only the recommended procedures and controls should be adopted. Properly controlled processing produces stable images, whereas improper control leads to instability or fading.

For permanent records, fixation and washing must be complete. In other words the final product should be free from residual silver and hypo salts. The American Standards Association and the National Bureau of Standards have established specifications for maximum allowable residual silver and hypo and tests for evaluating and controlling the processing operations. Similar standards have been or are being adopted in other countries.

Storage

Photographic films and prints, though stable, are sensitive to environmental conditions such as high humidity or variations in temperature, as well as to hydrogen sulphide and sulphur dioxide gases, hydrogen peroxide and certain organic vapours. They may also be damaged by water or fire. The planning of their storage should take these factors into consideration.

Storage in moist air and in an atmosphere of more than 50 per cent relative humidity should as far as possible be avoided. Relative humidity above 60 per cent encourages fungus growth, while very low relative humidity causes brittleness, curl and static charge. For long-term protection, the only practical solution is proper and controlled air-conditioning. Relative humidity between 40 and 50 per cent and a temperature of 20–22° C have been found to be the most suitable conditioning. Air-conditioning has also proved useful in removing harmful air contaminants.

To ensure safer preservation, microfilms should be stored in fire-proof and dust-proof cabinets, preferably made of steel and treated with non-corrosive, non-staining and non-combustible paint. The design of the cabinets should allow the free circulation of air in drawers and compartments. Such cabinets should conform to the requirements of the United States Fire Protection Association. To prevent water damage from fire-sprinklers and flooding of the storage area, they should be stored above ground level.

Microfilm reels are stored in specially designed metal cans, which may be sealed if desired with a good quality rubber base pressure sensitive tape. However, the use of rubber bands around microfilm reels should be avoided, because rubber may contain residual sulphur, which is harmful. Similarly, the use of adhesive tapes, tape splices, bleached paper or printed paper such as newspaper, around microfilm reels, have adverse effects and should be avoided.

Strips, sheet films and paper prints should be stored flat in separate envelopes which meet the specifications for the storage of negatives. The prints should not be interleaved with plastic sheets containing plasticizers as these may affect the image. Aluminium foil and to a lesser extent polyethylene have proved suitable for interleaving prints and negatives during storage.

The initial microfilm negative is set aside as a master copy, positive copies being made for reference or use. The master copy should be examined regularly for signs of deterioration or blemishes. At the first sign of deterioration in processed films, duplicates should be prepared and stored in a safe place under proper conditions.

BLEMISHES

In 1963 in the United States of America, microscopic blemishes were observed on microfilms of archive documents and other public records. These microscopic blemishes, known as J-type defects and sometimes referred to as 'measles', have been the subject of intense research by a number of institutions in the United States, including the Recordak Group, Xerox Corporation, University Microfilm Inc., Michigan, the National Bureau of Standards and the National Microfilm Association, etc. They are caused by oxidized grains of silver in the film coating which have moved or migrated in the emulsion and have been redeposited as fine but well-defined reddish particles, which appear on processed microfilm negatives and positives, after a period which may be as short as two years, in the form of (a) yellowish or reddish circular spots, varying in size from one- to six-thousandths of an inch; and (b) concentric light and dark rings. They also sometimes distort the recorded text, which appears lighter and broader as a result. In the case which we have mentioned, blemishes were mainly found on the leaders and trailers of each roll, i.e. the pieces of blank film at the beginning and the end, although 10 per cent of the rolls so affected showed more extensive damage, spots being found up to two or three feet inside the roll.

These blemishes are not confined to microfilms and have also been detected on other types of negative films. Studies show that they are caused by external influences.

The first and the most obvious source of the trouble seems to be in the storage. There is evidence that the deterioration could be due to peroxides, ozone and various contaminants found in an industrial atmosphere, such as sulphur dioxide, and possibly to atomic radiation. These defects or blemishes have been found to be most prevalent in films stored in conditions of high humidity or in a contaminated atmospheric environment. Microfilms stored in institutions which maintain strictly controlled environmental conditions in their vaults have been found to be almost free from these defects.

Another possible cause is over-exposure or careless processing. This suggestion is supported by observations that the spots are particularly evident (a) on leaders and trailers, which are often heavily exposed during document filming and therefore possess high average density; (b) on the extreme edge of positive microfilms; and (c) on scratches on the film. Low density areas, i.e. frames containing images, have been found to be comparatively less affected.

PREVENTIVE METHODS

One method of prevention is to store microfilms under proper environmental conditions. A constant temperature of 20–22° C and moisture content of 45 and 5 per cent relative humidity have been found to constitute ideal conditions for the storage of microfilms. Ideally, microfilm archives should be stored in an atmosphere of cool dry air, free from oxidizing gases or vapours. Another method involves the gold-toning of microfilms by a process which, it is claimed, can be applied in both high-capacity processing units and small processing machines, and which is considered to be the best protective treatment at present for microfilms, irrespective of the methods of storage and handling.

The process of gold-toning is simple, and the amount of gold required is very small. As pointed out earlier, the blemishes are produced by local oxidation of the silver grains, which subsequently migrate in the gelatine and are deposited in groups of fine particles. As a result of this migration, spotting occurs. Protective treatment with gold appears to prevent the formation of these spots. The microfilms are soaked in water, passed through a dilute solution of gold chloride and other chemicals in water, and finally rewashed in water. As a result, a continuous and microscopically thin layer of gold is deposited on each individual silver particle. This gold wash process is not unknown to photographers, who have been using it for some years to give added permanence to photographic prints.

Tests on gold-treated microfilms have revealed their superior resistance to laboratory-induced spots or fading. Eastman Kodak have published details of a gold-protective treatment for safeguarding films against oxidation, the effect of which is claimed to last for more than twenty years. Although a precious metal is involved, the process is relatively inexpensive, one ounce of gold being sufficient to treat several thousand rolls of microfilm.

Another process which has been investigated utilizes a gold-lacquer plastic coating which at the same time deposits gold on the image.

Sound recordings

Sound recordings are subject to deterioration both in storage and during playback. The mechanisms of degradation of each type of recording have been studied, and recommendations for proper storage and playback have been prescribed.

CAUSES OF DETERIORATION

Degradation in sound recordings, which may be physical or chemical, is a product of the process of manufacture, and the action of light, heat, moisture, dust and atmospheric contaminants. The changes produced are interdependent and occur simultaneously in the plastic material. Such changes cause permanent deformation, embrittlement, cracking, loss of adhesion between laminates or loss of strength.

Manufacture

The life-span of a plastic article under ideal conditions is built into the article during the process of manufacture. Uncontrolled variables such as the basic resin, the materials added to the basic resin to provide it with the desired properties, the presence of certain chemicals even in traces, together with changes in process techniques involving cycle time, temperature or pressure cause internal stress and changes in the retained solvent which, in their turn, initiate chemical degradation of the plastic.

Light and heat

Light, whether natural or artificial, has a deteriorative effect. All sound recordings are sensitive to ultra-violet rays and deteriorate on exposure to sunlight and artificial light rich in shorter wave lengths.

Heat causes both physical and chemical changes. Plastics have a high co-efficient of thermal expansion and low thermal conductivity, and their viscosity also changes with a change in temperature. Combination of all these factors results in changes in size and shape of the plastic and in consequent permanent deformation. It has been observed that chemical changes are accelerated by increase in temperature. For example, the reaction rate is approximately doubled by an increase in temperature of 8° C. On the other hand, low temperature creates problems, such as extreme brittleness, ice-crystal formation and failure due to the differing co-efficients of expansion of the constituent materials.

Moisture

Moisture is both a physical and a chemical agent of degradation. Changes in moisture content cause large dimensional changes in the plastic base and fillers and affects physical properties such as impact strength. Excessive moisture also brings about chemical change by hydrolysis or by catalytic or solvent action. In hydrolysis, water reacts directly with the plastic base. As a catalyst, it provokes other reactions. As a solvent, it facilitates reactions which can occur only in solution. In addition, moisture encourages the migration of compounds from one place to another within the material and in excessive quantities is also conducive to biological deterioration.

Dust

Dust and grit are responsible for both physical and chemical degradation in sound recordings. Physical damage is caused by scratching of the surface or embedment of dust particles on the surface. These affect the playback qualities. Furthermore, dust is not an inert material, and provides the acid radicals and metallic ions which act as catalysts for degradation processes. Dust films attract the moisture which is essential for starting chemical action on materials. Thermoplastics are electrostatically charged during the moulding process, and since they are poor conductors, the surface charge remains for a long time, and is moreover renerved during handling and playback. This charge attracts and retains dust on the surface.

Oxygen

Depending on the nature of the plastic material and on environmental conditions, oxygen may cause minor or serious chemical degradation. For example, chemical changes during the process of manufacture or as a result of exposure to light and heat provide sites for oxidative reactions which lead to degradation of the plastic. It has been observed that all modern plastic materials are quite stable to oxygen in the absence of light or excessive temperature, certain trace impurities and excessive moisture. It has also been observed that properly packaged materials are not affected even in heavily contaminated environments.

Fungal action

Fungi are a significant cause of deterioration of the organic ingredients used in sound recordings. They consume the plasticizer and manufacture various chemicals which affect the surface. They excrete both enzymes and acids which attack not only the materials on which they feed but other surrounding materials as well. The plasticizers, fillers and extenders found in the materials of sound recordings are excellent fungi nutrients. The basic resins, with the exception of cellulose nitrate and cellulose acetate, are fungi resistant, cellulose acetate being the most resistant of the cellulosics. Many of the packaging materials used in storage provide carbohydrates, proteins, waxes, cellulose and lignin for fungi nutrition.

Fungi require an adequate amount of moisture to be active and destructive. Most dusts and lints are to a certain extent hygroscopic and tend to maintain a higher moisture level on a surface than would otherwise exist there. Fingerprints also provide good culture media.

Other biological agents, such as bacteria and insects, do not appear to constitute a major threat to sound recordings.

Other factors

Degradation may also be induced by deterioration of the constituents of the plastic, such as plasticizers, fillers and extenders.

The physical properties of a basic resin are altered to those desired with the help of plasticizers, which may subsequently be lost by volatilization, extraction, exudation, wicking, chemical degradation or biological consumption. This loss provokes chemical degradation and results in damage to the plastic.

Fillers are used either to modify the physical properties of a resin, as in the case of shellac, or for purposes of economy, as in vinyl discs. These fillers are protected by their resin coatings, but may be attacked by any substance, such as moisture due to changes in humidity, which penetrates this coating.

An extender is an organic material blended with the basic resin. Extenders are less stable than the basic resin and reduce the potential storage life of the plastic. They are attacked by the agents which degrade other organic materials and resin, and are sensitive to the same environmental changes.

SHELF LIFE

Most sound recordings have been designed to provide playback qualities at low cost, and not for long-term storage. They are subject to both physical and chemical degradation as a result of deterioration in their constituent materials. At present, because comparatively little is known about the ageing of plastics, it is impossible to predict their potential shelf life with accuracy. However, studies do indicate a certain trend and provide some idea of their potential life.

Acetate discs

These have a limited shelf life because the material employed is known to be unstable. It has been observed that under normal storage conditions acetate discs of the older type have a maximum life of about fifteen years, while modern acetate discs survive for somewhat longer.

Shellac-type discs

Discs of this type are known to have survived for more than fifty years and appear to be in excellent condition. Others, however, have deteriorated in less than a decade. Generally speaking, it would appear that such discs have long storage life if properly protected against the harmful effects of moisture, heat, fungi, etc. Embrittlement is slow but progressive and is often detected in decreased flexibility or in wearing as a result of playback.

Vinyl discs

Vinyl discs resist chemical degradation in a normal storage environment. Improperly stored, however, they undergo physical damage and become so warped and deformed as to be unplayable. Such damage seems to be of far greater significance than chemical degradation. If kept properly, they could last a century.

Magnetic tapes

Magnetic tapes are subject to both phycisal and chemical degradation. Most of these tapes were not designed for long-term storage but for playback qualities at low cost. Their life is adversely affected by winding under tension, which creates radical pressures which diminish in intensity from the hub of the roll of tape outwards. This pressure causes longitudal warping. It has been observed that any unevenness in the distribution of stress throughout the tapes results in localized permanent deformation which impairs their playback qualities. Differences in the properties of the film base and the coating result in curl, i.e. transverse warping of the tape. Another cause of degradation is magnetization induced by temperature, the passage of time and AC and DC fields, which often results in print-through. If magnetic tapes are stored under optimum conditions, their actual life-span may be longer than that built in during their manufacture.

RECOMMENDATIONS FOR STORAGE

Phonogram discs

When storing records for a long period of time, a number of precautions must be taken to protect them from the deteriorative action of heat, light, moisture, atmospheric contaminants, etc. Temperature and humidity in the storage areas must be maintained at a reasonably constant level. The maintenance of a constant environment of 45–55 per cent relative humidity at a temperature of 20–22° C day in and day out necessitates the air-conditioning of the entire library. If this is not possible, efforts should at least be made to ensure that the playback and packaging rooms meet these standards, and that elsewhere the temperature and humidity are maintained at a reasonably constant level. The entire area should be dust free. Discs should be kept clean both for playback and storage by the use of material such as the Lektrostat Record Cleaning Kit manufactured by the Dexter Chemical Corporation (United States). During playback itself, ethylene glycol solution should be applied sparingly by a brush and mohair applicator pad. Dust control and cleaning by spraying, treated cloth, damped synthetic sponge or by radioactive ionization are not satisfactory.

In order to prevent fungal damage, the discs should be clean and packed for storage in packing material free from fungal nutrients. At the time of packing, the moisture on the disc surface should be below the level required for fungi to become active.

Care should be taken in lighting the stack area and playback and packaging rooms. Sunlight or artificial lighting of shorter wave lengths such as that provided by certain mercury vapour fluorescent lights should neither be allowed to penetrate these premises, nor used in them.

The grooved surfaces of the discs should never be touched with bare hands. Rubber gloves should be worn by persons handling the discs, which should be removed or inserted in the packages without touching the grooved surfaces or permitting them to slide against the packaging material. Modern commercial packaging materials for disc storage are all unsatisfactory in one respect or another. Proper packaging material should not only be resistant to the agents which cause degradation but should also protect the discs themselves from damage. Such material should present a smooth surface to the discs, so that they may be withdrawn and inserted without sliding contact between the disc and the package. The package should also have structural strength to help protect vinyl and shellac discs from warping. It should not itself deform and cause surface damage to the disc by high contact stresses. The most satisfactory packaging material appears to be a laminate of polyethylene, paperboard and aluminium foil.

Prior to insertion, the disc, and its envelope, should be placed in an atmosphere of 50 per cent relative humidity at 20° C. A conditioning room is recommended for this purpose. When the disc is exposed to an environment other than this, it should be conditioned for twenty-four hours before packaging. Relative humidity should never be higher than 50 per cent at the time of packing, as this may result in damage to the disc.

After packaging, the discs should be stored in a vertical position without pressure on the disc surface, and prevented from slipping from the vertical position. There are two methods for ensuring this. The first involves the use of a compartment shelf which can accomodate twenty discs. The shelf is either filled with packaged discs, or with a mixture of fillers and packaged discs, so that the discs remain upright and may be removed or replaced without exerting any force. The other method employs shelves slightly higher than the diameter of the discs. Metal strips fitted at the top and bottom of the shelves support each packaged disc separately in a vertical position.

Inspection for warping, fungus action or other visible evidence of deterioration should be carried out periodically. Whenever necessary, recordings should be re-recorded to ensure their preservation.

Magnetic tapes

The precautions necessary for preserving magnetic tapes are identical with those applied in the case of discs as far as temperature, humidity control, lighting and packaging are concerned. Additional care is, however, necessary when using and storing magnetic tapes. For example, the tapes should only be wound on metal reels with unslotted hubs. If the flanges of these reels are in any way deformed, they must be replaced.

Reels should be packaged in sealed metal cases or boxes made of a material such as polyethylene, cardboard paper, aluminium foil and polyethylene laminate. Tapes should be packaged only when they are in an atomosphere of 50 per cent relative humidity at 20° C. For storage purposes, the boxes should be stacked on edge in the shelves.

Packaging and playback rooms and stack areas should be maintained at the temperature and humidity recommended for discs. Rarely used and vulnerable tapes should be stored in special vaults at a temperature of 8–12° C, with 45–50 per cent relative humidity.

Stray external magnetic fields should be excluded from the stack, playback and packaging rooms as they adversely affect the magnetic tapes. All current-bearing wires have associated magnetic fields, and all the electric circuits should therefore be properly installed and balanced in such a way that the fields cancel each other out.

The playback of tapes should be restricted to the minimum necessary, since wear and tear do more to shorten the life of sound recordings than any other factor. Tapes suffer more damage from the handling required when loading and unloading the playback unit than from the actual playback itself. For this reason, care should be taken to avoid twisting, tearing or soiling the tape. Fingerprints on the tapes should be prevented by the use of gloves

The equipment used for playback should be separate from that used for recording in order to avoid accidental erasure during playback. Equipment and tape should be kept clean and dry to ensure proper reproduction and to avoid any damage to the recordings. Dust and particles of the tape coating often collect on the recording heads, where they not only affect the quality of the reproduction, but also abrade the tape.

The first and final fifteen feet of each tape should be left blank for inspection purposes. New tapes should be aged in the packaging room for six months before they are used for recording. Recorded tapes which have been exposed to other than the prescribed environments should be conditioned in the packaging room for six weeks prior to packaging.

Tapes should be inspected and rewound after each playback. In addition, they should be inspected every two years and re-wound so that the curvature of the base is reversed. Inspection should include spot-checks within the tape and close to the hub for coating adhesion or signs of delamination. Playback is not necessary during this inspection.

Re-winding will help to reduce creep-induced curvature and print-through. Regular inspection and re-winding will in addition limit the cumulative effects of print-through and will reveal the need for re-recording of the tape before deterioration has destroyed the information which it contains.

Storage shelves should be of wood or non-magnetizable metal and free from vibration or shock.

Potential longevity is a property incorporated in an article when it is manufactured. The best that can be done with existing sound recordings is to store them in the environment most conducive to attainment of their maximum life, and to re-record them before deterioration destroys their contents.

Appendix 1

Physical and chemical tests

Physical tests provide an idea of the durability of paper. Those commonly applied are:

Tensile strength

This is a measure of the resistance of paper to direct tension. Defined as the force required to break a strip of paper which has a specified length and a width of 15 mm, it is determined mechanically with Schopper or Elmendrof-type machines calibrated to measure the stretch undergone by the sample before it breaks.

Bursting endurance

This is measured in terms of pressure applied to a specific area of paper at the point of rupture. Mullen or Schopper-type endurance testers which give the readings directly are used for the purpose.

Folding endurance

This is measured in terms of the number of double folds the paper will endure before its tensile strength falls below a standard value of 1 kg. MIT or Schopper-type machines are used for the purpose. This is one of the most important tests and is frequently used for evaluating the durability of paper.

Internal tearing resistance

This is a measurement of the resistance of paper to tear, expressed in terms of the force required to extend a tear in the paper over a fixed distance, after the tear has been made by means of a cutter attached to the instrument. The Elmendrof Internal Tear Tester is used for this measurement.

Edge tearing resistance

This is the amount of force required to start the tear at the edge of the paper. It is probably more important than internal tearing resistance, which is the average force required to sustain the tear once it has started.

Before a paper sample is subjected to the above physical tests, it should be conditioned and tested according to the specifications and procedure issued by TAPPI (Technical Association for Pulp and Paper Industry) in the United States of America. Other countries have adopted similar specifications.

CHEMICAL TESTS

Alpha-cellulose content

Purity of cellulose has a direct bearing on the life of paper, and is determined by measuring the alpha-cellulose content of the sample. This is that part of the cellulose material in the paper which is insoluble in a 17.5 per cent solution of sodium hydroxide under certain specified conditions. Papers with high alpha-cellulose content contain high-quality rag or highly purified chemical pulps and are characterized by a high degree of stability.

Copper number

The portion of the cellulose which is hydrolyzed is a measure of impurity and is expressed in terms of copper number, which is defined as the number of grammes of metallic copper in cuprous oxide that is reduced by 100 grammes of disintegrated paper when treated with an alkaline solution of copper sulphate. The copper number is influenced by the presence of non-fibrous reducing agents. A low copper number is an indication of fibre stability.

Acidity

The acidity of paper is determined by its pH value, as measured by a pH meter. The degree of acidity or alkalinity is expressed on a pH scale from 0 to 14 in which the neutral point is 7. Values decreasing below 7 indicate increasing acidity, and values rising above 7 indicate increasing alkalinity. Papers with a pH value lower than 6 are unsuitable for permanent records. Determination of the other characteristics listed above will only substantiate this fact.

Accelerated ageing test

In this text, paper strips are heated in an oven at 100° C for 72 hours and then tested for folding endurance, which is much more susceptible than tensile strength to natural or accelerated ageing.

Appendix 2

Formulae and specifications for ink

Standard writing ink

Gallic acid	10 g	Tartaric acid	1 g
Ferrous sulphate	15 g	Soluble blue	3.5 g
[Water to make 1 litre]			

Standard copying and record ink

Tannic acid	23.4 g	Hydrochloric acid	25 g
Gallic acid	7.7 g	Carbolic acid	1 g
Ferrous sulphate	3 g	Soluble blue	3.5 g
[Water to make 1 litre]			

Standard fountain-pen ink

Tannic acid	4.5 g	Hydrochloric acid	6 g
Gallic acid	1.5 g	Phenol	1 g
Ferrous sulphate	1 g	Soluble dye	1 g
[Water to make 1 litre]			

SPECIFICATIONS

Ferro-gallo tannate fountain-pen ink (0.2 per cent iron content)

1. Total solids g/100 ml maximum	2.5
2. Iron content as Fe g/100 ml minimum	0.2
3. Ratio of ethyl acetate extract to iron content minimum	3
4. Iodine absorption by ethyl acetate extract percentage by weight minimum	5

5. Corrosion, percentage by weight, maximum 5
6. Hue and colour as desired

Blue black ink for permanent records

1. Total solids g/100 ml, maximum 6.5
2. Iron content as Fe, g/100 ml, minimum 0.4
3. Ratio of ethyl acetate extract to iron content 3 to 7
4. Iodine absorption by ethyl acetate extract per cent
   by weight, minimum 500
5. Corrosion per cent by weight, maximum 8
6. Hue and intensity of colour as desired

Appendix 3

Pastes

Dextrine paste

Dextrine	2.5 kg	Safrol	40 g
Water	4 kg	Barium carbonate	40 g
Oil of cloves	40 g		

Add dextrine slowly to hot water (90° C) and stir vigorously to prevent formation of nodules and ensure thorough mixing of dextrine. Then add barium carbonate, stir and finally add oil of cloves and safrol. Complete preparation of paste by cooking over fire for from six to eight minutes.

Thin starch paste

Starch	250 g	Safrol	40 g
Water	5 kg	Barium carbonate	40 g
Oil of cloves	40 g		

Preparation as for dextrine paste. (Starch may be replaced by wheat flour).

Starch paste

| Starch | 200 g | Copper sulphate | 2–3 g |
| Water | 1 l | Glycerine | 2 g |

The paste is prepared in the normal manner. Glycerine is added after the paste has been cooked and then thoroughly mixed. (Starch may be replaced by wheat flour.)

Wheat paste

| Wheat flour | 250 g | Formalin | 10 drops |
| Water | 1 l | | |

Formalin is added after the paste has been cooked.

Rice paste

| Rice flour | 250 g | Water | 2.5 l |

Mix the flour with a small amount of cold water to form a thick cream. Bring the rest of the water to a rolling boil and pour about half into the cream while stirring vigorously. When the mixture has become smooth add more boiling water to obtain the desired consistency and set aside to cool.

Another paste for repair work

| Rice paste | 80–85 per cent | Polyvinyl alcohol (medicine hydrolysis and medium degree of polymerization) 15–20 per cent |

[Ration of paste to water, 1 : 4]

First dissolve the polyvinyl alcohol in a little cold water to make a smooth paste. Add the rest of water to make a 15 per cent solution. Polyvinyl alcohol will dissolve completely if treated in a double bath.

Make the starch into a smooth paste with a little water and mix the two solutions well. Pour in boiling water with constant stirring. Continue heating on the double bath, stirring occasionally. When the paste is translucent to clear in colour it is ready. Add an appropriate disinfectant and mix thoroughly.

Appendix 4

Leather dressings

Neat's foot oil, pure 20° C cold test	25 per cent by weight
Lanolin anhydrous	17.5 per cent by weight
Japan wax, pure	10 per cent by weight
Sodium stearate, powdered	2.5 per cent by weight
Water, distilled	45 per cent by weight

Melt lanolin, wax and castor oil. Add water and stir vigorously. Finally add sodium stearate.

Lanolin anhydrous	55 per cent by weight
Sperm oil	25 per cent by weight
Japan wax, pure	15 per cent by weight
Sodium stearate, powdered	5 per cent by weight

Melt lanolin and wax. Mix with sperm oil. Add sodium stearate, mix and shake vigorously.

Neat's foot oil pure	60 per cent
Lanolin anhydrous	40 per cent

Melt in a double boiler and let cool before using.

Potassium lactate	7 per cent
Potassium lactate 50 per cent solution	2 ounces
Distilled water	1 pint
Para-nitrol phenol	0.05 ounce

Anhydrous lanolin	7 ounces	Beeswax	0.5 ounce
Cedarwood oil	1 ounce	Hexane	11 ounces

Appendix 5

Equipment for repair and binding

The equipment recommended for repair and binding work by a staff of one, four or ten is as follows:

Material	Staff		
	One	Four	Ten
REPAIR WORK			
1. Plates for paste, 15 cm diameter	1	4	10
2. Cups for dextrine paste, 10 cm diameter	1	4	10
3. Painting brush, 25 mm–37 mm	1	4	10
4. Scissors, 20 cm, pointed end	1	4	10
5. Knives, 7.5 cm blade	1	4	10
6. Paper cutting slice, 17 cm pointed	1	4	10
7. Steel/plastic scale, 100 cm	1	4	10
8. Measuring square	1	1	2
9. Vessel for preparing paste	1	1	1
10. Vessel for preparing dextrine paste			
11. Enamelled trays	2	4	8
12. Electric irons	1	2	3
13. Glass topped tables	1	4	10
14. Drying racks	1	1	4
BINDING WORK			
1. Lying press	1	2	4
2. Press boards, 40 cm	1 pair	2 pairs	5 pairs

Material	Staff		
	One	Four	Ten
3. Backing boards, 40 cm	1 pair	2 pairs	5 pairs
4. Card cutter, 45 cm or large	1	1	3
5. Electric gluepot (one point), AC 200/250 volts	1	1	2
6. Backing hammer (Cobbler's hammer), 45 grammes	1	2	5
7. Scissors, 25 cm (for cutting cloth and leather)	1	2	5
8. Knives, 8 cm blade	1	4	10
9. Leather paring knife	1	1	3
10. Firmer chisel, 5 cm blade, 15 cm blade	1	1	3
11. Bodkin	1	1	3
12. Paper cutting-slice, steel, 18 cm	1	4	10
13. Measuring square	1	1	2
14. Glue bushes, round	1	1	5
15. Needles	12	12	36
16. Nipping press, small	1	4	10
17. Nipping press, big	1	2	4
18. Gold lettering equipment	1	1	1
19. Paper cutting machine	1	1	1
20. Ordinary tables	1	4	10

LABORATORY EQUIPMENT

1. Working bench	1	—	—
2. Fume cupboard	1	—	—
3. Balance, ordinary	1	—	—
4. Balance, analytical	1	—	—
5. Water distillation unit	1	—	—
6. pH meter (Beckman or Pye model)	1	—	—
7. Microscope (Bauch and Lomb or Carl Zeiss)	1	—	—
8. Water bath	1	—	—
9. Hot plates	4	—	—
10. Muffle furnace	1	—	—
11. Electric mixer	1	—	—
12. Folding endurance machine	1	—	—
13. Ultra-violet lamp	1	—	—
14. Grafflex camera	1	—	—

Material	Staff		
	One	Four	Ten
15. Tanks for deacidification, electrically, heated	2	—	—
16. Support for washing	4	—	—
17. Large trays	8	—	—
18. Steel wire-net plates	10 pairs	—	—
19. Plastic wire-net plates	10 pairs	—	—

Appendix 6

Norms of output

The following norms are typical of those adopted for use at Florence (output relates to one person per day):

Washings/ deacidification	400 sheets	Stitching	640 sheets
Minor repairs	120 sheets	Binding	
Tissue repair	50 to 70 sheets	Tooling	2 to 3 volumes
Sizing	400 sheets	Solvent lamination	10 volumes
Guarding	480 sheets	(cellulose acetate, tissue and acetone repair)	80–100 sheets

Appendix 7

Some addresses

TISSUE PAPER

Federal Republic of Germany
Oskar Vangerow, Munich.

Japan
International Inspection Service, Central P.O. Box 1539, Tokyo.
Naohache Usami, Tokyo.

United Kingdom
Lawrence & Co., London.
Charles Morgen & Co. Ltd, Gateway House, Watling Street, London,
    E.C.4.
Wiggens Teape & Alex Pirie (Export) Ltd, Gateway House, London
    E.C.4.

United States
Andrews/Nelson/Whitehead Inc., 7 Laight Street, New York, New York
    10013.
John A. Manning Paper Company, Troya, New York.
Yasutomo & Co., 24 California Street, San Francisco, Calif.

CHIFFON OR SILK

France
Lyon Nouveautés Textiles, 10 Place Tolozan, Lyon.
Sauzet et Caponat, 68 Rue de l'Hôtel de Ville, Lyon.

India
Government Silk Weaving Factory, Raj Bagh, Srinagar, Kashmir.

United Kingdom
Combier Silk Ltd, Langham House, 308 Regent Street, London, W.1.

United States
Transparo Company, P.O. Box 838, New Rochelle, New York.

HANDMADE PAPER

France
Rougier et Plé, 13–15 Bd des Filles du Calvaire, 75 Paris-3ᵉ.

India
Khadi and Village Industries Commission, Bombay.

Sweden
Edvard Schneidler A.B., Malmskillnadsgatan 54, Stockholm.

United Kingdom
J. Barcham Green Ltd, Hayle Mill, Maidstone, Kent.
W. S. Hodgkinson & Co. Ltd, 1 Tudor Street, London, E.C.4.
Wiggins Teape and Alex Pirie (Export) Ltd, Gateway House, 1 Watling
    Street, London E.C.4.

United States
Andrews/Nelson/Whitehead Inc., 7 Laight Street, New York, N.Y.

CELLULOSE ACETATE FILM

Formula P–911

Belgium (general agents for Europe)
Amcel Europe, 251 Avenue Louise, Brussels.

France
Celanese Corporation of America, 8 Place Vendôme, 75 Paris-2ᵉ.

Federal Republic of Germany
Plastica Repenning K.G., Anderalstr., 26–Hamburg.

Hong Kong
Yuen Hing Hong & Co. Ltd, P.O. Box 2016.

Italy
Soc. Usvico, Vla Generale Albricci 8, Milano.

United Kingdom
Celanese Corporation of America, 49 Old Bond Street, London, W.1.

United States
Celanese Plastic Company, 744 Broad Street, New York, N.J.
Celanese Corporation of America, 180 Madison Avenue, New York 16,
    N.Y.

Formula 88 CA–148

France
Du Pont de Nemours (France) S.A., 9 Rue de Vienne, 75 Paris-8ᵉ.
Société de Chimie et d'Entreprises, 55 Rue La Boétie, Paris.

Switzerland
Du Pont de Nemours International, S.A., 81 Rue de l'Aire, CH 1211, Genève 24.

United Kingdom
Du Pont Company (United Kingdom) Ltd, 18 Bream's Buildings, Fetter Lane, London E.C.4.

Federal Republic of Germany
Du Pont de Nemours (Deutschland) GmbH, Bismarckstrasse 95, 4000 Düsseldorf.

United States
E. I. Du Pont de Nemours Inc., Wilmington 98, Del. (88 CA–48 formula.)

Note: Cellulose acetate film is available in roll form as well as in reams of various sizes. In roll form the cost is much less.

LAMINATION EQUIPMENT

Flat-bed or hydraulic press

United States
Baldwin-Lima-Hamilton, Department 1565, Industrial Equipment Division, Philadelphia, Pennsylvania.
Drake Corporation, 641 Robbins Road, Grand Haven, Michigan 49417.
Eire Foundry Company, 12th and Cranberry Streets, Eire, Pennsylvania 16512.
Emry Company Inc., 11411, Bradley Avenue, Patomia, California 91331.
The French Oil Mill Machinery Company, 1058 Greene Street, Piqua, Ohio 45366.

Rotary or cylinder press

Federal Republic of Germany
K. Hennecke, Birlenghoven, Siegkreis.
Erwin Kampf, Maschinenfabrik, Postfach 64, D–5286, Bielstein, Rheinland.

United States
The Arbee Company Inc., 6 Carlemont Road, Bernadeville, New Jersey 07924.
W. J. Barrow Restoration Shop, State Library Building, Richmond, Virgina 23219.

Solvent lamination machine

France
M/s Omnia Industrie, 8 Cité de Hauteville, 75 Paris-10e.

Yugoslavia
Mašino-Impex Laminator (Impregnation), Zagreb, Varsvs Rq–9, P.O. Box 02–822.

FUMIGATION EQUIPMENT—VACUUM TYPE

United States
American Machine and Foundry Company, Tobacco Group, Richmond, Virginia. (Guardite Corporation.)
J. P. Devine Manufacturing Company, Pittsburgh, Pennsylvania.
Minnesota Mining and Manufacturing Company, Medical Products Division, St Paul, Minn. 65119.
Vacudyne Corporation, 375 East Joc Orr Road, Chicago Heights, Chicago, Ill.

For other equipment such as humidifiers, vacuum cleaners, adhesives, leather, cloth and other binding and repair equipment, ultra-violet lamps and photographic equipment, fungicides, insecticides, etc., local dealers should be contacted. Such equipment is now available in almost every country.

Bibliography

AGARWALD, O. P.; BISHT, A. S. Non aqueous deacidification and conservation of an Indian illustrated Mss. leaf. *Proceedings of the IV Seminar of Indian Association.* p. 25–8. 1969.

Air conditioning and lighting from the point of view of conservation. *Museum journal,* vol. 63, nos. 1, 2, 1963.

ALMELA MELIA, J. *Manual de reparación y conservación de libros, estampas y manuscriptos.* Mexico, Pan American Institute of Geography and History. 1949. (Publication no. 95.)

AMERICAN PULP AND PAPER ASSOCIATION. *The directory of paper and papermaking terms.* 3rd ed. 1957.

American standard methods for predicting the permanency of silver images of processed films. New York, United States Standards Institute, 1948.

ANDERSON, A. R.; THOMAS, J. M. *Encyclopaedia of chemical technology.* 2nd ed., p. 832–51. New York, J. Willey & Sons, 1963.

Die Archivtechnische Woche der Archivschule, Marburg, Veröffentlichungen der Archivschule Marburg, Institut für Archivwissenschaft, 1957.

ARMITAGE, F. D. The cause of mildew and methods of preservation. *Printing, Packaging and Allied Trades Research Association, Bulletin no. 8,* Leatherhead, 1949.

BANKS, P. N. Paper cleaning. *Restaurator,* vol. 10, 1969, p. 52–66.

BARROW, W. J. Block writing ink of the colonial period. *The American archivist* (Washington), vol. 11, 1948, p. 291–307.

——. *Procedures and equipment in the Barrow method of restoring manuscripts and documents.* Richmond, Va, 1952.

——. *Manuscripts and documents. Their deterioration and restoration.* Charlottesville, Va, 1955.

——. *Deterioration of book stocks, causes and remedies.* Richmond, Va, Virginia State Library, 1959. (Publication no. 10.)

——. *The manufacture and testing of durable book papers.* Richmond, Va, Virginia State Library, 1960. (Publication no. 13.)

——. *Permanent durable book paper.* Richmond, Va, Virginia State Library, 1960. (Publication no. 16.)

——. *Permanence and durability of the book.* Richmond, Va, Virginia State Library. 5 vols: vol. I, *Two year research programme,* 1963; vol. II, *Test data of naturally aged paper*, 1964; vol. III, *Spray deacidification*, 1964; vol. IV, *Polyvinyl acetate (PVA) adhesives for use in library bookbindings*, 1965; vol. V, *Strength and other characteristics of book papers*, 1800–1899, 1967.

BARROW, W. J. Archival file folders. *The American archivist* (Washington), vol. 28, 1965, p. 125–8.

——. *The Barrow method of restoring deteriorated documents*, Richmond, Va, Barrow Research Laboratory, 1966.

BARROW, W. J.; SPROULL, R. C. Permanence in book papers. *Science*, vol. 129, 1959, p. 1075–84.

BAYNES-COPE, A. D. The non-aqueous deacidification of documents. *Restaurator*, vol. 1, 1969, p. 2–9.

BEADLE, C. The recent history of paper making. *Journal of the Royal Society of Arts*, 46, 1898, p. 405–17.

BELANKAYA, N. G. *Methods of restoration of books and documents*. Washington D.C., Office of Technical Sciences, United States Department of Commerce, 1964. (OTS 64–11054.)

BELANKAYA, N. G.; STRELTSOVA, J. N. *New methods for the restoration and preservation of documents and books*. Washington, D.C., National Science Foundation, 1964.

BELJAKOVA, L. A. Gamma-radiation as a disinfecting agent for books infested with mould spores. *Microbiologiya*, vol. 29, 1960, p. 762–5.

——. *Collection of materials on the preservation of library resources*. Vol. 1 Moscow, Lenin State Library, 1964.

BELJAKOVA, L. A.; KOZULINA, O. Book preservation in U.S.S.R. libraries. *Unesco bulletin for libraries*, vol. XV, 1961, p. 198–202.

BHARGAVA, K. D. *Repair and preservation of records*. New Delhi, National Archives, 1967.

BHOVMIK, S. K. A non aqueous method for the restoration of Indian miniature paintings. *Studies in conservation*, vol. 12, 1967, p. 116–17.

BIBIKOV, N. N.; FILIPPOVA, N. A. The electrochemical method of restoration of library materials. *Art and archaeology technical abstracts*, vol. 6, no. 2, 1966.

BLOMQUIST, R. F. *Adhesives past, present and future*, Philadelphia, American Society of Testing Materials, 1963.

BLUM, A. *On the origin of paper*. Translation from the original in French by H. M. LYDENBERG, New York, R. R. Bowker Co., 1934.

BRETT, C. H. *Thysanurans: damage by and control of silverfish and firebrats, pest control*. p. 75–8. 1962.

British Standards recommendation for storage of microfilms, BS 1153. 1954.

BRITT, K. W. *Handbook of pulp and paper technology*. New York, N.Y., Reinhold, 1964.

BUCK, R. P. An experiment in cooperative conservation. *Studies in conservation*, vol. 2, no. 3, 1956.

Buildings and equipments for archives. *Bulletin of the U.S. National Archives*, vol. 6. (Washington).

CASEY, J. P. *Paper making*. New York, N.Y., Inter Science Publishers, 1952. 2 vols. Climatology and conservation in museums. *Museum*, vol. XIII, no. 4, 1960.

COCKERELL, D. *Book binding and the care of books*. 5th ed. London, Pitman, 1953.

COCKERELL, S. M. *The repairing of books*. London, Sheppard Press, 1958.

COLHOUN, J. M. The preservation of motion picture films. *The American archivist* (Washington), vol. 30, 1967, p. 517–25.

COLLIS, I. P. The use of thymol for document fumigation. *Journal of the Society of Archivists*, vol. 4, no. 1, 1970, p. 53–4.

The conservation of cultural property with special reference to tropical conditions in museums and monuments. Paris, Rome and New York, 1968. (International Center for the Study of the Preservation and the Restoration of Cultural Property, no. 11.)

Copying, Kodak data book no. M 1, Eastman Kodak Co., 1968.

CRABTREE, J. I., EATON, G. T.; MUCHLER, L. E. Elimination of hypo from photographic images. *Journal of the Society of Motion Picture Engineers*, vol. 35, 1940, p. 484–500.

CUNHA, G. D. M. *Conservation of library materials*. Metuchen, N.J., Scarecrow Press, 1967.

DADIC, V.; RIBKIN, T. Techniques of delaminating polyethylene laminates *Restaurator*, vol. 1, no. 3, 1970, p. 141–8.

DAHL, S. *History of the book*. Metuchen, N.J., Scarecrow Press, 1958.

DIEL, E. *Book binding: its background and technique*. New York, N.Y., Reinhold, 1946. 2 vols.

DIRINGER, D. *The hand produced book*. London, Hutchinson, 1953.

DUPUIS, R. N. Evaluation of Langwell's vapour phase deacidification process. *Restaurator*, vol. 1, no. 3, 1970, p. 149–62.

EDE, J. R. Steel shelving for record storage. *Journal of the Society of Archivists*, vol. 2, no. 1, 1961.

EDE, J. R.; LANGWELL, W. H. *Sulphur dioxide and vapour phase deacidification*. Conference at the International Institute for Conservation of Historic and Artistic Works, London, 1968.

——. *Vapour phase deacidification of books and documents*. Conference at the International Institute for Conservation of Historic and Artistic Works, London, 1968.

ELLIS, R. *The principles of archive repair*. London School of Printing and Graphic Arts, 1951.

Etat des microfilms de sécurité conservés aux Archives Nationales. Paris, 1962.

EVANS, D. M. The protection of books against insects: a short review of existing methods. *Printing, Packaging and Allied Trades Research Association bulletin no 9*. Leatherhead, 1949.

EVANS, J. Report of the Committee on Deterioration of Paper. *Journal of the Royal Society of Arts*, vol. 46, 1898, p. 597–601.

EVANS, L. *Ancient paper making*. London, 1896.

FARADAY, M. On light or ventilation. *The repertory of patent inventions and other discoveries and improvements*, vol. 2, 1843, p. 174–81 and 238–50.

FELLER, R. L. The deteriorating effect of light on museum objects. *Museum news*, no. 43, 1964.

FILIPPOVA, N. A. Methods of removing ink spots from paper. *Art and archaeology technical abstracts*, vol. 6, no. 2, 1966.

FLEETWOOD, G. The conservation of mediaeval seals in the Swedish A. Riksarkiv. *The American archivist* (Washington), vol. 12, 1949, p. 164–74.

FLIEDER, F. Etude des blanchiments chimiques des papiers anciens. *Bulletin de l'Association Technique de l'Industrie Papetière*, vol. 4, 1960, p. 173–84.

——. Protection des documents d'archives contre les effets climatiques des pays tropicaux. *Manual d'archivistique tropicale.* p. 105. (Publié sous la direction d'Y. Perotin.) Paris and The Hague, Mouton & Co., 1966.

——. *Lutte contre les moisissures des matériaux constitutifs des documents graphiques, procédés employés en France.* Paris, 1961. (Compte-rendu IIC.)

FOWLER, G. H. Maps. *British Records Association Technical Bulletin*, no. 16, 1946.

FUSSLER, H. H. *Photographic reproduction in libraries*, Chicago, University of Chicago Press, 1942.

GAIROLA, T. R. Preservation of parchment. *Journal of Indian museums*, 1958–60.

GALLO, F. *Biological agents which damage paper materials. Recent advances in conservation.* Ed. by G. Thompson. IIC Rome Conference, 1961. London, 1963.

——. About the conservation of microfilms. *Art and archaeology technical abstracts*, vol. 6, 1966.

GAWRECKI; DRAHOSLAV. *Compact library shelving.* Trans. from Czech by S. Rehase. Chicago, Ill., American Library Association, 1968.

GEAR, J. L. Comments of Mr Kathpalia's article. *The American archivist* (Washington), vol. 21, 1958, p. 275.

——. Lamination after 30 years: record and prospect. *The American archivist* (Washington), vol. 28, 1965, p. 293–7.

GETTENS, R. J. The bleaching of stained and discoloured pictures on paper with sodium chlorite and chlorine dioxide. *Museum*, vol. 5, 1952, p. 116–30.

GUNTHER, A. Microphotography in the libraries. *Unesco bulletin for libraries*, vol. XVI, no. 1, 1962.

GRANT, J. *Books and documents: dating, permanence and preservation.* London, 1937.

——. *The records of Virgenic Com. of London.* Vols. 1–4. Washington, Government Printing Office, 1906–35.

GREATHOUSE, G. A.; WESSEL, C. J. *Deterioration of materials—causes and preservative techniques.* New York, N.Y., Reinhold, 1954.

GROVE, L. E. Paper deterioration. *College and research libraries*, vol. 25, 1964, p. 365–74.

GWAM, L. C. Construction of archive buildings. *Manuel d'archivistique tropicale*, Paris and The Hague, Mouton & Co., 1966. (Publié sous la direction d'Y. Perotin.)

HAMILTON, C. E. *A handy guide to papermaking.* Berkeley, Calif., The Book Art Club, 1948.

Handbook for library binding, Boston, Mass., Library Binding Institute, 1963.

HANSEN, F. S. Resistance of paper to natural ageing. *Paper industry and paper world*, vol. 20, 1939, p. 1157–63.

HARRISON, L. S. *Report on the deteriorating effects of modern light sources.* New York, N.Y., Metropolitan Museum of Art, 1954.

HEAUSER, E. *Chemistry of cellulose*, 1944.

HENN, R. W.; WIEST, D. G.; MACK, B. D. Microscopic spots in processed microfilm: the effect of iodine. *Photographic science and engineering*, vol. 9, 1965, p. 167–73.

HENN, R. W.; WIEST, D. G. Properties of gold-treated microfilm images. *Photographic science and engineering*, vol. 10, 1966.

HENN, R. W.; MACK, B. D. A gold protective treatment for microfilm. *Photographic science and engineering*, vol. 9, 1965, p. 378–84.

History of technology, London, 1956.

HORTON, C. *Cleaning and preserving bindings and related materials.* American Library Association, 1967. (LTP publication no. 12.)

HUDSON, F. L.; MILNER, W. D. Technical notes. *Journal of the Society of Archivists*, 1957, p. 172.

HUNTER, D. *Paper making through eighteen centuries.* New York, N.Y., W. E. Rudge, 1930.

——. *Paper making. The history and technique of the ancient craft.* 2nd ed. New York, N.Y.. Alfred A. Knoff, 1957.

Inspection of processed photographic record films for ageing blemishes. *N.B.S.*, 1964.

ISO recommendations for storage of microfilms.

JARRELL; HANKINS; VEITCH. The effects of deorganic acids on the physical properties of waterlay rag board paper. *U.S. Dept. of Agriculture technical bulletin*, vol. 334, 1934.

——. Deterioration of book and record papers. *U.S. Dept. of Agriculture technical bulletin*, vol. 541, 1936.

——. Deterioration of paper as indicated by gas chamber tests. *U.S. Dept. of Agriculture technical bulletin*, vol. 605, 1938.

JENKINSON, Sir H. Some notes on preservation, moulding and casting of seals. *Antiquaries journal*, vol. 4, 1924, p. 388–403.

——. *Manual of archive administration*, London, P. Lund Humphries & Co., 1937.

——. The principles and practice of archive repair work in England. *Archivum*, vol. 2, 1952, p. 31–41.

JOSHI, K. L. *Paper making in India*, Poona.

JUDD, D. B. *Radiation hazard of museum light sources.* NBS, 1953. (Report no. 2254.)

KANE, L. M. A guide to the care and repair of manuscripts. *Bulletin of the American Association for State and Local History*, 1966.

KATHPALIA, Y. P. Care of books in libraries. *Indian pulp and paper*, vol. 9, 1955, p. 147–54.

——. Hand lamination cellulose acetate. *The American archivist* (Washington), vol. 21, 1958, p. 271–74.

——. Deterioration and conservation of paper. Part I: Biological deterioration.*Indian pulp and paper*, vol. 15, 1960, p. 117–25.

——. Trends in restoration. *Indian pulp and paper*, vol. 16, 1961, p. 203–8.

——. Science and paper preservation. *Indian pulp and paper*, vol. 17, July 1962.

KATHPALIA, Y. P. Deterioration and conservation of paper. Part II: Chemical deterioration. *Indian pulp and paper*, vol. 17, 1262.
——. Deterioration and conservation of paper. Part IV: Neutralization. *Indian pulp and paper*, vol. 17, 1962, p. 245–51.
——. Deterioration and conservation of paper. Part V: Restoration of documents. *Indian pulp and paper*, vol. 17, 1963, p. 565–73.
——. Synthetic materials for preservation. *Indian pulp and paper*, vol. 20, 1965.
——. Preserving the heritage. *Indian pulp and paper*, vol. 20, 1965.
——. Synthetic fibres for preservation of paper. *Indian pulp and paper*, vol. 20, 1966.
——. Restauration des documents. *Manuel d'archivistique tropicale*. p. 123. Paris and The Hague, Mouton & Co., 1966. (Publié sous la direction d'Y. Pérotin.)
——. India–7 and solvent lamination. *India pulp and paper*, vol. 21, 1966.
——. Preservation of sound recordings. *Indian pulp and paper*, vol. 22, 1967.
——. Consultant report on flood damaged records in Florence and Venice. Unesco, Paris, 1970.
KEALLY; MEYER, H. C. Air-conditioning as a means of preserving books and records. *The American archivist* (Washington), vol. 12, 1949, p. 280–2
KECK, S. A method of cleaning prints. *Technical studies in the field of fine arts*, vol. 5, 1936, p. 117–26.
KIMBERLY, A. E. ; EMLEY, A. L. *A study of deterioration of book papers in the libraries*. NBS, 1933. (Misc. Publication, 140.)
KIMBERLY, A. E.; SCRIBNER, B. W. *Summary report of National Bureau of Standards Research on preservation of records.* NBS, 1937. (Publication 154.)
KOWALIK, R.; SADURSKA, I. Microorganisms destroying leather book bindings. *Acta microbiologica Polonica*, vol. 5, 1956, p. 285–90.
LACUNER, H. F.; WILSON, W. K. Photochemical stability of papers. *Journal of research* (NBS), vol. 30, 1943, p. 55–74. (NBS.)
LANGWELL, W. H. The permanence of paper records. *Library Association records*, vol. 55, 1953, p. 212–15.
——. *The conservation of books and documents*. Pitman, London, 1957.
——. The Postlip Duplex Lamination Process. *Journal of the Society of Archivists*, vol. 2, 1964, p. 471–6.
——. The vapour phase deacidification of books and documents. *Journal of the Society of Archivists*, vol. 3, 1965, p. 137–8.
——. The protection of papers and parchemin against dampness in storage. *Journal of the Society of Archivists*, vol. 3, 1965, p. 82–5.
——. Recent developments in Postlip lamination process. *Journal of the Society of Archivists*, vol. 3, 1968, p. 360–1.
——. Method of deacidifying paper. *Journal of the Society of Archivists*, vol. 3, 1969, p. 491–4.
LE GEAR, C. E. *Maps, their care, repair and preservation in libraries*. Washington, D.C., Library of Congress, 1956.
LEIGHTON, J. On the library, books and bindings: Pertaining with report to their restoration and preservation. *Journal of the Royal Society of Arts*, vol. 7, 1859, p. 209–15.

LEMONOVA, G. V. Toxicity of cyclohexylamine and docyclohexylamine. English translation in *Federation Proceedings, translation supplement*, vol. 24, 1965, p. 96–8.

LEWIS, A. W. *Basic bookbinding*. London, 1962.

——. *Synthetic materials used in conservation of cultural property*, Rome, International Centre for the Study of the Preservation and the Restoration of Cultural Property, 1965.

LEWIS, C. M.; OFFENHAUSER, W. H. *Microrecordings: industrial and library applications*. New York, N.Y., Interscience Publishers, 1956.

LEWIS, H. F. The deterioration of book papers in library use. *The American archivist*, vol. 22 (Washington), 1959, p. 309–22.

LEWIS, L. L. Air conditioning in museums. *Museum*, vol. 10, no. 2, 1957.

LI-SHU-HUA. *The spread of the art of paper making*. Taipei, National Historical Museum, 1960.

LODOLINI, A. *Miscellanae di Scritti Vari in memorda di Alfonso Gallo*. p. 519. Florence, Olschki. 1956.

LONGO, L. Experiments on a method for cleaning discoloured paper mss. *Bolletino del Istituto di Patologia del Libro*, vol. 18, 1959, p. 3–4.

LUCAS, A. *Ancient Egyptian materials and industries*. 3rd ed. Edward Arnold & Co., 1948.

LUNAR, P. Paper permanence. *TAPPI standards*, vol. 52, 1969, p. 796–803.

LYDENBERG, H. M.; ARCHER, J. *The care and repair of books*. 3rd. ed. New York, N.Y., R. R. Bowker & Co., 1945.

MACCARTHY, P. Vapour phase deacidification. A new preservation method. *The American archivist* (Washington), no. 32, 1969, p. 333–42.

Manuscript repair in European archives. *The American archivist* (Washington), vol. 1, p. 14, 51, 363.

Microfilm preservation. *Chemistry* (Washington), vol. 37, 1966, p. 28–9.

MINOGUE, A. E. The repair and preservation of records. *National Archives of U.S.A.*, *bulletin*, no. 5, 1943.

MITCHELL, C. A.; HEPWORTH, T. C. *Inks, their composition and manufacture*. 4th ed. London, 1937.

Mould deteriorations on treated and untreated reclaimed fibreboards. 1944. (United States Forest Products Lab. report.)

Mould growth report. United Kingdom, Signal Research and Development Establishment, 1945.

MURRAY, J. *Practical remarks on modern paper with an introductory account of its former substitutes; Observations on writing inks, the restoration of illegible manuscripts and the preservation of important deeds from the effects of damp*. London, T.Cadell, 1829. Also see his *An account of the Phormium Tenax or New Zealand flax*. London, Henry Renshaw, 1836.

NATIONAL BUREAU OF STANDARDS. *Protective display lighting of historical documents*. 1953. NBS, Circular 538.

NELSON, C. E. *Microfilm technology engineering and related fields*, McGraw-Hill, New York, N.Y., 1965.

New methods for the restoration and preservation of documents and books. Moscow, 1960. English translation available from Office of Technical Services, Department of Commerce, Springfield, 1964.

NIUKSHA, U. P. A microscopic study of paper pigmented by the *Gymnoasius Setotus* fungus. *Microbiologiya*, vol. 29, 1960, p. 133–6.

PAPRITZ, J. *New methods, new materials and new results in the restoration and conservation of archives and in documentary phototechniques since 1950.* Göteborg, 1960. (Report to International Congress of Archives.)

PINA; ROUSSET. Construction of libraries in tropical climate. *Unesco bulletin for libraries*, vol. XV, no. 5, 1961.

PLENDERLEITH, H. J. *The conservation of prints and drawings.* Oxford, University Press, 1937.

——. *Technical notes on unwrapping of Dead Sea Scrolls. Discoveries in the Judean Desert.* Clarendon Press, London, 1955.

——. *Conservation of antiquities and works of art: treatment, repair and restoration.* London, Oxford University Press, 1956.

PLENDERLEITH, H. J.; WERNER, A. E. Technical notes on the conservation of documents. *Journal of the Society of Archivists*, vol. 1, no. 7, 1958, p. 195–201.

PLUMBE, W. J. *The preservation of books in tropical and subtropical countries.* London, Oxford University Press, 1956.

PRAVILOVA, T. A. *Ageing of paper.* Washington, D.C., United States Department of Commerce, 1964. (Available as OTS 64–11 034 from the Office of Technical Sciences.)

PRAVILOVA, T. A.; ISTRUBCINA, T. W. *The bleaching of documents on paper with sodium chlorite.* Moscow, U.S.S.R. Academy of Sciences, 1962.

——. *Preservation of paper documents by the buffering method in preservation of documents and papers.* United States Department of Commerce, 1968. (T.T. 67–5–1400.)

Preservation and storage of sound recordings, Washington, D.C., Library of Congress, 1959.

Preservation of leather book bindings. No. 69, 1933. (United States Department of Agriculture leaflet.)

PRICE, D. *Detergents.* New York, N.Y., Chemical Publishing Co., 1952.

Probleme der Archivetechnik. Munich, 1958.

Protection of cultural property in the event of armed conflict, Paris, Unesco, 1955.

Protection of records. Boston, Mass., National Fire Protection Association, 1963. (No. 132.)

Protection from fire. *The American archivist*, vol. 1, 1938, p. 179; vol. 11, 1948, p. 165; vol. 14, 1951, p. 157; vol. 16, 1953, p. 145–53.

Publications biological scientific. Vol. 1, p. 299. University of California, 1940.

PUTMAN, G. H. *Books and their makers during the Middle Ages.* New York, 1962. 2 vols.

RAFT, R. A. V.; HERRICK, I. W.; ADANES, M. F. Archives document preservation. *Northwest science*, vol. 40, February 1966.

The restoration system. p. 1–33. Biblioteca Nazionale Centrale di Firenze, 1968.

SANCHEZ BELDA, L. *Nuevos methodos tecnicos, nuevos materiales (. . .) en el campo de la restauracion*, Direccion general de Archivos y Bibliotecas, 1961.

——. Construction of archives buildings in the last ten years. *Unesco bulletin for libraries*, vol. XVIII, no. 1, 1964.

SANTUCCI, L. *Recent advances in conservation: the application of chemical and physical methods to conservation of archival materials.* p. 39–47. London, Butterworths, 1963.

SANTUCCI, L.; WOLFF, C. Rigener Azione dei Documenti IV. *Bolletino del Istituto di Patologia del Libro.* 1963.

SAX, N. J. *Dangerous properties of industrial materials.* 3rd ed. New York, Reinhold Book Co., 1968.

SCHELLENBERG, T. R. *Modern archives.* Chicago, Chicago University Press, 1956.

SCHIERHOLTZ, O. J. *Process for the chemical stabilization of paper and paper products.* (United States Patent no. 2, 033, 452 of 1936; also British Patent no. 443, 534 of 1936.)

SCRIBNER, B. W. *Protection of documents with cellulose acetate.* 1940. (NBS, publication M 168.)

SKORDES, G. The parchment stretcher at the Maryland Hall of Records. *The American archivist* (Washington), vol. 9, 1946, p. 330–2.

SMITH, R. D. *The preservation of leather book bindings from sulphuric acid deterioration.* University of Denver, 1964. (Thesis for Master's Degree.)

——. Paper deacidification. A preliminary report. *Library quarterly,* vol. 36, 1966, p. 273–92.

——. Paper impermanence as a sequence of pH and storage conditions. *Library quarterly,* vol. 39, 1969, p. 153–75.

——. New approaches to preservation. *Library quarterly,* vol. 40, 1970, p. 139–71.

SNYDER, T. E. *Our enemy, the termites.* New York, Comstock Publishing Co., 1948.

Stains on negatives and prints. Eastman Kodak Co., 1950. (Kodak Data Book no. 1–18.)

Standard requirements for photographic filming enclosures for storing processed photographic films. United States Standards Institute, New York, N.Y., 1948.

Standard specifications for photographic films for permanent records. New York, N.Y., United States Standards Institute, 1957.

Standard specifications for safety photographic films. New York, N.Y., United States Standards Institute, 1965.

Standards for the protection of records. Boston, Mass., National Fire Protection Association, 1967.

STOLOW, N. The action of environment on museum objects. Pt. II: Light. *Curator,* vol. 9, 1966, p. 298–366.

Storage and preservation of microfilms. Eastman Kodak Co., 1965. (Kodak Data Book no. P–108.)

Storage of processed colour films. Eastman Kodak Co., 1962.

Technical bulletin of British Paper and Board Manufacturers' Association, vol. 29, 1952, p. 21, 30; 1953, p. 2.

Theory and practice of book binding. Washington, D.C., United States Government Printing Office, 1950.

THOMPSON, Sir E. M. *An introduction to Greek and Latin palaeography.* London, Oxford University Press, 1912.

——. Parchment and vellum. *Encyclopaedia Britannica,* 1945.

THOMSON, G. Visible and ultraviolet radiation. *Museum journal*, vol. 57, 1957, p. 27–32.

TITUS, A. C. *Fungus resistance of untreated materials*, New York, N.Y., GEC, 1945.

TOTTLE, H. F. Strong-room climate. *Archives*, vol. 2, 1956, p. 387–402.

TSIEN, T. H. *Written on bamboo and silk: the beginnings of Chinese books and inscriptions.* Chicago, Ill., University of Chicago Press, 1962.

U.S. Government Printing Office technical bulletin, vol. 22, p. 94.

VEITCH, F. P. *Suitable paper for permanent records.* p. 261–6. Washington, D.C., United States Government Printing Office, 1908. (Yearbook of Department of Agriculture.)

VERY, H. R. *Microcopying methods*, London, Fountain Press, 1963.

VOORN, H. In search of raw materials. *Paper maker*, vol. 30, 1952, p. 47–52.

WACHTER, O. *On the stretching and flattening of old parchment.* Stuttgart, Allgemeiner Anzeiger für Buchbindereien, 1958.

——. *Parchment restoration.* Stuttgart, Allgemeiner Anzeiger für Buchbindereien, 1962.

WARDLE, D. W. Public Record Office: The Repository. *Archivum*, vol. 7, 1957.

WATSON, A. *Hand bookbinding*, New York, N.Y., Reinhold, 1963.

WERNER, A. E. The lamination of documents. *Problems of conservation of museums.* Paris and London, Eyrolles and Allen & Unwin, 1969. (Works and publications no. 8, of the International Centre for the Study of the Preservation and the Restoration of Cultural Property, ICOM Committee for Conservation.)

——. The conservation of leather, wood, bone, and ivory and archival materials. *The conservation of cultural property.* p. 282–90. Paris, Unesco, 1968. (Museums and monuments, XI.)

WESSEL, C. J. Environmental factors affecting the permanence of library materials. *Library quarterly*, vol. 40, 1970, p. 39–84.

WILSON, W. K.; FORSHEE, B. *Preservation of documents by lamination.* 1959. (NBS monograph no. 5.)

YABROVA, R. R. *Removal of dyes from paper.* Moscow, Department for Book Preservation and Restoration, Lenin Library. English translation published in *Collection of materials on preservation of library resources.* Washington, D.C., 1964. (Israel programme for Scientific Translation for the National Science Foundation and the Council of Library Resources, no. 2 and 3.)

——. *The prevention of ageing of books and newspapers.* (Available as OTS 64–11053 from the Office of Technical Sciences, Washington, D.C., 1964.)

[B] COM. 72/**XXIV**.3/A